STO

FRIEI

OF ACPL

W9-DBC-605

LANDS BEYOND

OTHER BOOKS BY **L. SPRAGUE de CAMP**

FICTION:

LEST DARKNESS FALL

THE INCOMPLETE ENCHANTER (with Fletcher Pratt)

THE LAND OF UNREASON (with Fletcher Pratt)

THE CARNELIAN CUBE (with Fletcher Pratt)

DIVIDE AND RULE

THE WHEELS OF IF

THE CASTLE OF IRON (with Fletcher Pratt)

GENUS HOMO (with P. Schuyler Miller)

THE UNDESIRED PRINCESS

ROGUE QUEEN

NON-FICTION:

INVENTIONS AND THEIR MANAGEMENT (with Alf K. Berle)

THE EVOLUTION OF NAVAL WEAPONS

LOST CONTINENTS

OTHER BOOKS BY **WILLY LEY**

THE LUNGFISH AND THE UNICORN

BOMBS AND BOMBING

THE DAYS OF CREATION

SHELLS AND SHOOTING

ROCKETS

THE LUNGFISH, THE DODO AND THE UNICORN (revised and enlarged edition)

THE CONQUEST OF SPACE (with Chesley Bonestell)

DRAGONS IN AMBER

ROCKETS, MISSILES AND SPACE TRAVEL (revised and enlarged edition)

LANDS

BEYOND

by L. Sprague de Camp and Willy Ley

RINEHART & CO., INC.

NEW YORK

TORONTO

398.2
D35

BLACK & GOLD

Grateful acknowledgment is made to the following publishers for permission to quote excerpts from their publications:

George G. Harrap & Company, Ltd., London, for excerpts from *The Odyssey*, translated by H. B. Cotterill, 1912.

Harvard University Press for excerpts from Pliny's *Natural History*, Loeb Classical Library, translated by H. Rackham, and for excerpts from *Plato's Timaeus* and *Critias*, Loeb Classical Library, translated by R. G. Bury.

The Macmillan Company, New York, for an excerpt from *The Iliad*, translated by Smith and Miller, Copyright 1944 by the Macmillan Company.

The Technology Review, edited at the Massachusetts Institute of Technology, for permission to use an expanded version of "The Great Dream" by Willy Ley, which appeared in the April and May, 1951, issues and for the Ptolemy, Idrisi and Quadus maps which were adapted from the original sources by the M. I. T. Illustration Service.

Columbia Publications, New York, for the use of the articles "The Mislaid Tribes," published in *Future Fiction* for May, 1921, and "The Mountain of Light," published in *Science Fiction Quarterly* for August, 1921.

PUBLISHED SIMULTANEOUSLY IN CANADA BY

CLARKE, IRWIN & COMPANY, LTD., TORONTO

COPYRIGHT, 1952, BY L. SPRAGUE DE CAMP AND WILLY LEY

PRINTED IN THE UNITED STATES OF AMERICA

ALL RIGHTS RESERVED

LIBRARY OF CONGRESS CATALOG CARD NUMBER:—52-5577

Contents

802519

LIST OF ILLUSTRATIONS

LANDS BEYOND

Introduction

THREE COLOSSAL FIGURES STRIDE ACROSS THE LANDSCAPE OF THE mind of early man: the warrior, the wizard, and the wanderer. The warrior or war chief protects the folk from material foes, human and animal. The wizard or priest-magician defends them against supernatural dangers: he defeats demons and witches, assures the fruitfulness of men, beasts, and crops, cherishes the tribal lore, and teaches the young what will happen to them if they defy the rules. And lastly the wanderer, the wayfarer, brings goods to trade and news of far and fantastic places to entertain.

In competing for prestige and power, all of these public figures are wont to make much of their importance and to magnify the perils and hardships of their occupations. While the warrior may try to double the size of the lion he has slain or the number of Philistines he has routed, his hyperbole is limited by the fact that his feats are usually performed before witnesses. The wizard, whose foes are often invisible, is in somewhat better case, but even his style is bound to be cramped by the presence of friends and neighbors who knew him when.

The traveler, however, has a virtual *carte blanche*. He has been where his hearers have not, and in case of argument he commands that crushing rejoinder:

"I was there!"

No wonder "traveler's tale" has come to mean an elaborate lie or a fantastic exaggeration! And one traveler's tale paves the way for the next, for when one is brought up to believe that beyond the horizon lie the perilous seas of faery lands forlorn, infested by demons, dragons, and men whose heads do grow beneath their shoulders, a tale that confirms this belief will find readier acceptance than one that refutes it.

The traveler himself was often the best argument for the truth of his narrative, for the ruggedness of early travel called for a good all-around man to endure its adversities. He had to combine the brawn and agility of the warrior with the guile and glibness of the wizard, in order to repel assault, to flee catastrophe, and to ingratiate himself with strangers who would just as lief eat him as not. Courage and resource he needed, but strict truthfulness he would find more a handicap than an asset.

Furthermore he needed a burning curiosity as to what lay beyond the horizon. Without such curiosity he would probably never have been able to suppress his atavistic fears of the unknown long enough to have become a voyager in the first place. While most early travel was undertaken for purposes of colonization or trade (shading betimes into plain piracy) the true-born traveler had to have some motive besides mere avarice to spur him on.

Now, the land beyond the real horizon is probably much like the land you are standing on, but if you travel beyond the horizon often enough you will reach a land that *is* different. How different you won't know until you get there; it may prove a place of heavenly delight or of hellish horror.

So it is not surprising that throughout history the explorer, the seafarer, has been an even greater hero than the warrior and the wizard. The fighter might be brave and strong, but he faced a known danger: another warrior or a dangerous beast. The magician dealt with dangers which, while unknown to the masses, were presumably known to him, and on his own ground.

But the traveler faced perils unknown even to him: devouring monsters, fierce people not altogether human, and the wrath of strange gods. He accepted the risks of driving snowstorms and blinding fog, deadly calm and monsters of the deep, violent winds and jagged cliffs, sucking swamps and burning deserts, the Mountain of Lodestone and the Jellied Sea, the impenetrable seaweeds and the great whirlpool near the world's rim.

And when he returned you may be sure that he did not understate the dangers he had undergone. By making the most of them, on the contrary, he could expand his ego, justify the high prices he wanted for his trade goods, and discourage possible competitors from horning in on his territory. The Phoenicians elevated such individual business acumen to a principle; they spread a whole family of horror tales around the Eastern Mediterranean about the more or less fictitious dangers outside the Pillars of Herakles.

However, such stories were seldom pure fabrications.

Real dangers did exist, and it was easier to exaggerate them than to think up purely imaginary ones—though an especially gifted liar might sometimes do the latter, too. The traveler would often repeat accounts of things that he had not seen himself but had heard of from other travelers, and such yarns grew with every telling. Or he might indulge in the old human weakness for repeating an anecdote he had heard, making himself the hero. Or he might convey a false impression because he had no exact words to fit the thing that he was describing, or the treacheries of translation from one language to another might give rise to an honest misunderstanding.

How do you describe something the like of which you have never seen or heard of, anyway? The Northerners who encountered their first elephant or flying fish were in that position; so were the Southerners who saw their first iceberg or aurora borealis, and the landsmen who met their first octopus or oceanic tide.

To sum up: The deliberate bragging and lying of returned explorer-heroes, the cunning horror myths sown to enhance the value of trade goods, the difficulties of description and translation, all worked together through the centuries to create a series of half-mythical worlds somewhere in the dimly known lands beyond the horizon of reality, in a belt surrounding the known.

For to early man the world comprised a little patch of the known surrounded by a ring of the unknown, and beyond that you came to the edge of the world, where the world-island ended or the sky-bowl came down to meet the ground. The wizards, keepers of the tribal lore, wove rumors of unknown lands into the tribal myths, combining them with their traditional tales of gods, monsters, and heroes. When travel familiarized the people with the surrounding unknown belt, these beliefs had become part of the nation's sacred literature and were not to be questioned. The monsters and prodigies must exist—but farther away than had been thought. Therefore the makers of myths combined the existing myths with rumors about the new unknown belt encircling the old to construct a new mythos. And so on. . . .

As a result, these half-imaginary worlds of geographical legend, once conceived, showed an amazing vitality, for people are much readier to embrace an attractive or exciting belief than to give it up. If a later traveler failed to find a particular prodigy, that must be because he had not gone far enough, or had gone in the wrong direction, or had not gone at all but was jealously trying to discredit his intrepid predecessors by malicious lies.

Moreover, until very recent times there was always plenty of blank space on the map marked "unknown" wherein elusive marvels could be located. As Plutarch remarked:

> . . . geographers crowd into the edges of their maps parts of the world which they do not know about, adding notes in the margin to the effect that beyond this lies nothing but sandy deserts full of wild beasts, unapproachable bogs, Scythian ice, or a frozen sea . . .
>
> Plutarch, *Theseus*, 1.

In time the hunt for wealth, the pursuit of political boundaries, and at last the search for scientific fact filled in our knowledge of the world so that hardly any part of it is really unknown any more. In this process the worlds of geographical legend, after having been whittled down and shunted all over the map, have finally been pushed off the globe altogether.

Still, as we can restore a dinosaur from its bones, so can we re-create these imaginary worlds from their traces in literature, folklore, and figures of speech. And a fascinating business it is. As with the restorations of fossil animals, some cases are so well established and present only such minor difficulties that the "restoration" may be considered correct. In other cases conjecture has had to fill in some minor gaps and it is possible that detail may have to be changed later because of further research or chance discoveries. Finally there are cases where we have only fragments—tantalizing glimpses—which we cannot restore to coherent wholes because key pieces are missing.

However, in general it is now not only possible to write the story of exploration from the point of view of who discovered what and when. It is also possible to write the same story from the point of view of what people wanted or hoped to find.

And at the beginning of all the places people wanted to find there is the land described by Plato . . .

CHAPTER I

The Land of Longing

IF ONE WERE ASKED TO PRONOUNCE A MAGICAL NAME, A SINGLE word known to every listener, a word of splendor and of mystery, a word which means many different things to many different people, that word would and could only be: *Atlantis.*

The very sound of the name "Atlantis" evokes visions of something wonderful, something glittering and golden in the immensity of a wide blue sea, far from the daily life of which everybody is an active part but which many profess to abhor.

Because Atlantis has come to mean so many different things to so many people it is no wonder that the number of books and pamphlets dealing with it is enormous. An estimate made in 1938 stated that a complete library on Atlantis would comprise some 1700 titles; the number has indubitably grown larger since then. An interesting and rarely mentioned point about this large volume of literature is that about 1650 of the 1700 titles originated during the last two centuries. But unlike other long and involved stories which have been much discussed during the same interval, the story of Atlantis has a specific and well-defined beginning.

It goes back in a straight and unbroken line to the works

of a Greek philosopher of the fourth century B.C. His original name was Aristokles, but that is a name known only to a few specialists. To the public he is known as Plato, a nickname meaning "broad-shouldered," which was either invented by his friends and accepted by the bearer or possibly even picked by the man himself. The man called Plato was born probably in 427 B.C.; the year of his death is 347 B.C. For a time he traveled a great deal, but most of his life was spent in Athens, where he finally founded a school of philosophy which is the first known university of written history. Called simply the Academy, it flourished until 529 A.D. when it was closed by Justinian. Plato's teacher was the famous Socrates; the even more famous Aristotle was his pupil.

Most of Plato's philosophical writings revolved around one idea: the State. The State as it should be ideally, and what should be done to make the existing states approach the ideal. In external form all his works have a form which is called "dialogues," although "discussions" would be a better term, with Plato's master Socrates presiding. The most famous and in every respect the "main work" of Plato is the dialogue *The Republic*. The two dialogues which interest us here are called *Timaios* and *Kritias;* the titles refer to characters in the discussions. Both these dialogues were late works, but not his latest; *The Laws* was written or at least completed after Plato put his *Kritias* aside unfinished. It is these two dialogues, the finished (and polished) *Timaios* and the unfinished and strictly unpolished *Kritias* which comprise the first and original source on Atlantis.

Plato's account of Atlantis—we'll go into detail later—is a story of a lost civilization on a large sunken island. Consequently the ones who later evinced a profound and often all-consuming interest in Atlantis can be divided into several large categories. Some looked mainly for a lost civilization and often did not care whether the land in which they thought they had discovered it still existed, or even whether it was, or ever had been, an island. Others looked for a lost small continent, and were often not overly concerned with the question of whether its probable civilization matched the dialogues. Some, of course, looked for such a civilization on such a continent, generally willing to sacrifice one or two minor items as allegory. Others, looking for the same lost civilization on the same lost continent, were also ready to give up minor items, but very often they considered just those items incidental which the other group considered essential. Hence, of course, the 1700 titles in 1938.

To all those who wanted to take the material in the two dialogues literally it was disconcerting to learn that Plato was not only the first source but, under strict judgment, the only one. It was even more disconcerting how little attention had been paid to Atlantis by Plato's classical colleagues. Aristotle (who, after all, was Plato's pupil) implied that Atlantis was a fiction or allegory, while Strabo the geographer was cautiously noncommittal. Pliny the Elder, while mentioning Atlantis, carefully added "as far as we can believe Plato." Since Pliny was writing an encyclopedia he could not just drop the whole thing, but he was not obliged to accept responsibility. And Plutarch did likewise, speaking of "the history or fable of Atlantic island."

One might say that most classical authors agreed with Aristotle, mostly by way of not mentioning Atlantis at all. This has led a few modern Atlantists, annoyed by classical neglect of their pet theory, to assert that this "attitude was directly caused by Aristotle's overwhelming influence." Which just proves that most Atlantists, in spite of their wide reading, are hazy about cause and effect and the interrelationships of history. The overwhelming influence of Aristotle's works did exist for a number of centuries, but that was in Christian countries beginning early in the thirteenth century. By that time, in those countries, Aristotle replaced Plato as "the philosopher."

Among the classical writers the question consisted of the simple choice of either accepting Plato's story more or less literally and of believing in a former island-continent in the ocean west of Spain, or else taking the whole as a philosophical allegory. The alternative of believing the story but doubting its geography and generally "explaining" it came later, though quite early. The first—or at least one of the first—to treat it in this manner was one of the early Christian writers, Kosmas Indikopleustes ("he-who-traveled-to-India") who identified Atlantis with the paradise of the Bible and who "recognized" in the ten princes of Atlantis the ten generations of Man between Adam and Noah.

After America was finally discovered, a few learned men began to wonder whether Plato might have "meant" America. It seemed to fit so well: a large continent far to the west, with teeming civilizations, native princes and kings, strange dresses, and gold—gold everywhere, on costumes, weapons, and temples. Except: all this was still there while Plato had written that it was destroyed. Atlantis probably was something else; one might be able to find it by hard thinking. It was then that "Atlantean Research" began in all its fearful contortions.

A learned Swede, Olaus Rudbeck by name, spent many years writing a heavy folio volume which was finally published under the title *Atlantica* in 1675 in Upsala. In that volume Rudbeck "proved" that Atlantis was actually southern Sweden and that the palace described by Plato had been in Sweden too, situated (strange coincidence) in the vicinity of

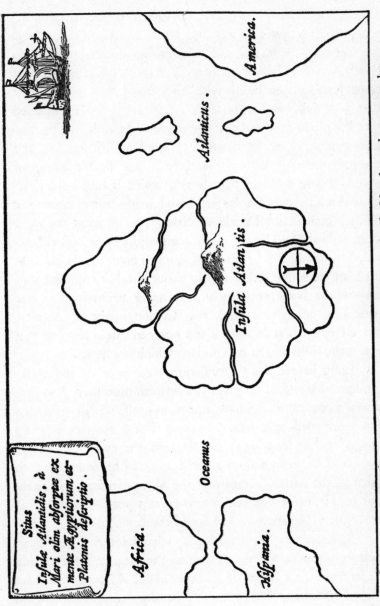

FIG. 1. Atlantis, as it was pictured in 1678 in the book *Mundus subterraneus* by Athanasius Kircher. Note that north is at the bottom of the map.

Upsala. Only ten years later came Georg Kaspar Kirchmaier with his *Exercitatio de Platonis Atlantide*. He did not root for Germany as the place of Atlantis, but decided in favor of South Africa. Followed an interval of about one century, then came Jean Sylvain Bailly with his *Lettres sur l'Atlantide de Platon et l'ancienne histoire de l'Asie* (1779). He explained that Plato had reported that the sea near Atlantis had become unnavigable. This "obviously" referred to drifting ice, and the remains of Atlantis, "therefore," must be the group of islands to the north of Scandinavia which is called the Svalbard Archipelago, the largest island being Spitsbergen. But Bailly's compatriot Delisle de Sales, who, during the same year, published a *History of All the Peoples of the World*, decided that only the Caucasus Mountains could be Atlantis. In his book he spoke rather rudely about another compatriot of his—whose book apparently was never printed—who had been silly enough to think that Ceylon might be Atlantis. Since Ceylon is at least an island one can't help but feel that it was the sillier of the two notions which saw print.

Long before these speculations kept printers and bookbinders occupied, if not happy, a Spanish missionary had produced a contribution which, useless in itself, was to open up a few more roads in several directions. The missionary was one Diego de Landa, who in the days of the conquest became Bishop of Yucatán and considered it one of his main duties to burn all the native literature of the Mayan Indians. He could not read it, of course, but he was certain just the same that it was full of "superstition and lies of the devil."

Subsequently he acquired a belated interest in Mayan culture and wrote a big treatise on the subject, the *Relación de las Cosas de Yucatán or Account of the Affairs of Yucatán*. When preparing for this work he decided that he should learn the Mayan system of writing. In addition to his native Spanish he must have known Latin, and may have learned some Hebrew and possibly even a little Greek. All these languages write with letters expressing sounds. One could easily memorize that where Latin used a "g," Greek used a *gamma* and Hebrew a *gimel*, just different symbols for the same idea. That there might be a different method of writing was a thought which never occurred to him.

So, in all probability, he hauled in some literate Maya (who had all reason to feel apprehensive about the summons), explained what he wanted, and snapped:

"Qué es A?"

Mayan writing, of course, was essentially ideographic like modern Chinese writing, with a few phonetic elements thrown in. The poor Maya, expecting to be sentenced to the stake for heresy at any moment, thought the terrible old man wished to know the sign for *aac* ("turtle") and drew it—a picture of a turtle's head.

"Qué es B?"

Well, *be* is Mayan for "road," so Landa's informant drew the ideograph for "road": an outline of a human footprint between two parallel lines. And so on through the Spanish (but not Mayan) alphabet, until Landa had twenty-seven signs and a few compounds, most of which did not mean at all what he thought they did. He did get the correct explanation of the Mayan numerals and of the Mayan calendar. But then the *Relación* was lost until in 1864 a diligent if erratic French scholar, the Abbé Brasseur de Bourbourg, found an abridgment in the library of the Historical Society of Madrid. Abbé Brasseur was overjoyed, thinking that he had come across the Rosetta Stone, the key, to Mayan writing. He undertook to translate one of the few surviving Mayan books, the Troano Codex, by means of Landa's "alphabet" and much imagination. The result was an incoherent description of a volcanic catastrophe.

In the Codex there were two symbols faintly resembling the M and U of Landa's "alphabet," and Brasseur, unable to account for them otherwise, assumed that they represented the name of the land destroyed by the volcanic catastrophe which he had read into the Codex. And that is the true, original, and only origin of the word *Mu*.

Other scholars soon found that trying to translate Mayan writing by Landa's "key" resulted in sheer gibberish. And although they lacked the help which Landa had had, they at least knew that they were dealing with ideographs and not letters. By a vast amount of work over three-quarters of a century they did discover the meaning of somewhat over a third of the Mayan ideographs. Knowing only four words out of every ten does not make for easy reading, but one can at least find out what a manuscript is about, and it is now evident that Brasseur's "translation" is entirely wrong. The Troano Codex is actually a portion of a treatise on Mayan astrology and has nothing to do with volcanic eruptions or earthquakes.

Many, though, continued to take Brasseur's translation seriously even after it had been discredited. One was that extraordinary character Ignatius Donnelly, a Philadelphia lawyer who moved to Minnesota in his youth and led an active political career there. He was elected Lieutenant Governor of Minnesota at the age of twenty-eight, served two terms in Congress, and helped found the Populist Party. In addition he wrote many books, including several science-fiction novels, one of which, *Caesar's Column*, sold a million copies. Two books which were not meant to be fiction were *The Great Cryptogram*, in which Donnelly popularized the Baconian theory, and *Atlantis: The Antediluvian World* which appeared in 1882 and started the modern version of Atlantist cultism.

Donnelly eloquently argued that all the ancient civilizations, including those of the Mayas and Aztecs, were derived from Atlantis. This has become the major tenet of most Atlantists since then; they all decided that civilization is so hard to invent that it could have happened only once. Donnelly had collected a vast mass of argument and alleged fact, with much emphasis on certain customs found among primitive groups in both the New and Old Worlds. It so happens that Donnelly's book is practically a solid mass of mistakes of fact and errors of interpretation, but that did not stop it from running through more than fifty editions. It is still available.

Donnelly's contemporary, Augustus Le Plongeon, another major contributor to the stream of Atlantist theory, bears the distinction of being the first to excavate Mayan ruins in Yucatán. A French physician, distinguished by a magnificent beard down to his waist, Le Plongeon wholeheartedly accepted Brasseur's French version of the Troano Codex. From it and from some pictures he found on the walls of Chichén Itzá he built a romantic tale of the rivalry of the two princes Coh ("Puma") and Aac ("Turtle") for the hand of their sister Móo, Queen of Atlantis or Mu. Puma won, but was murdered by Turtle. Then, as the continent sank, Móo fled to Egypt where, under the name of Isis, she built the Sphinx* as a memorial to her late husband. She founded the Egyptian civilization which Atlantists, in spite of the clearest evidence to the contrary, consider as having sprung full-blown from nothing.

Brasseur, Donnelly, and Le Plongeon were careless as investigators, negligent in their logic, and given to believing

* Probably a monument to King Khafra of the Fourth Dynasty.

whatever pleased them. But they could all still claim to have been merely mistaken. The next major contribution to Atlantist theory, however, was an outright hoax of the baldest kind. Atlantists hailed it when it was new, and many continued to cling to it even after it was exposed.

The perpetrator of the hoax was Dr. Paul Schliemann, grandson of the great Heinrich Schliemann who dug up Troy. In 1912 the younger Schliemann, tired of being a little man with a big name, gave the New York *American* a sensational story of how his grandfather left secret papers instructing him to break open an owl-headed vase. This Schliemann did and found therein valuable archeological specimens, some of them square coins of platinum-aluminum-silver alloy and other objects bearing the inscription, in Phoenician characters, "From the King Cronos of Atlantis." Schliemann added that he had confirmed the former existence of the continent called Atlantis by the Greeks and Mu by the Mayas by reading the Troano Codex in the British Museum. (But the Codex was in Madrid all the time and Schliemann's version of it was that of Le Plongeon!) He had also read, he said, a 4000-year-old Chaldean manuscript which had been preserved, of all places, in a Buddhist Temple in Lhasa, Tibet.

The article ended with the announcement of further revelations. Apparently Schliemann had thought that his, or rather his grandfather's, names would cause immediate and unquestioning belief. But it didn't. The inconsistencies were so obvious, the assertions of accomplishment so incredible, and the logical slips so conspicuous that only hopeless credophiles could swallow it. In addition to all this Dr. Dörpfeld, who had been an assistant of the elder Schliemann, declared that the famous archeologist had not even been interested in Atlantis.

Finally, James Churchward, a small wraithlike Anglo-

American in his seventies at the time, burst into print with *The Lost Continent of Mu* in 1926, followed by several other Mu books. Churchward called himself "Colonel" and claimed to have traveled widely in Central America (where he was once attacked by a flying snake!) and Asia. He expanded upon the yarns of Le Plongeon and Schliemann by claiming to have read the Naacal* tablets in India or Tibet and by assuming two lost continents: Atlantis in the Atlantic and Mu in the Pacific, confusing the preceding generation of Atlantists by appropriation of the name Mu.

Churchward stands about midway between the more fantastic Atlantists of the Le Plongeon variety and the occultists, who had meanwhile pushed their way into the lost-continent domain. Churchward not only placed his Mu where the occultists had put "their" Lemuria; he also shared the favorite occultist obsession of being able to read the symbols of an ancient people by sheer mental concentration. He claimed that in the old Muvian alphabet the rectangle had stood for the sound we now write "M." Hence the rectangle symbolized the name Mu—being utilized by its very shape to indicate Muvian culture. Now the ordinary building brick is "significantly" bounded by rectangles or Muvian "M's," which needless to say opened wide vistas. Wherever you had a rectangle, you had Mu. In addition to that he misquoted Plato and printed footnotes reading "Greek record" or even "various records." Of course he denied evolution—an almost infallible sign of charlatanism—and held that Man was created fully civilized. As for the disappearance of continents, that was simple: they had been supported by gas-filled chambers which at one time collapsed.

Now for the part played by the occultists in the development of the Atlantis theme. First, paleontologists had mean-

* The Naacals, according to Le Plongeon, were Mayan adepts.

while postulated a lost continent of their own which they called "Lemuria." The idea had originated with the Austrian geologist Melchior Neumayr, while the name had been invented by the British zoölogist Philip Sclater and popularized by the German Ernst Haeckel. This was in the 1860's and 70's, when scientists were first trying to draw maps of the earth at former geological periods. Now, there is a group of primitive relatives of the monkeys called lemurs. At present they are especially abundant on Madagascar, but they occur in India too. Because of this distribution of the lemurs, and because of some other evidence which pointed in the same direction, a kind of land bridge between India and South Africa via Madagascar was assumed. It was this hypothetical subcontinent (which was believed to have disappeared late in the Cretaceous period, or about 60 million years ago in modern dating) that was called Lemuria. Modern geologists are not so sure any more whether this geological Lemuria actually existed, but for a time it was widely accepted in scientific circles.

The idea of Lemuria was picked up by that impressive old she-warlock Helena P. Blavatsky, the founder of Theosophy, and incorporated along with Atlantis (which she got from Donnelly) into her own gaudy cosmogony. According to her works and those of her disciples there is going to be a total of seven Root Races on earth, each with seven subraces. The Third Root Race fitted nicely on Lemuria; Madame described the Lemurians as gigantic apelike men, hermaphroditic and oviparous, some with four arms and some with a third eye at the back of their heads. They came to a sad end. Madame Blavatsky, who was then no longer very young herself, was certain that their downfall was caused by their discovery of sex. But in spite of this discovery, which for some reason was not forgotten, the Fourth Root Race on At-

lantis did well for a long time. In the descriptions of their ac-
tivities, in which a number of occultists engaged—notably
Scott-Elliot—they gradually acquired warships with guns and
searchlights, troop-carrying reaction-propelled aircraft, black
magic, the transmutation of metals, telepathy, priests in
silken gowns and mistresses with transparent veils and jewel-
covered golden clogs.

Lemuria, it must be added, was moved in the course of
this development. Madame Blavatsky, being eager to re-
inforce her own word with quotations from contemporary
geological literature, had left Lemuria in the Indian Ocean.
But her successors felt that the Pacific was a much larger
ocean, capable of accommodating a much larger continent. It
also afforded an opportunity of declaring that the Easter Island statues were actual and life-size portrait busts of the original inhabitants. Hence the occultists' "Lemuria" in the Central Pacific, where for geological reasons any continent, past
or future, is most unlikely.

If this sounds like the last word in "Inner Show" accom-
plishments, it is merely because whoever thinks so has not
read a book by Karl Georg Zschaetzsch. Its title: *Atlantis, die
Urheimat der Arier* (*Atlantis, the Original Home of the
Aryans*, 1922). Atlantis was inhabited by perfect people
who were perfect because they were vegetarians. Their first
imperfection consisted, evidently, in deviating from the vege-
tarian diet. And then a non-Aryan girl by the name of Heid
either invented or imported the art of fermenting drinks.
This, according to Zschaetzsch, is the true meaning of the
apple which Eve handed her husband. It was a fermented
apple! Because of this discovery Atlantis was destroyed by a
collision with the *tail* of a comet. Now the tail of a comet,
although it is huge, is so tenuous that it could be stuffed into
a five-gallon jug if compressed to the average density of iron.

Zschaetzsch did not know this—but evidently when you are actively visualizing things knowledge is merely a handicap.

So the collision with the comet's tail set the earth afire. Atlantis burned and only three people survived: an old man, a small girl, and a pregnant woman. Fleeing from the fire they discovered a cold geyser which squirted its water into the boughs of a large tree. The old man noticed that a snake and a she-wolf disappeared among the roots of the tree and reasoned that there was a cave among the roots. Inside, the woman died and the old man went outside to get cold water; a small meteorite fell from the sky and burned out one of his eyes; but the she-wolf suckled the child. This event, deeply buried in "racial memory," later appeared piecemeal in legends as: the Christmas star, the Tree of Life, the ash Yggdrasill, the spring Mimir, one-eyed Wotan, and Romulus and Remus.

If one looks over the development of the story from Rudbeck to Zschaetzsch, one might be justified in simply giving up. It seems, and actually is, impossible to make any sense out of such an enormous accumulation of supposition, commentary, cross- and counter-commentary and piled-on private beliefs and prejudices.

But when we turn back to Plato himself we find that most of the perplexities just disappear; after the occult horror chambers of black magic and primal races the actual reading of the *Timaios* is like a pleasant breeze from the sea on a sunny day in the company of rational people.

The *Timaios* is a treatise on Pythagorean philosophy, written as a discussion between Socrates and three of his friends: Timaios, Kritias, and Hermokrates. The "fictitious date" is about 421 B.C., when in real life Socrates was not yet fifty and Plato was a small child. The day of the discussion is allegedly the day following the dialogue of *The Republic*, though actually a number of years intervened between the writing of the two.

After the speakers recall the discourse of Socrates on the previous day, Hermokrates (a former Syracusan general) remarks that the other three also have something to say, especially Kritias, who has already "mentioned to us a story derived from ancient tradition." The others press Kritias (an uncle or cousin of Plato and a scoundrelly politician in real life) for details, and presently he begins:

> Listen then, Socrates, to a tale which, though passing strange, is yet wholly true, as Solon, the wisest of the Seven, once upon a time declared. Now Solon . . . was a relative and very dear friend of our great-grandfather Dropides; and Dropides told our grandfather Kritias—as the old man himself, in turn, related to us—that the exploits of this city in olden days, the record of which had perished through time and the destruction of its inhabitants, were great and marvelous . . ."
>
> *Timaios*, 20D-E

"This city" is, of course, Athens, and to begin a story by assuring the reader that every word of it is true is an old literary device. Kritias goes on to tell how his grandfather once expressed regret that Solon had never, because of the press of public business, completed the epic poem he had begun on a tale that he had picked up in Egypt, whither he had gone to escape the unpopularity that he had incurred by reforming the Athenian constitution.

Solon, says Kritias, arrived in Saïs in the Delta during the reign of King Amasis. There he became involved in a discussion of ancient history with the priests of the goddess Neïth or Isis, whom the Greeks identified with their own Athena. When Solon tried to impress the Egyptians by telling them some of the Greek legends, like the Flood of Deukalion and Pyrrha, the oldest priest laughed at him, saying:

> O Solon, Solon, you Greeks are always children. . . . You are young in soul, every one of you. For therein you possess not a single belief that is ancient and derived from old tradition, nor yet one science that is hoary with age. And this is the cause thereof: There have been and there will be many and divers destructions of mankind, of which the greatest are by fire and water, and lesser ones by countless other means."
>
> *Timaios*, 22B-C

These passages illustrate what specialists have known all along: that Plato was (to our mind) careless with the use of facts. Since he wanted to express abstract ideas, he did not handle facts with precision; the ideas did not depend on these particular facts, so there was no need for exactness. Solon's actual trip, for example, took place between 593 and 583 B.C. whereas Aahmes II, the Egyptian king mentioned, did not ascend the throne until 570. Also the theory of recurrent catastrophes was not Egyptian but Babylonian. It gained more currency later when a Hellenized Babylonian priest named Berossos established a school on the island of Kos where he taught the Babylonian science of (apparent) planetary movements and the Babylonian pseudo-science of astrology. That Babylonian ideas had filtered into Greece before Berossos can be seen from the *Timaios* itself, because Plato followed the Babylonian custom of naming a planet after a god: he refers to Mercury as "Star of Hermes" instead of using the old Greek name of *Stilbōn*, "twinkling star."

Although Plato may not have actually confused Egyptian and Babylonian beliefs, he found the transposition convenient for story purposes. Nor is this a unique case about which one may have doubts. In another dialogue, the *Phaidros*, he used a myth about an exchange between the Egyptian god "Theuth" (the ibis-headed Tehuti or Thoth, the Egyptian god of wisdom) and "King Thamos." But "King Thamos" is not an Egyptian king at all, but the Babylonian vegetation-god Tammuz.

The priest goes on to say that ". . . at one time, Solon, before the greatest destruction by water, what is now the Athenian state was the bravest in war and supremely well organized in all other respects. . . ." In fact, according to Solon's Egyptian priest (in reality, of course, Plato) "the goddess who is the common patron and protector and educator of both our cities" founded both of them, Athens "9000 years ago" (that is around 9600 B.C.) and the Egyptian city "8000 years ago," which explains the many resemblances between the two peoples.

The destruction by water referred to is the Flood of Deukalion and Pyrrha, already mentioned—with many parallels elsewhere, including the Flood of the Bible—while the dates mainly serve the purpose of pricking the pretensions of the Egyptians to being the oldest of mankind. Apparently the Greeks were tired of this claim, so Plato found this way out: the Egyptians did have the older tradition because there had been no Flood in Egypt. The original proto-Athenians had been destroyed by the Flood, but they were an even thousand years older. The fact is that the Egyptians had some 3000 years of recorded history in Plato's time and the Greeks hardly 800 even if one accepted all legends as history.* Having settled the priority of the Greeks, Plato let the priest go on:

> Many, in truth, and great are the achievements of your State, which are a marvel to men as they are here recorded; but there is one which stands out above all both for magnitude and for nobleness. For it is related in our records how

* The traditional date of the Trojan War was about 1200 B.C., but this tale is so largely fictional that we cannot infer anything about the date of the real war or wars upon which it may be based. Reliable, authentic Greek history starts only about 650 B.C., just before Solon.

once upon a time your state stayed the course of a mighty host, which, starting from a distant point in the Atlantic Ocean, was insolently advancing to attack the whole of Europe, and Asia to boot. For the ocean was at that time navigable; for in front of the mouth which you Greeks call the Pillars of Herakles there lay an island which was larger than Libya and Asia together* and it was possible for the travellers of that time to cross from it to the other islands, and from the islands to the whole of the continent over against them which encompasses the veritable ocean.

Timaios, 24D-25A

Just what Plato had in mind when he spoke of the Atlantic Ocean and the continent beyond is not quite clear to this day. Of course the continent beyond the Atlantic is America, and much ink has been spilled in trying to prove that the Phoenicians or somebody had crossed the Atlantic before Plato's time and brought back word of the wild lands on the other side. However, from what we know of classical ships and navigation, such a feat would, by any reasonable calculation, have been quite impossible. The classical war galleys could not have accomplished it because they could not carry enough food and water for their rowers, and the sailing merchant ships could not have done it because they were so rigged that they could not tack against the wind. They also lacked a compass to guide them during overcasts. While an accidental one-way trip under special storm conditions cannot be ruled out completely, a premeditated round trip was an impossibility.

But there are two other answers. One is geographical, the other more mythological. The geographical reasoning could proceed as follows: outside the Strait of Gibraltar there were a number of islands somewhere and, according to Plato, one could go from island to island and finally reach a continent. If one started somewhere near Gibraltar, say in

* This means North Africa and Asia Minor combined.

southern Spain, one would, after a long sail, first reach Madeira and then the Canary Islands. After that one would reach the African continent. The direction of such a trip would be essentially southward, but Plato does not mention any direction. And even if he had mentioned one it would still be possible that he was uncertain about the true direction.

The truth, however, is probably that Plato just continued the tradition of the *Odyssey*. Several centuries before Plato, Homer had sent his hero Odysseus to the "Ocean Stream" in the Far West, named for the sea-god Okeanos, Poseidon's father-in-law. Geographically this corresponded to the Atlantic, but the Greeks of that period did not have the mental picture which is evoked by that name in our minds. To them the *oikoumēnē*, the known world (the lands bordering the Mediterranean), was surrounded by an enormous river—at least that word probably comes closest to their idea —and the river, naturally, had to have a further bank. This was the outer continent, stretching away to Zeus alone knew where. Later, when the Atlantic became better known, it continued to be called Okeanos until about the fifth century B.C., the time of the great historian Herodotos. He not only realized clearly that it was an "ocean" (in our sense); he was also the first to use the name "Atlantic," although other terms like "Great Sea" and "Western Ocean" long continued to be used.

Plato knew, of course, that there was a wide sea to the west of the Pillars of Herakles, but he may just have carried on the tradition of "the other bank." He is not concerned with it in any way; the story centers on one of the islands:

> Now in this island of Atlantis there existed a confederation of kings, of great and marvelous power, which held sway over all the island, and over many other islands also and parts

of the continent; and moreover, of the lands here within the Straits they ruled over Libya as far as Egypt and over Europe as far as Tuscany.

Timaios, 25A-B

The names Atlantis and Atlantic are both derived from Atlas, whom Homer had called

. . . Atlas, the wizard of bale, who of every ocean knoweth the watery depths and alone upholdeth the pillars soaring aloft and keeping the earth and heaven asunder.

Odyssey, I, 52-55

The word translated by Cotterill as "upholdeth" is, in the original, "has" *(echei)* which may, depending on circumstances, mean "possess," "has charge of" or "holds up." Originally Atlas was probably thought to be in charge of the all-important pillars; later it was asserted that he, because he had taken part in the rebellion of the Titans, had been condemned to hold up the heavens and had become a pillar himself.* Simultaneously Atlas had been moved from Greece to the farthest known West and then a legend was invented or adapted, telling how Perseus, by showing the head of the gorgon Medusa to the poor giant, had transformed him into a mountain. Why Atlas's name was applied to the main mountain range of Morocco is not really known, but there are some suspicions. One of the reasons was indubitably the location of these mountains. They were in the Far West where, according to ancient belief, anything was possible.

Another reason may be derived from several old stories. Herodotos had told about the tribes of the Atlantes who ate no living things and never dreamed, and of the Atarantes who had no personal names and cursed the sun. Later, during the second century B.C. one Dionysios Skytobrachion wrote a

* Because this is difficult to picture the customary statue of Atlas shows him, not upholding the heavens, but shouldering the earth.

long poem purporting to give the mythology of the Atlantioi of the same region, indubitably the same people Herodotos had named. It seems likely, therefore, that the area was inhabited by a tribe with peculiar customs and with a tribal name which reminded Greek-speaking listeners of the name Atlas.

Atlantis, considered as a word, is simply a feminine noun derived from Atlas; the meaning can be roughly expressed as "daughter of Atlas." In mythology Atlas has seven daughters, called the Atlantides, which is just the plural of Atlantis.

After this linguistic interlude let us return to Plato's account:

> So this host, being all gathered together, made an attempt one time to enslave by a single onslaught both your country and ours [meaning Athens and Egypt] and the whole territory within the Straits. And then it was, Solon, that the manhood of your State showed itself conspicuous for valor and might in the sight of all the world. For it stood preeminent above all in gallantry and all warlike arts, and acting partly as leader of the Greeks, and partly standing alone by itself when deserted by all others, after encountering the deadliest perils, it defeated the invaders and reared a trophy; whereby it saved from slavery such as were not yet enslaved, and all the rest of us who dwell within the bounds of Herakles it ungrudgingly set free.
>
> *Timaios*, 25B-C

The story of the surpassing Athenian valor is one more item designed to bolster Greek self-esteem against the Egyptian claims of superior age and wisdom, which must have annoyed the Greeks considerably. Plato attacks these claims from two directions. First he asserts that Athens is actually 1000 years older even if it had to suffer destruction in the intervening time. Now he adds that the Egyptians would all be slaves if it had not been for Athenian military prowess. His hearers would be perfectly willing to believe him because of a then recent event, which probably was in Plato's mind too. The Greeks had warred against both the Persians and the Carthaginians, and both these wars had come to a smashing climax in 480 B.C. when on one and the same day the Greeks of Greece broke the Persian sea power at Salamis while the Greeks of Sicily defeated the Carthaginians in a great land battle at Himera.

> But at a later time there occurred portentous earthquakes and floods, and one grievous day and night befell them, when the whole body of your warriors was swallowed up by the earth, and the island of Atlantis was in like manner swallowed up by the sea and vanished; wherefore also the ocean at that spot has now become impassable and unsearchable, being blocked up by the shoal mud which the island created as it settled down.
>
> *Timaios*, 25C-D

As the Mediterranean Sea lies in one of the world's major earthquake zones, Plato was familiar with earthquake damage. He even accepted certain erroneous ideas about earthquakes that were widely believed until recently: for example that they open cracks in the ground large enough to swallow a city or an army. They do open cracks, but only the sort a man might break his leg in if he were careless. A couple of violent quakes had shaken Greece in Plato's own lifetime—and that means also the lifetimes of his listeners, who were therefore acquainted with earthquakes. Of the earlier of these two quakes Plato probably had no direct memory, for it took place when he was about one year old. (The other took place in 373 B.C.) The first of these two quakes set up an earthquake wave or tsunami that *inundated the small Greek island of Atalantë*. This event has been described by Thucydides in his *Peloponnesian War* (III, 1, xxxix) in terms which, to us, sound irresistibly like an earlier version of Plato's Atlantean catastrophe:

At about the same time, while the earthquakes prevailed, the sea at Orobiai in Euboia receded from what was then the shore line, and then coming on in a great wave overran a portion of the city . . . In the neighborhood also of the island of Atalantë, which lies off the coast of Opuntian Locris, there was a similar inundation, which also carried away a part of the Athenian fort there, and wrecked one of the two ships which had been drawn up on the shore.

It would be nice if one could prove that Plato had read Thucydides. We know that his pupil Aristotle did, and it is probably the least far-fetched of any Atlantean theory to assume that the master knew the books the pupil knew.

By now we have most of the essential elements of the Atlantis story, as given in *Timaios*, together. The great age of original Athens or "proto-Athens" as an answer to Egyptian haughtiness, the military exploits of the Greeks as partly the same thing, partly as a reference to then recent major military victories. The name of Atlantis as a derivation from the name Atlas; the location in the Far West from the general location of the Atlas mountains; and the ocean is also named after Atlas. And the inundation of Atlantis as a reference to the actual inundation of the actual island of Atalantë.

Two geographical points still need clearing up. The actual mountains which now bear the name of Atlas are not particularly tall and differ in appearance from the Atlas which classical authors described as a single tapering peak so tall that its summit was always hidden by clouds. We'll return to this mountain in Chapter VIII. At this point it may only be mentioned that there is one which fits the old descriptions much better than the present Atlas mountains. But the problem of the proper identification of "Atlas" has no direct bearing on the Atlantis story.

The great mud shoals supposedly blocking navigation west of Gibraltar are a different matter. If there were any such mud shoals, one may wonder whether Europe did not extend farther to the west in early historical times than it does now. But any topographical map of the North Atlantic shows that there are not even any reasonably shallow sections in the sea there. In fact the water is over a mile deep most of the distance from the coast of the Iberian peninsula to the Azores. And from what we know about the rate at which geological movements take place, we can be sure that if such a shoal had existed in Plato's time it would still be very strongly in evidence.

As a matter of fact, we know a lot more about geology now than in Plato's time, particularly about the movements of the earth's crust that result in the raising of lands out of the sea and their sinking back into it. And from this knowledge we can be reasonably sure that no continent ever disappeared in the course of a single earthquake as asserted by Plato, or even in the course of a number of earthquakes over a period of centuries. Earthquakes and volcanic eruptions do sometimes cause land areas to sink—but only small areas, say the size of Manhattan Island; not areas of continental size. And while large areas have risen and sunk throughout geological time, as a result of continuous movements of the crust, such movements over any large area average only a fraction of an inch a year. For a whole continent to sink beneath the waves, the material underneath has to go somewhere, which takes millions of years. So even if a continent once existed in mid-Atlantic (which appears unlikely), it must have disappeared millions of years ago, before man evolved from his branch-sitting flea-scratching ancestors, and therefore it could not have supported a human civilization.*

* For a fuller discussion of the complex and controversial subject of the geological aspects of the lost-continent question, see Chap. vii of co-author de Camp's *Lost Continents*.

However, in classical times such shoals were widely believed in; Aristotle and the geographer who borrowed the name of the explorer Skylax both mentioned them. Much of the big to-do about these shoals may have been part of the careful and apparently quite systematic horror propaganda put out by the Phoenicians. The Phoenicians were very well aware of the fact that much of their influence and even more of their fortune rested on the fact that the trade route through the Strait of Gibraltar was theirs alone. To keep it, they not only made laws and enforced these laws by military might, they also told all and sundry how terrible things were in, around, and outside the Strait. Both sea monsters and elemental dangers threatened the traveler, and among the elemental dangers were these shoals.

But it seems that the Phoenicians rarely invented any of their tales out of whole cloth; there was usually something behind the tale. In this case the tale may refer either to the silting up of the estuary of the Guadalquivir River in Spain, or else it might originally have been inspired by the "Phantom Shoals" off the African coast near Cape Arguin.

In this area powerful currents so change the location of extensive sandbanks from one tide to the next that the mariner never knows whether he might not run aground in a place where there was clear deep water yesterday. Aristotle said that the shoals provided a great catch of tuna and that does fit the "Phantom Shoals," even if not the Phantom Shoals alone.

There is nothing else about Atlantis in *Timaios*. The speaker, Kritias, alludes to the ideal *Republic* described previously by Socrates, tells that he lay awake during the night recollecting the story as he heard it from his grandfather in his youth, and adds:

And the city with its citizens which you described to us

yesterday, as it were in a fable, we will now transport hither into the realm of fact; for we will assume that the city is that ancient city of ours, and declare that the citizens you conceived are in truth those actual progenitors of ours, of whom the priest told.

Timaios, 26C-D

The precise meaning of that sentence is obscure, but it certainly looks like a broad hint that, as many Platonists have suspected and as Aristotle seems to have understood, the Atlantis story was essentially a fictionized version of Plato's *Republic*. The remainder of the *Timaios* drops the Atlantis story and is given to a discourse on the nature of man and of the universe according to the Pythagorean philosophy, delivered by the character after whom this dialogue is titled.

Now we come to the sequel, the unfinished dialogue *Kritias* in which Kritias begins to tell in detail the Atlantean story which he had merely outlined in *Timaios*. That the dialogue was not finished is testified by Plutarch (*Solon*). It is not a case of a missing fragment; what Plato wrote we have. That he abandoned the dialogue at just the point he did abandon it is not at all surprising.

After a long-winded apology Kritias begins:

Now first of all we must recall the fact that 9000 is the sum of years since the war occurred, as is recorded, between the dwellers beyond the pillars of Herakles and all that dwelled within them; which war we have now to relate in detail.

Kritias, 108 E

Here is another one of Plato's inconsistencies, proving that this dialogue was never given its final polish and also that Plato's dates are not to be taken seriously. In *Timaios* Plato said that Athens was *created* 9000 years before; now he asserts that Atlantis *sank* 9000 years before. But there was that invasion which the newly created city could not very well be expected to stop almost singlehanded, and elsewhere Plato even says that "many generations" intervened between the two events. 802519

Kritias gives a brief résumé of his Atlantis story as told in *Timaios*, mentioning once more the "barrier of impassable mud" left by the sinking of Atlantis, then goes on with a detailed account of the proto-Athens against which Atlantis fought. When the gods were dividing up the earth after the creation, Athena and Hephaistos got Athens, and the former set up the Athenian state along the lines of Plato's *Republic*. The state was ruled by a communistic military caste and everybody was brave, handsome, and virtuous, just as the Red Army is described in *Pravda* and the Nazi S.A. used to be described in the *Völkischer Beobachter*. Nature also lived up to regulations, and the Greek peninsula was covered with deep fruitful soil in which grew official lush vegetation and which produced abundant crops according to plan.

That there never was such a prehistoric state is obvious. The institutions ascribed to proto-Athens are so patently those of the *Republic* (which in turn was an idealization of the authoritarian, rigid, militaristic Lycurgan constitution of the Sparta of Plato's own day) that no such coincidence is even remotely possible. Furthermore, Greece happens to have been so exhaustively picked over by archeologists that any remains of any reasonably large prehistoric city could not have escaped detection.

Then Kritias proceeds to describe Atlantis. As Athena received Athens, so Poseidon obtained Atlantis. Here dwelt the girl Kleito, daughter of the "earthborn" Leukippe and Euenor. Poseidon, filled with desire for Kleito, made her a home on the island, consisting of a hill with two springs, one hot, one cold, and surrounded by alternate rings of land and water, two of the former and three of the latter. Here he begat on Kleito five pairs of twin sons, the eldest being named Atlas. (Plato is taking very considerable liberties with the traditional Atlas myths in this story.) When they grew up, Poseidon divided Atlantis among his sons to rule as a confederacy of kings, of whom Atlas was to be the high king.

The land was exceedingly rich:

> . . . the island itself furnished most of the requirements of daily life—metals, to begin with, both the hard kind and the fusible kind, which are extracted by mining, and also that kind which is now known only by name but was more than a name then, there being mines of it in many places of the island, I mean *oreichalkōn* which was most precious of the metals then known, except gold. It brought forth in abundance all the timbers that a forest provides for the labors of carpenters; and of animals it produced a sufficiency, both of tame and wild. Moreover it contained a very large stock of elephants; for there was an ample food-supply not only for all the other animals which haunt the marshes and lakes and rivers, or the mountains or the plains, but likewise also for this animal, which of its nature is the largest and most voracious.

Kritias, 114E-115A

Plato's "orichalc" is a bit of a puzzle. A few commentators have tried to make out a case for amber, mostly on the grounds of its high value, but most are convinced that the reference is to an alloy. Just what it is supposed to be is hard to say, and the translation of the Greek word as "mountain bronze" is no help. Now the ancient world knew two alloys, bronze and *ēlektron*, or electrum. Bronze is an alloy of copper and tin, while electrum is an alloy of gold and silver.* Orichalc

---

* Brass is a copper-zinc alloy, but metallic zinc was not known till the Renaissance. The nearest the ancients got to brass was an alloy of copper with *cadmia*, a crude mixture of the oxides of several metals including zinc.

may have been a copper-silver alloy—we would now call it silver bronze—which would have many uses. But this is conjecture; the fact is that the ancients were incorrigibly inconsistent in their technical nomenclature.

As for the elephants of Atlantis, they are probably based upon the fact that elephants of a now extinct subspecies used to roam Morocco. Plato probably had heard about them and since, to him, Morocco was in the Far West too, there was no reason in his mind why there should not be elephants everywhere in the West.

Plato then lists the many food plants that grew in Atlantis and tells how Atlas and his descendants built the city of Atlantis on the south coast of the island. They interconnected Poseidon's rings of land and water by means of bridges and canals, built a royal palace on the central island, and bordered the waterways with walls of black, red, and white stone.

> And they covered with bronze, as though with a plaster, all the circumference of the wall which surrounded the outermost circle; and that of the inner one they coated with tin; and that which encompassed the acropolis itself with orichalc which sparkled like fire.
> The royal palace within the acropolis was arranged in this manner. In the center there stood a temple sacred to Kleito and Poseidon, which was reserved as holy ground, and encircled with a wall of gold; this being the very spot where at the beginning they had generated and brought to birth the family of the ten royal lines. Thither also they brought year by year from all the ten allotments their seasonable offering to do sacrifices to each of those princes. And the temple of Poseidon itself was a stade in length, three plethra in breadth [approx. 303.5 x 607 ft.] and of a height which appeared symmetrical therewith; and there was something of the barbaric in its appearance. All the exterior of the temple they coated with silver, save only the pinnacles, and these they coated with gold. As to the interior, they made the roof all of ivory in appearance, variegated with gold and silver and orichalc,

and all the rest of the walls and pillars and floors they covered with orichalc. And they placed therein golden statues. . . .

Kritias, 116B-117D

And so on, and so on. Gold and silver and orichalc; orichalc, silver, and gold. Indicative of wealth, but also indicative of a plentiful supply of metals, presumably in the vicinity as Plato has specifically said earlier. Having finally finished with the marvels of Atlantean architecture, Plato goes on to describe the racetracks, the parks, drill grounds and other public works, and then proceeds to the harbor. "And the shipyards were full of triremes and all the tackling that belongs to triremes . . ."

It is notable that the only two pieces of machinery mentioned by Plato are the trireme (*triērē*, supposedly invented by Ameinokles of Corinth about 700 B.C.) and the chariot. We don't know when the latter was invented, but chariots are not very well possible without domesticated horses or asses, and in 9600 B.C. these animals were not yet domesticated, especially in western Europe.

After describing a ceremony involving the capture and sacrifice of a bull in the enclosure of Poseidon, Plato proceeds to tell of the gradual decline of the Atlanteans. They deteriorated because "the portion of divinity within them was now becoming faint and weak through being ofttimes blended with a large measure of mortality, whereas the human temper was becoming dominant . . ."

And Zeus, the god of gods, who reigns by law, inasmuch as he has the gift of perceiving such things, marked how this righteous race was in evil plight, and desired to inflict punishment upon them, to the end that when chastised they might strike a truer note. Wherefore he assembled together all the gods into that abode which they honor most, standing as it does at the center of all the Universe, and beholding all things

that partake of generation; and when he had assembled them
he spake thus:

Kritias, 121B-C

This is the very end of the dialogue. That Plato stopped
writing at this point originally is quite understandable. When
one is about to announce the judgment of the highest god
one naturally wants to think carefully first; maybe sleep first
to gather both thoughts and strength. That he never touched
the dialogue afterwards and wrote the *Laws* instead will become understandable upon examination of everything that
went before.

Plato had very successfully written himself into a corner from which he could not escape. In *Timaios* he had told
how the earthquake destroyed both the proto-Athenian army
and all of Atlantis. He had to do that because neither of
them existed any more. But then he had proceeded along a
line which was supposed to reveal the ways of the gods to
mortals. Zeus had decided to chastise the Atlanteans to re-
form them. However, it had already been said that they had
been destroyed utterly, not merely chastised. And what had
they really done wrong? As far as the listener could tell
they had been merely human, certainly no worse than any
of the peoples or races that were still around. So where was
the divine justice? Another writer might have had the way
out to have Zeus chastise them first and then have later a destruction due to blind chance. But to Plato that would have
seemed like the materialism of Demokritos and his followers, of which he sternly disapproved. Being old, Plato simply
put his *Kritias* aside, unfinished because he did not know how
to finish it.

The main new element in the *Kritias,* as compared with
the *Timaios,* is the very minute description of the city, a de-

scription which does sound as if he had had a model to go by. Naturally one should not expect the model to correspond to the description in every respect; Plato did not write a street guide with detailed information about the public works. But one might hope for a city which was located a long distance to the west from Greece, which was a harbor town in a country where metal was abundant. And, if possible, a city generally known to the Greeks through intermediaries and tradition.

Such a city actually existed, and it was known to the Greeks both through intermediaries and through their own literary tradition. It has been said earlier that Plato is the first source for Atlantis and according to strict judgment the only one.

However, it seems that the actual city which served as a model for his fabulous metropolis had served as a model before, for the same purpose. At first glance the similarities between Plato's Atlantis and Homer's Scheria are considerable, and a more careful comparison enhances these similarities. And both are quite similar to the actual ancient city of Tartessos on the shores of the Atlantic near modern Cadiz in metal-rich Spain. Tartessos—the Biblical Tarshish, Jonah's destination—was located at the mouth of the Guadalquivir River. The affinities of the Tartessians are not known for sure. A line in the *Odyssey* states that the "Scherians" looked different from the Greek Odysseus. The writer Arrian thought that the Tartessians may have been Phoenicians, but it seems as if Tartessos and Phoenician Gades (Cadiz) were competing trade centers. They may have been Cretans.

The city of Tartessos flourished as a trading and mining center for an unknown number of centuries. About 500 B.C. it disappeared—just how or why, no man now knows.

The similarities between historical Tartessos, Homeric

Scheria, and Platonic Atlantis have been carefully compiled by the German geographer Dr. Richard Hennig. The following table is a condensed version of Dr. Hennig's compilation; the main difference between the three is that Atlantis is supposed to have been on an island; Homer's Scheria (never mind what some schoolbooks say, read the *Odyssey* directly) is *not* specified as having been on an island but near a large river which suggests a mainland; while the real Tartessos may, at best, have been situated on an island formed by various arms of the Guadalquivir.

TARTESSOS:	ATLANTIS:	SCHERIA:
Located in the extreme west of Europe. Very rich city.	Island to the west of Gibraltar, old and rich country.	In the extreme west, at "the end of the world," prosperous.
Near mouth of large river but not directly at the seashore.	Main city not directly at the seashore, near a canal.	Scheria near mouth of large river, but not visible from the sea.
Trade activities involved much sailing, unknown whether they built their own ships.	Harbor and shipyards full of triremes.	By definition the best sailors in the world, having the fastest ships, "do not care about quivers and bows."
Shape of city unknown. Flourished for a long time.	High walls and towers although no enemy ever threatened Atlantis.	"Towering walls . . . a marvel to behold," even though "no enemy ever designs to disturb our peace."
Main building not known in detail, said to have been "towering" (on a hill?)	Castle elaborate and of barbaric splendor, see earlier quote.	The castle has brazen walls, silver doors with golden handles, bronzen the threshold.
The "Temple of Herakles" is mentioned	Splendid Temple of Poseidon.	Temple of Poseidon, on a square "fitted

		with flagstones hauled from the quarries and deeply imbedded"; a paved street was the height of luxury then.
in one breath with Tartessos and Gades.		
This temple is credited with two wells, one warm, one cold.	Temple of Poseidon with two springs, one warm, one cold.	Two springs in the castle garden.
Tartessos and Gades two cities, near each other.	Atlas and Gadeiros, twin sons of Poseidon, Atlas high king over nine other kings.	Alkinoös, grandson of Poseidon, high king over twelve other kings.
Tartessos apparently not trading directly with the Mediterranean oikoumenë.	No trade contact between Atlanteans and Greeks.	Scherians "dwell apart . . . nor ever doth visit us other of mortals."
Large plain in back of the city, mountains in the north.	Mountains in the north, south of the mountains large plain.	Scheria near a plain which is suitable for carts and chariots.
Ten-foot tide in the mouth of the Guadalquivir.	———	River is stemmed by tidal action when Odysseus reaches it.

One, two or even three such striking similarities could be coincidences; ten are too many. Tartessos was obviously the model for Atlantis, some of the features possibly derived from Homer. It is also to be noted that the *Odyssey* does not treat Scheria as a place of past glory, for it still existed. But in Plato's time Tartessos was a memory—like Atlantis. A few items may or may not fit: we have no idea whether the bull-killing ceremony was a Tartessian custom or not. But it was a custom on Minoan Crete, which also resembled Tartessos-Scheria-Atlantis in being a sea power. Plato may well have filled in some detail which was missing in the traditions known to him from the otherwise generally similar Crete.

And here the story of Atlantis stops somewhat abruptly,

just like the *Kritias*. There was the fabulous city in the Far West, there was the Babylonian belief in catastrophes, there was the inundation of Atalantë which looked like an example, there was the actual Greek double victory against overwhelming odds . . . and there was, by no means least, Plato's conviction about the way a state should be run. They all flowed together into a tale of great impressiveness and lasting charm.

But the continent of Atlantis would never have appeared on any map of the real world, no matter when drawn.

CHAPTER II

The Long Homecoming

AT THE BEGINNING OF THE STORY OF EXPLORATION STAND A few terse travel reports and a gigantic epic, the prototype of all sea stories.

The reports are those of a couple of Egyptian and Hebrew trading ventures. Thus in 1492 B.C. (remarkably coincident date!) Queen Hatshepsut of Egypt sent a fleet to Punt, on the Red Sea, and in the next century Rameses III dispatched a force into the Nubian Desert. Then, in the tenth century B.C. Shelomoh ben-Dawid, or Solomon son of David, King of Judah and Israel, formed a profitable partnership with King Hiram of Tyre. They built a fleet in the Mediterranean and sent it on three-year round trips to Tarshish in the Far West for "gold, and silver, ivory, and apes, and peacocks" (*1 Kings* x, 22). They built another fleet at the head of the Red Sea and sent to Ophir for gold. Hiram furnished "shipmen that had knowledge of the sea" (*1 Kings* ix, 27) while Solomon supplied a guard of his warlike subjects.

The location of "Ophir" is still in doubt and subject of much inconclusive discussion. But as for Tarshish the answer is furnished by the next main source for ancient knowledge of geography, the epic mentioned in the opening paragraph: the *Odyssey* of Homer. The *Odyssey* is almost our only source of knowledge of what the Greeks believed about the world they lived in during the early centuries of the first millennium before Christ—beliefs, moreover, which were based mainly on secondhand accounts derived from the same Phoenician "shipmen that had knowledge of the sea."

But you cannot say *Odyssey* without drawing a deep breath first.

Barring the Bible, no other work of ancient literature has been reissued so many times in its original language, has been translated wholly and in part, in prose and in rhymes, in hexameters like the original and in free verse, into all the important and some of the unimportant languages of to-day. The translations alone would fill the bookshelves of a small room, and the commentary would require a whole library. The work has furnished the common noun "siren" to the English language, in which "odyssey," "Circe," "lotus-eater's life," "Trojan horse" and "between Scylla and Charybdis" have become worn-out figures of speech. Names from the *Odyssey* have been freely bestowed upon modern people and things: "Ulysses Grant," "Ithaca, New York," "H.M.S. *Calypso*," not to mention the names of several hundred minor planets and a few craters on the moon.

Students of history, literature, philology, mythology, and archeology have argued endlessly whether Homer lived, whether he was one man or a dozen, whether he was an original poet or a mere compiler, where he came from, how much he knew, what variety of Greek dialect he used, whether he could write or composed by memory, and so on. Nor do the countless disputes over his works show any signs of dying down.

In classical times people took it for granted that the *Iliad* and the *Odyssey* had been composed by a blind poet from Ionia (the west coast of Asia Minor) named *Homēros* who had wandered about the blue Aegean Sea singing lays to the tune of his lyre. They attributed his birth to a dozen

FIG. 2. Sketch map of southern Italy and Sicily, showing the locations of places identified with some of the early adventures of Odysseus.

different cities and dated it anywhere from 1159 to 685 B.C. Although some spurious "biographies" of Homer circulated, there was no "hard" knowledge of his life beyond what little could be inferred from the poems. And while the Greeks and Romans produced a vast literature of commentary on these epics, few took seriously the contention of the *chōrizontes* or "separatists" like Xenon that the two poems were by two different authors.

Then in 1795 Friedrich August Wolf of Halle and Berlin startled the academic world by asserting that "Homer" was not a man at all, but the collective name adopted by or applied to a whole school of poets who composed a series of heroic lays not combined into the present *Iliad* and *Odyssey* till the time of Peisistratos, a dictator of Athens in the sixth century B.C. The uproar caused by this pronouncement still resounds. Among modern Homerists some insist on one Homer, a few believe in two, and some in an indefinite number. And those who believe in more than one Homer disagree as to which author wrote what part of the epics and when the parts were assembled into their present form.

At any rate, the works deal with events supposed to have taken place back in the thirteenth or twelfth century B.C.: events mainly fictional, though no doubt based upon some few scraps of historical fact, could we but filter them out. As to when they were composed, parts of them go back to around 900 B.C. or earlier. The poems are thought to have taken at least rough shape in the eighth century B.C. and to have acquired their modern form (save for minor variora) in the time of Peisistratos, around 530 B.C. You might call Peisistratos the "publisher" of the first complete, definitive edition.

Both poems deal with one of the major themes of Greek myth: the Siege of Troy. They do not however deal exhaustively with it; the *Iliad* confines itself to the story of the Wrath of Achilles at the Siege, while the *Odyssey* narrates the Homecoming of Odysseus. These poems, furthermore, were but two out of eight or more comprising the Trojan cycle of epics, which included others like the *Sack of Ilion* and the *Homecomings*. There were in addition several other whole cycles like the *Argonautika* and the *Herakleia*. None of these many epics, alas, has come down complete except the *Iliad* and the *Odyssey*, which survived by virtue of having been picked for public recitation at the festival of the Panathenaia during the fifth century B.C. Many fragments of the other epics, some attributed to Homer and some to other more or less legendary bards like Stasinos, have come down as quotations, and we know their plots from the many later Greek plays, poems, and mythological treatises based upon them.

While men of letters generally praise the *Iliad* as the more artistic of the two epics, the *Odyssey* is far more important to the study of geographical legends. The significant part of the *Odyssey* (from our point of view) comprises only four out of the twenty-four books: Books IX to XII, the *Tales of Odysseus at the Court of King Alkinoös*, as Victor Bérard (who contributed fifteen volumes to the library of Homeric commentary) called them. It is these "Tales" which we think of when the *Odyssey* is mentioned, because they contain the liveliest and most imaginative parts of the epic and because they mirror the geographical lore of the period of their composition, the beliefs of the Greeks about "the inmost sea of all the earth"—the Mediterranean.

To give you an idea of the setting of the "Tales": Odysseus,* King of Ithaka, has played an active part on the side of the Achaeans (Greeks) at the Siege of Troy; he it was who devised the final stratagem of the Trojan Horse. Now that

---

* The Greek name *Odysseus* developed into the Latin *Ulyxes* or *Ulysses* via intermediate forms like *Olysseus*.

Troy has fallen, he sets out for home with twelve ships, but is blown out of his course . . . and ten years later shows up alone and destitute in the country of the Phaiakes or Phæacians whose king, Alkinoös (Latin, *Alcinoüs*), he entertains with an account of his previous adventures. This king sends him home in a ship, and with the help of the gods Odysseus regains his kingdom.

The actual structure of the epic is more complicated than that: It starts with the conference of the gods on the question of what to do about Odysseus, then shifts to Ithaka where Penelopeia, the wife of the hero, is standing off a horde of suitors who are besieging her, and tells much of the story in flashbacks. Our main concern, however, is with the four books wherein Odysseus regales the court of Alkinoös.

To identify the places mentioned in the *Tales* (on the supposition that the poet had real places in mind) and to explain the hero's adventures have been favorite hobbies of scholars over the last twenty-five centuries. It is a fascinating but treacherous pastime, for it is fatally easy to find places to fit "Homer's" poetical descriptions and assume that those are they—ignoring the fact that others have fitted the allusions just as well to other locations.

The Greeks themselves, who began the pastime, added to the confusion because when they went forth from the Aegean they were always on the lookout for places that corresponded to Homer's descriptions, and when they found them they applied the names from the *Odyssey* forthwith. Hence later scholars, coming upon these names, thought they had found the places mentioned in Homer because they "still bore the same name." Actually it worked the other way round: the poet had invented names for places described to him, and centuries later his admirers had plastered these names on any sites that seemed to fit his specifications.

Moreover, the local inhabitants of these places developed a fondness for "Odysseus slept here" legends as tourist-bait, until by Roman times it was believed that Odysseus had founded Lisbon and had voyaged as far north as Scotland.

When Odysseus was sitting among the Phæacian lords at the banquet table of Alkinoös, the latter observed that his strange guest wept when the bard Demodokos sang of the fall of Troy, and eloquently urged Odysseus to tell his story: "Had you some valiant kinsman by marriage who fell at Troy, one next to your own blood relations?"

Odysseus at last confessed his identity and began his tale: After leaving Troy his fleet lands on the Thracian coast, where they raid the city of the Kikones for loot, this being in an age when international aggression was perfectly proper if you could get away with it. Although the attack is successful, the men get drunk and give the Kikones time to rally, and as a result are driven back to their ships with loss. Then:

> Verily now had I come unscathed to the land of my fathers
> Had not the stream of the sea and the roll as I rounded Maléa
> Carried me, under the stress of the Boreas, south of Kythera
> Hence nine days I was borne by the ruinous blast of the storm-winds
> Over the teeming deep. On the tenth day we arrived at the mainland
> Land of the Lotus-eaters whose food is the fruit of a flower . . .*

Considering all Homer's data: the point of departure, the general direction ("Boreas" from the North or Northeast, blowing ships that could not sail close-hauled but only before the wind) and the time involved, the land of the Lotophagoi is obviously somewhere along the North African coast be-

* *Odyssey*, IX, 79ff. Nearly all the quotations from the *Odyssey* in this chapter are from the Cotterill translation (London: 1912) which uses the original meter and keeps each word in the line where Homer put it.

tween the Gulf of Sidra in Libya and the Gulf of Qabès in Tunisia. The ancients, in fact, were sure that it was the Island of Jerba in the Gulf of Qabès, and they may have been right as to the general if not the specific locale.

> Now, whoever did eat of the fruit honeysweet of the lotus
> Felt no longer the wish to return nor tidings to carry
> Caring for naught but to stay with the Lotus-eaters for ever . . .

The "lotos" was not one of the pond lilies now called by that name, but the jujube: the fruit of a small tree, *Zizyphus spina* or one of its relatives, which looks something like a large date and is still relished in those parts.

It is not surprising that the men wish to stop for a while, since they have just been blown for nine tempestuous days across the sea in the little cockleshells that passed for ships in those days, without adequate provisions, protection, or sleeping accommodations. When they are rested, however, the "magic spell" is broken and off they go.

So far we have followed our guileful hero's footsteps with fair confidence that we knew where we were, but how much farther can we continue to do this? We don't really know, except in a vague way, just how far Homer's accurate geographical knowledge extended.

We do know pretty well what sort of picture of the world was held by the Greeks in the sixth century B.C., the century of Peisistratos the tyrant and of Hekataios the first Greek geographer. We also know that early in the first millennium B.C., after the fall of the Cretan civilization, the Greeks were a pretty barbarous lot who knew little enough geography. They did not begin to colonize outside the Aegean until the eighth century B.C., and did not definitely penetrate the western Mediterranean until the seventh, and settle there permanently until the sixth. As for map knowledge, there is no evidence that Homer was at all map-conscious, for Greek cartography only began in earnest with the world map of Anaximandros in the sixth century B.C.

Furthermore it would normally be a safe assumption that their geographical knowledge expanded continuously during this era, from 1000 to 500 B.C. But in this case the expansion may not have been uniform; there may have been an actual recession after Homer as a result of the rise of Carthage, which enforced its claim to a commercial monopoly in the western Mediterranean by the brusque but effective method of drowning the crews of any non-Carthaginian ships found in those waters.

Opinions on Homer's wisdom have varied widely ever since ancient times. Anti-Homer classical writers like Kallimachos of Kyrenë tended to restrict Homer's knowledge to the eastern Mediterranean, while those of the pro-Homer party like Strabo affirmed that the poet had known the lands and seas all the way from the Atlantic to the Black Sea. These Homerophiles reacted to criticism of Homer as do Fundamentalist Christians to criticism of the Bible, and sought like Bérard and others in modern times to identify all the places mentioned in the poems.

The argument has come right down to modern times: Samuel Butler even wrote a book to prove that a young lady of Drepanum (modern Trapani) in Sicily wrote the *Odyssey*, putting herself in as Nausikaä, and that all the places in the poem are Sicilian. Others have averred that Odysseus made his journey around the Black Sea instead of the Mediterranean, or that he got as far as the British Isles, or that all the places in the *Odyssey* are wholly fictitious.

Disregarding these eccentric speculations and making what use we can of Homer's use of names and descriptions, it seems likely that he knew the Aegean Sea and its shores and islands well from firsthand acquaintance. He had a fairly reliable secondhand knowledge of such surrounding areas as Egypt, Thrace, and the west coast of Greece, though he makes mistakes in describing them. Further to the west he has a vague and garbled knowledge of southern Italy and Sicily—not from Greek sources, for Greeks had not gone thither yet, but from the Phoenicians. (Bérard thought he even used a Phoenician *periplous* or sailing guide as an aid in plotting his story-line.) He has heard of the tribes of that region, the Sikeloi and Sikanioi, but has no clear concept of the shape of their lands—whether they are islands or parts of the mainland.

And west beyond this Homer's knowledge gets thinner and more dilute until one can barely detect the connection between romance and reality.

Odysseus leaves the land of the Lotophagoi and after an unspecified but seemingly short voyage:

> Unto the land of the Kyklops, a race overbearing and lawless
> Soon we arrived. Here, trusting the favor of powers immortal
> None with his hands e'er planteth a plant or tills with the
> ploughshare
> Yet untilled and unplanted, behold, all groweth in plenty
> Wheat and barley and vine . . .
>
> *Odyssey*, IX, 106ff.

Looking around for hosts or for loot they enter a large cave. With the coming of darkness the Kyklops appears, a giant with one large round eye (*ōps kyklias*) in the middle of his forehead, and an antisocial disposition. He is Polyphemos, the "much-discussed one," driving in his flock of giant sheep.

If the audience snickered at the name, it sat up with shock as the rhapsode continued: The Kyklops, despite Odysseus' appeal to his better nature, catches up two of the men, slams them against the floor, and munches the bloody bodies.

Then he settles down to sleep after closing the cave entrance by a boulder too heavy for human hands to move.

Next morning two more are devoured; then the Kyklops leaves, carefully closing the cave behind him. Odysseus and his men sit around gloomily, pondering plans to escape.

That night Odysseus offers Greek wine to Polyphemos, so heavy that the Greeks always mix it with water, but Odysseus prudently refrains from mentioning this custom. In the ensuing conversation Odysseus, asked his name, replies:

"Nobody called me my mother, and nothing but Nobody call me all my companions . . ."

The Kyklops, failing to recognize the ruse, answers with Kyklopean delicacy that as a special favor, now, then, Nobody, you shall be the last to be eaten.

After eating two more men and drinking the wine the giant falls into a drunken sleep, belching and vomiting, tossing and moaning. Odysseus and his men, stiffening their sinews with the courage of despair, heat a pole in the fire and thrust it into the monster's eye, pressing and drilling. The giant leaps up, his eye socket sizzling, and his roars bring the other Kyklopes to the cave, where they call in to ask what the racket is all about. Polyphemos, in a wonderful passage of rising anxiety, screams that Nobody has tried to kill him, not by strength but by craft. The others shake their heads and shamble off, muttering that if Nobody has tried to kill you the pain must come from Zeus; offer a prayer to thy sire, earth shaking Poseidon . . .

Next morning Odysseus and his men escape with the sheep. Aboard ship Odysseus mischievously shouts his real name to Polyphemos, who hurls a mountaintop at him but, being blind, misses.

Where are we now?

A tradition almost as old as the *Odyssey* itself insists that the land of the Kyklopes was Sicily. Virgil spoke of *Aetnaeos Cyclopas,* showing that he thought Polyphemos a personification of Mount Aetna which, towering up from the shore of the sea, fits Homer's description of Polyphemos quite well. The one big eye could be the crater, and the roaring and stone throwing suggest an eruption. The caves, the statement that the Kyklopes "dwell apart on the crests of the mountain," and the marvelous fertility of the soil all fit.

It happens that Homer also mentions Sicily under its old name of Sikania, without indicating any connection between it and the Kyklopes. But in the state of his knowledge that is not surprising. One Phoenician could tell him about the land of the Sikanioi and another about the land of the roaring volcano without bothering to inform him that they were one and the same.

Fleeing from the land of the Kyklopes, the adventurers seem to bid farewell for a while to bad fortune. They arrive in what may be called a neutral port:

> Now did we come to the isle Aeolian, home of the monarch
> Aiolos, Hippotas' son, by the gods everlasting belovèd.
> This is an island that floats, and a rampart is builded around it,
> Bronzen, unbroken; and sheer from the water the precipice
> rises.
>
> *Odyssey,* X, 1-4

Aiolos, the poet says, receives Odysseus with great cordiality. Being the dispenser of winds he assures Odysseus' safe return by putting into a bag all the winds but the Zephyr which was to blow the wanderers home, and giving the bag to Odysseus with instructions to open it after reaching his destination.

Poseidon, however, has listened to his blinded son's

prayers for vengeance. When the ships are in sight of Ithaka he craftily arouses the curiosity of Odysseus' men about the bulging bag while their chief is asleep. Suspecting treasure they open it—and out rush the howling winds to sweep the ships to sea again. After a stormy voyage they find themselves back at the island of Aiolos, who is much disconcerted to see them again so soon. When Odysseus explains, Aiolos refuses any further help to men evidently hated by the gods, and sadly the ships set sail once more.

Now, what is the island of Aiolos?

As those who denied any geographical basis for Homer's concepts have pointed out, real islands do not float. On the other hand tradition long identified Aiolia with the Lipari Islands off the west coast of southern Italy, where Mussolini used to confine his political enemies.

Richard Hennig, going on from there, made a plausible identification with one of these islands: that called Volcano (ancient Thermessa), an upstanding volcanic cone with a smoke plume still used by fishermen to tell the direction of the wind. Aiolos's name "dispenser of winds" could refer to a belief that the winds come from the cone. Volcano's steep, almost unscalable ring-wall of rock discolored by sulphur with a metallic sheen also fits Homer's sheer bronze wall encircling the island.

And the island does float—or at least parts of it do! The outer surface consists partly of pumice, a spongy, porous lava full of imprisoned gas bubbles. If stones from the island would float it was a natural inference that the island itself did too.*

Before we press this identification too far, however, there

* During World War II some American sailors on an island in the southwest Pacific got a shock. Wishing to mark a shoal with a buoy, they roped a boulder they found on shore to a log they picked up and dropped them into the water at the right place—and the rock floated while the log sank. The boulder was pumice, the log ironwood.

is one catch to take into account. Homer makes the West Wind waft Odysseus eastward for nine days to within sight of his homeland, which fits the Lipari Islands fine as to distance and latitude—except that he would have to sail right across southern Italy, mountains and all: a task to daunt even such an accomplished mariner as Odysseus the son of Laertes!

Evidently, then, either Aiolia was not one of the Lipari Islands or Homer had no clear idea of the distribution of land masses in the Italo-Sicilian region. And the latter seems the more plausible. Homer was in much the position *vis-à-vis* the western regions as an educated European was with regard to the Americas about the year 1500. The latter knew that Columbus and others had found new lands across the Atlantic, and had even heard some particulars about these places and their people, but he did not know whether these new lands were continents or islands only, and, if the former, whether Asia had been attained or wholly new lands discovered.

> Six days long did we voyage, the nights no less than the day-
> time
> Till, on the seventh, we came to the mountainous stronghold
> of Lamos
> Laistrygonian Telepylos, where shepherd to shepherd
> Calls as one comes home with his flock and the other is
> starting.
>
> *Odyssey*, X, 8off.

This is the land of the giant Laistrygones, to whom the Greek sailors mean but one thing: food. Hordes of the giant cannibals set upon the visitors and hurl boulders down upon the ships, which are all wrecked except that of Odysseus, whose men row frantically to safety. Describing this ill-mannered country further, Homer says:

> Here might twofold wages be won by a man that was sleep-
> less

Once as a herd of kine, once white flocks tending as shepherd
Such in the land is the nearness of night and of day in their
    courses.
Now when at last we had come to the glorious haven (around
    it
Both to the right and the left is a cliff's precipitous rampart
Two bluff headlands as well just opposite one to the other
Out to the mouth of the haven and make right narrow the
    entry) . . .

Odyssey, X, 84ff.

The Laistrygonian Coast has long been a stumbling block
to commentators. Although tradition claims the harbor of Sicilian Leontini as the Telepylos ("Wide-gates," referring no
doubt to the headlands), six days' sailing sounds long from
Volcano to Leontini—though of course the fleet may have
meandered a bit. Some recent Homerists have pointed out
that the description of the harbor fits Balaklava on the Crimean shore of the Black Sea, where the Light Brigade
charged. No doubt it does; but another commentator sailed
up and down the Mediterranean and came home with a list
of some fifteen other places the description fits too.

While Bérard was sure Sardinia was meant, others, taking their cues from the lines about the herdsman's double
wages, moved the Laistrygonian Coast out of the Mediterranean and Black Seas entirely. That statement, they said, must
refer to the Far North where the nights are short enough in
summer to speak of a "nearness of night and of day in their
courses." The Greeks might have known of conditions in the
Far North because after all they had amber from the shores
of the Baltic and North Seas. Why, even Krates of Mallos,
around 170 B.C., identified Laistrygonia with "Thule". . . .

However, we may safely discard this theory as nonsense.
Even though the Greeks (like the Cretans before them) knew
amber that had come down over trade routes from Pomerania
and Denmark, there is no evidence that any single merchant

made the whole trip; rather the stuff was passed from hand to hand. And if Homer had meant to describe the short nights of the North he would probably have spoken of the nearness of the days to each other. The lines probably refer to a custom of grazing sheep and cattle on the same pasture, the cattle by day and the sheep (whose woolly coats protect them from mosquitoes) by night.

The old tradition that put the Laistrygones in Sicily gets support from another quarter: an explanation that also disposes of the Kyklopes, advanced by the great European paleontologist Professor Othenio Abel of Vienna.

Here is the story: About the middle of the fourteenth century Giovanni Boccaccio (he of the *Decameron*) announced in his *Genealogia Deorum* that the remains of Polyphemos had been found in a cave near Trapani in Sicily, thus vindicating Empedokles of Agrigentum who in 440 B.C., trying in his turn to defend Homer, claimed that a race of giants once dwelt in Sicily. These bones, Boccaccio wrote, indicated giants 300 feet tall.

The bones were carefully saved and 300 years later the learned Jesuit, Athanasius Kircher (who had theories on everything under the sun), examined them and announced that Boccaccio had exaggerated: the giants were only thirty feet high. Otherwise, however, he confirmed Boccaccio, who confirmed Empedokles, who confirmed Homer.

"Polyphemos" is now unhappily lost, though we know what the bones were from similar blunders elsewhere in Europe and similar finds in Sicilian caves. They were the bones of elephants.

During the Pleistocene period, of several hundred thousand years ago, Europe was inhabited at various times by several species of elephant, rhinoceros, and hippopotamus. There were three species of elephant, whose ranges moved

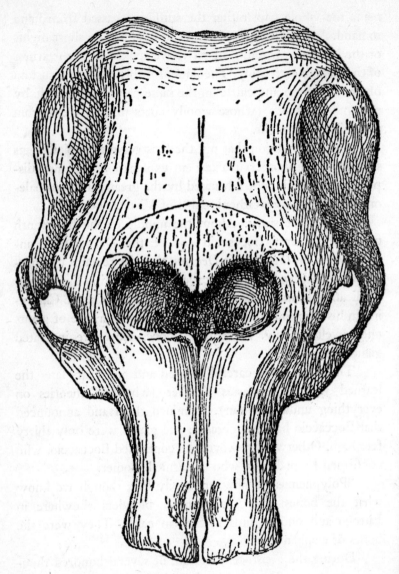

FIG. 3. Elephant's skull without tusks, head-on view (after Othenio Abel).

north and south as the climate varied: the smallish woolly mammoth (*Elephas primigenius*), which the Aurignac men drew with such verve on cave walls, in the North; and in the South two: *Elephas meridonalis* and *Elephas* (or *Paraloxodonta*) *antiquus*, which looked respectively rather like the modern Asiatic and African elephants but bigger.

Whenever the bones of any of these beasts were found during historic times they were always ascribed to giants or dragons until a whole collection of Biblical, mythological, and specially invented giants accumulated. The great Cuvier in his *Récherches sur les ossemens fossiles* (1824) devoted considerable space to debunking these giants.

Now, Abel first pointed out just why these "giants" were believed to be Kyklopes. Though most people nowadays know an elephant's skull when they see it, imagine that you are looking at one without ever having heard of an elephant. It does look rather like a human skull on a vast scale, doesn't it? Not a very prepossessing sort of man, but still more like a man than like a wolf or cow or any other of the animals with which a European of Homer's time would be acquainted. And when you look at the thing from the front, you are struck by the fact that instead of two eye sockets where you would expect them, there is a single hole that looks like two sockets merged together in the middle of the forehead. Actually this hole is the nasal opening, the real eye sockets being around to the sides where they cannot be seen from in front.

Naturally the Mediterranean sailors of 2,500 to 3,000 years ago, not being osteologists, took these skulls for those of one-eyed giants five or six times the size of normal men. Even a simple sailor could see that these giants must have been hideous beings, with their low crania, monstrously wide bony noses, narrow pointed chins, huge tusks, and single eyes in the middle of their foreheads. When they got home it was the most natural thing in the world to report these giants, not as mere bones, but as live and ferocious monsters by whom the valiant voyagers just escaped being eaten.

This explanation applies not only to the Kyklopes but also to the Sicilian Laistrygones. Except for the single eye, the Laistrygones are virtual duplicates of the Kyklopes, with their size, cannibalism, and habit of hurling rocks at ships. Such duplication is common in mythology: For instance the episode in *Genesis* xii, where Abraham tries to pass his wife off as his sister but is found out, is repeated with only minor changes in *Genesis* xx, and again (with Isaac as the protagonist) in *Genesis* xxvi. It was to be expected that the giant reports should be confused and that those who stayed home should try to group them into Kyklops stories and Laistrygon stories, using the "single eye" as the distinguishing mark, just as Europeans long tried to distinguish the unicorn from the Indian rhinoceros, both originally one and the same beast.*

After this disaster Odysseus and his surviving comrades pass on to a more enchanting scene—literally enchanting, for their remaining ship reaches Aiaia, the island of the beautiful witch Kirkë, daughter of the Sun and granddaughter of the other sea-god Okeanos.

This time, save for a casual mention of cliffs and an oak forest on the island, there is nothing to tie the site of the episode to any real place. In fact Aiaia seems to be one of the few places Homer invented out of whole cloth.

True, the Italians, backed by Bérard, claim that Monte Circeo (a mountain on the Italian coast south of Rome which looks like an island from the sea) is Aiaia. Others identify it

* For the whole story of the unicorn legend, see Chapter i of co-author Ley's *The Lungfish, the Dodo, & the Unicorn.*

with Malta or with an island at the head of the Adriatic Sea. But so sparse are the clues this time that to make Aiaia a real place you have to assume that, because Homer used real places as a basis for some incidents in the *Odyssey*, he must have used real places for *all*, and could not have imagined one if it suited him. Which is not only bad logic but also a libel against the Greek imagination.

Kirkë, you remember, turns Odysseus' companions into swine, but their leader rescues them with the aid of a magical herb he gets from Hermes. After the spell is broken they all stay on the island, loafing, for a year. (Their early conflict seems to have been forgiven and forgotten, for from other sources—not the *Odyssey*—we learn that Odysseus begat a son Telegonos upon Kirkë. Like the Greek gods, the Greek heroes never passed up an amatory opportunity.)

At last the wanderers begin to yearn for home again. Kirkë gives them what help she can: Although she cannot send them home directly against the wishes of the higher god Poseidon, she warns Odysseus of the troubles in wait for him and advises him to go farther on to the entrance of Hades, where the ghost of the seer Teiresias will give him further directions.

Whither? It is usually assumed that the witch directs him westward, though actually she tells him that Boreas (the North Wind) will bear him along. Moreover she instructs him: ". . . when by your ship you have crossed the Ocean Stream, beach your barque by the deep, eddying flood upon the rugged shore, at Persephone's grove of tall poplars and seed-shedding willows, and you yourself go into the dismal domain of Hades."

You can easily see that Homer's places are becoming more and more hazy with distance. His voyagers are nearing the very rim of the world, where the sun plunges into the sea at night and where the dead pass underground. As far as this never-never land corresponds to anything in the real world, Odysseus was nearing the Atlantic Ocean.

Set was already the sun and darkened was every roadway
Ere to the bounds we arrived of the fathomless stream of the
   ocean
Here the Kimmerian people inhabit a land and a city.
Shrouded in darkness of mist and of cloud, since never upon
   them
Glorious Helios looks down with his radiant daylight
Neither whenever he mounteth the starry expanses of heaven
Nor as again to the earth he returns and from heaven de-
   scendeth;
Ever a darkness of death o'erhangs these pitiful mortals.
                                             Odyssey, XI, 12ff.

Following Kirkë's directions they land and, by necromancy, conjure up the spirits of their former comrades at the Siege of Troy. Here the ghost of fleet-footed Achilles* makes his mournful remark that he "had rather be a poor man's serf than king over all the dead."

Where are they?

The mention of the eternal fog of the region may refer either to a section of the Moroccan coast noted for dense fogs in summer and fall, Pliny's *Mare tenebrosum*, or it might simply mean the normal weather of the Atlantic. For as you pass out of the Strait of Gibraltar to westward, you go from one climatic zone to another and much cloudier one. To a sailor accustomed to the cloudless Mediterranean summers, the Atlantic with its frequent overcasts and storms any time of year would seem a fearsome place, especially in the centuries before the invention of the compass enabled mariners to orient themselves regardless of clouds.

* The Greek form is *Achilleus*.

And who are the "Kimmerian people"? It is very odd that Homer should bring them in at this point. History does know such a people, the Gimri or Gimirai, steppe-dwelling nomads akin to the Persians who swept from their homeland north of the Black Sea into Asia Minor in the seventh century B.C. Now, if Homer's Kimmerioi and the Kimmerioi or Cimmerians of later historians are the same, Homer must have been pretty far off in his directions to put those Easterners in the Far West. Perhaps he had heard the name without knowing in which direction these barbarians dwelt.

Or there is one other remote possibility. The Greeks got their tin from Britain via various intermediaries, and it is just barely possible that the name of the Keltic British tribe of the Cymry may have come to Homer's ears and been confused with the eastern Gimri.

After a brief return from the Ocean Stream to Aiaia, Odysseus sets forth on a series of adventures that again take him into the Far West—or at least that is the impression. Kirkë warns him that he must first pass the rocks of the Sirens, three sea nymphs who will try to lure him to disaster with their song. This peril they will surmount by stuffing their ears with wax. If Odysseus wishes to hear the songs without losing his life, he should have his men bind him to the mast with unplugged ears, and with orders that, should he command them to release him, they should only tie him the tighter.

Now, there are three rocks off the coast of Italy, in the Bay of Salerno, within sight of the coast. Tradition claims that these rocks, once owned by the Russian dancer Leonid Massine, are the Sirens' rocks. They were certainly dangerous once because during the thirteenth or fourteenth century the largest of them, significantly named Briganti, was a pirate base. A few years ago it was reported that human bones had been found in caves in these rocks, and imaginative Italian writers asserted that these bones might "prove" the legend of the Sirens. Well—we don't know how old these bones really are, and almost every island in the Mediterranean has been used as a pirate base at some time or other. Still, it's a suggestion.

Then Kirkë advises Odysseus to avoid the Planktai or Clashing Rocks, a feature boldly borrowed by Homer from the older epic of the *Argosy**, and which properly refers to the Bosporus at the entrance to the Black Sea. Instead he shall take a course between

> . . . twain rocks, one reaches to heaven
> Lifting a sharp-peaked crest, and a cloud aye hangeth around it
> Blue-black, never receding—nor ever the cloudless aether
> Lieth about this peak in the season of summer and autumn
> Nor might ever a mortal ascend or ever descend it
> Nay, not e'en if his hand and his feet were twenty in number.
> Such is the slippery smoothness thereof, as of stone that is polished.
> Right in the midst of the rock there gapeth a shadowy cavern
> Turned to the gloom of the west—t'ward Erebus—even the quarter
> Whither the hollow ship ye shall steer, o noble Odysseus.
> Never a man in the prime of his strength from his hollow vessel
> Launching a shaft from a bow could reach to the mouth of the cavern.
> Here inhabiteth Skylla, a howling and horrible monster. . . .
> *Odyssey*, XII, 73ff.

* As Homer refers to the *Argosy*, the Argonautic legend cycle must be at least as old as the Trojan. However, the oldest complete versions we have are those of Pindar (fifth cent. B.C.) and Apollonios Rhodios (third); both very late, by which time the story had been so euhemerized or rationalized that there is not much geographical legend left in it.

After describing Skylla, Kirkë goes on:

Now for the second rock,—it is lower to look at, Odysseus;
Nigh to the other it lies; 'twere easy to reach with an arrow.
Growing thereon is a fig-tree tall with luxuriant leafage.
'Neath it the deep black water is swallowed by mighty
    Charybdis.
Thrice in the day doth she swallow it down and thrice she
    rejects it.

Odyssey, XII, 101-110

Charybdis is evidently a whirlpool.

There was a widespread theory that the Passage of Skylla
and Charybdis was the Strait of Messina between Italy and
Sicily, for the latter does contain a harmless little eddy, the
Garofalo Whirlpool, which sometimes scares people in small
boats by spinning their craft round and round before they
can row clear. But the likelier explanation is Strabo's: that
Homer was describing the Strait of Gibraltar, which has a lot
of really dangerous whirlpools. The "thrice a day" refers not
merely to whirlpools, but to those caused by tides, "thrice"
being a simple error for "twice." Homer, remember, knew
nothing about tides, since those in the Mediterranean for the
most part amount to a few inches, and such little tides are
not noticeable unless you already know about them and know
where to look for them.

At Gibraltar, on the other hand, ten-foot tides are normal, and the worst of the whirlpools, west of Tarifa, can
bother even small steamers. Moreover Gibraltar has "twain
rocks"—the 1,400-foot Rock of Gibraltar of smooth limestone,
with a big cave beyond bowshot on its western side; and opposite it on the African side the 2,830-foot Jebel Musa
("Mount Moses") with an almost constant cloud plume at its
peak. Which certainly looks as though Homer had had a
rather complete description to go on, even if he or his informant did mix up the features of the two mountains, so that the

Rock is made the taller of the two and given the cloud plume. As to the location of the whirlpool on the south side, whereas the main one today is on the north, that might be another mistake, or it might be that the whirlpools have changed their patterns in the last thirty centuries.

Skylla, the other monster, was not as some have thought another whirlpool. Kirkë describes her in terms that leave little doubt:

> . . . but her form is a sight portentous that no one
> E'er would gladly behold, not even a god if he met her
> Round her a dozen of feet she is always waving suspended
> Six long and sinuous necks outstretching before her and each
> one
> Beareth a head terrific with teeth in a threefold order
> Many and thickly arrayed, where gapes death's cavernous
> blackness.
> Up to the midmost parts she is hid in the depths of the cavern
> Whilst from her lair in the fearful abyss six heads she ex-
> tendeth
> Hunting for fish at the foot of the rock and peering around
> it . . .
>
> *Odyssey*, XII, 87ff.

Here we have an attempt to describe a giant octopus in terms that do not quite fit because the describer has never seen one and the right terms have not yet been invented. The six "necks" are tentacles—octopodes commonly anchor themselves by two or three of their eight tentacles while snatching at their prey with the rest—and the "teeth in threefold order" are the rows of sucking disks. That a large octopus is a sight nobody would ever gladly behold has been asserted by many who have seen them; Kirkë could have gone on to mention, besides the writhing arms, the lidless, slit-pupiled eyes, the chameleonlike changes of color, the parrot beak in the midst of the tentacles, and the ink sac with which the octopus blackens the water when frightened. These creatures do occur around Gibraltar: Pliny the Elder had a report of a monstrous one caught there in his own time. And while they do not usually attack men, they can be dangerous if cornered or harpooned. Of course real octopodes do not live out of water, but they do lurk in underwater caves to pounce out upon the passing crab.

This account also provides a small datum of Greek dietary history. Homer's heroes live on a diet of bread, roast meat, and little else; Alkinoös personally serves Odysseus with a saddle of pork. The Greeks of the classical period (especially the Athenians) were, on the contrary, great eaters of sea food, which probably included the octopus and its cousin the squid. These mollusks are highly relished by modern Mediterranean peoples (as you can check by going to an Italian restaurant) and despite their horrific appearance are quite edible. Evidently the octopus had not yet become a fixture in the Greek menu when the *Odyssey* was written, or Homer would probably have recognized Skylla for what she was.

Next Kirkë says:

> Isle Thrinakia next shalt thou reach, where pasture in numbers
> Cattle of Helios and the fat-fed flocks of the sun-god
> Seven the droves of kine and seven of fair-fleeced fatlings
> Fifty in every flock. 'Tis a race that has never an offspring
> Nor do they dwindle and die. . . .
>
> *Odyssey*, XII, 127-131

If they leave these cattle alone, says Kirkë, they will get to Ithaka, but if they injure any of them all will perish save Odysseus, and he will have a terrible time getting home.

Everything turns out as predicted. After passing through the Strait, where Odysseus sacrifices six of his men to Skylla rather than lose the whole ship to Charybdis, they reach Thrinakia and land to rest. Then adverse winds hold them there for a month while provisions dwindle. Finally the men get so hungry that when Odysseus is absent they butcher and eat some of the Sun's cows. A week later the storm abates and they put to sea, but a bolt of lightning shatters the ship. Odysseus alone survives by clutching a piece of the mainmast, and after nine days afloat drifts ashore on Kalypso's isle of Ogygia.

Thrinakia is a puzzle. It has been identified with Sicily (once called "Trinacria" from its triangular shape) and with various places in Italy, none of which fits if we are right in thinking that our hero reached it after sailing west through the Strait of Gibraltar. Perhaps it is entirely fictional. The only clue to its nature is not geographical but mythological: Helios has 350 immortal cattle, which would be the number of days in the year as the Greeks originally counted it. So Thrinakia becomes a symbol in a calendar myth!

In the case of Ogygia we are on slightly firmer ground. Athena has already described it at the very beginning of the *Odyssey*, when she is urging Zeus to let poor Odysseus go home:

> Far from his home on a sea-girt isle; 'tis the navel of ocean
> Even this isle is well-wooded, whereon has a dwelling the goddess
> Daughter of Atlas, the wizard of bale, who of every ocean
> Knoweth the watery depths, and alone upholdeth the pillars
> Soaring aloft and keeping the earth and heaven asunder.
> *Odyssey*, I, 50-54

Several lines make it clear that this island was a long way from known countries. Thus when Hermes arrives at Ogygia with Zeus's message to Kalypso, he explains:

> Zeus hath commanded me hither to come, and I came, but unwilling.
> Who would willingly cross such spaces of salt sea water
> Terrible, endless! and never at hand was a city of mortals.
> *Odyssey*, V, 99-101

Evidently such a long flight without emergency landing fields was too much for him. The name of this island "in the very center" (literally "boss" or "navel") "of the sea" gives a further clue to its location: Ogygia appears to be from the Semitic (Phoenician) root *og*, "circle," the source also for the Greek word *ōkeanos*, whence our "ocean." Lewi, an expert in both Hebrew and Latin, translated the derived form *ogeg* or *hogeg* as "the water that forms a circle"; hence "Ogygia" is "the island in the circling ocean," the merry-go-round Ocean River.

Judging from the general description of a well-wooded subtropical island in the ocean, then, Ogygia (where Odysseus now spends nine homesick but not uncompensated years with the nymph Kalypso) would seem to be neither Malta nor Cape Japygia in Italy (as has sometimes been supposed) but Madeira, known to the Phoenicians along with the Canaries. Here our hero languishes in durance de luxe until Zeus orders his fair-haired captor to let him go. (A modern would suspect that if Odysseus had really wished to get away he could have found means to do so before this; but it is not fair to pick logical flaws in a work written before logic was invented.)

The Madeira-Ogygia theory is also confirmed by Odysseus' sailing directions to his next stop:

> Keeping the raft to her course by the helm with the skill of a
>   sailor
> Seated he steered (nor for a moment did drowsiness fall on
>   his eyelids)
> Holding the Pleiads in view and the autumn-setting Boötes,
> Holding moreover the Bear, that is called by the name of the
>   Wagon.
> (Ever she circles around and around on the watch for Orion,
> Having alone of the stars no share in the baths of the ocean.)
> Her—since thus had commanded the beautiful goddess
>   Kalypso

Voyaging over the ocean he steadily held on his left hand.
Seven and ten was the number of days that he voyaged the
    waters,
Till on the eighteenth day he beheld far shadowy moun-
    tains. . . .

Odyssey, V, 270-279

Some decades ago Drs. Hennig and Erpelt set the Düssel-
dorf planetarium back to 800 B.C., as of the latitude of
Madeira, and found that Ursa Major, the Bear, did not touch
the horizon in its circles, and that Boötes and the Pleiades
emerged at the same point in east-northeast, the direction of
the nearest point on the Iberian mainland when coming from
Madeira. And a primitive vessel would in fact require eighteen days for the trip, though we need not believe that our
hero stayed awake the whole time. So, however tenuous the
thread connecting Homer's Ogygia with reality, the other end
of that thread would seem to be belayed fast to Madeira.

When Odysseus is in sight of land, his enemy Poseidon,
returning from a visit to the Aithiopes (Ethiopians, "Burnt-
faces") spies him and wrecks his raft. Odysseus is drowning
when the nymph Leukothea "of the beautiful ankles" takes
pity on him and lends him her veil as a magical life preserver.
By strenuous swimming through a savage surf the Wanderer
makes "the mouth of a fair-flowing river," where the river-
god, in answer to his prayer

. . . slackened the might of its billowy current
Spreading before him a calm; and the deity brought him to
    safety
Unto the beach at the mouth of the stream. . . .

Odyssey, V, 439ff.

When the exhausted hero has crawled out of the water
and got his wind back, he casts Leukothea's veil into the water,

and "a great wave bore it down the stream" to its owner.

So comes "god-like, long-tried Odysseus" to the land of the "oar-loving Phaiakes," the world's most accomplished sailors, who "live farthest away on the loud-surging sea, and none else of mortals mingles with" them; who "care not for bow or quiver, but for masts and oars and trim ships, with which they rejoice to cross the foaming sea." These are no ordinary ships, but magical:

Yet swift as a bird or a thought is the speed of their vessels.
Odyssey, XIII, 242

Homer here tells us a bit more about these Phaiakes or Phæacians: Once they had dwelt in "spacious Hypereia, near the overbearing Kyklopes" who raided them until their king, godlike Nausithoös (a son of Poseidon) led them to their present land of Scheria "distant from wheat-eating men." So far this makes little sense, since the only Hypereia ("Uppertown") known to history is a fountain in the town of Pherai in southwestern Thessaly, near Iolkos of Argonautic fame; nowhere near Kyklopean Sicily.

At any rate Nausithoös now was deceased and:

With god-given wisdom Alkinoös reigned in his stead.

The day after the Wanderer's escape from the sea, Athena inspires the king's daughter, white-armed Nausikaä, to go with her maidens to the river with the palace laundry. After the wash they amuse themselves with a ball game until their chatter awakens Odysseus, who, holding a bush in front of his nakedness with un-Hellenic modesty, appeals to them for help. After the first fright they give him clothes and tell him to follow them back to town.

Odysseus does so, much impressed by the lofty wall, the

spacious harbor, the splendid temple of Poseidon, and the megalithic assembly place. At the king's palace his breath is fairly taken away by the lavish decorations: walls and threshold of bronze, golden doors, silver doorposts, and inside golden statues of youths holding torches.

Alkinoös (portrayed as a jolly old *bon vivant*) receives his visitor with right royal hospitality. Odysseus learns that the Phaiakes are, like the Kyklopes, related to the gods, and that the farthest land they had visited was the island of Euboia off the east coast of Greece, whither they had once taken Rhadamanthos to visit a cousin. In Greek myth this Rhadamanthos had been a brother of King Minos of Crete. Because of his integrity the gods had made him, after his death, one of the judges of the dead and let him live in the Elysian Fields, which were, like Ogygia and the land of the Kimmerioi, somewhere in the Far West. The Phaiakes lead a luxurious life, fond of "the feast, the lyre, the dance, change of raiment, warm baths, and love."

Next day Alkinoös gives a party for the stranger, in the course of which Odysseus tells the story of his adventures since leaving Troy. The day after, Alkinoös sends his guest (who has politely declined an offer to become his son-in-law) on his way with rich presents in one of the Phaiakes' magical ships.

> Steadily onward she flew; not even the falcon that soareth,
> Swiftest of birds in the air, might vie with the ship in her swiftness
>
> *Odyssey*, VII, 36f.

At such a speed they reach Ithaka in a single night, and the sailors put the sleeping Odysseus ashore and return to Scheria, where Poseidon spitefully turns their ship to stone and threatens to "overshadow their city with a great mountain." This threat causes the Phaiakes to give up their friendly habit of ferrying strangers home.

Now, where is Scheria, the land of the Phaiakes?

Scheria has been located in as many different places as any of Homer's creations, and in almost as many as Plato's Atlantis: in Palestine, Tunisia, Sicily, Gades, the Canary Islands, or even the island of Socotra in the Arabian Sea.

One of the most widespread and long-lived opinions on this subject originated somewhat as follows: Two thousand years ago a clever fisherman or peasant on a Mediterranean isle had the bright idea that he and his friends and relatives could live better with less work if they could convince others that their home was an important place in the *Odyssey*. In mulling over such thoughts he looked across the blue water at a small island in the distance. From certain angles, he noted, the small island looked like a ship. Like a ship of stone.

And at that instant one of the big frauds of history was conceived. There was the stone ship of the Phaiakes; and thus the island of Kerkyra (Latin, *Corcyra*) off the coast of Epeiros, modern Corfu, became Scheria.

For two thousand years tourists, believing the story, came to gape at the alleged home of the Phæacians. Even in the present century the story had enough vitality to incite Kaiser Wilhelm II, in line with his maritime ambitions, to build his summer castle on the former home of the world's greatest seafarers.

This in spite of the many lines in the *Odyssey* that make Scheria's remoteness as plain as possible, as when Odysseus in Phæacia says "far is my homeland," which he could hardly do if he were in Corfu almost in sight of his home islands. And there are other "stone ships": near Malta, near Cadiz (called "La Galera"), and even in this country.

But there are simple indications of the whereabouts of Scheria. The reversal of the river when Odysseus swims into it looks like a description of the tides, which means the Atlantic Ocean. The lavish metallic furnishings point to a mining country: specifically to southwestern Spain, still an important mining center.

Everything, in fact, suggests the city of Tartessos—a city as mysterious in fact as the Scheria legend is in fiction. Tartessos lay near modern Cadiz, on a flat sandy coast beaten by high

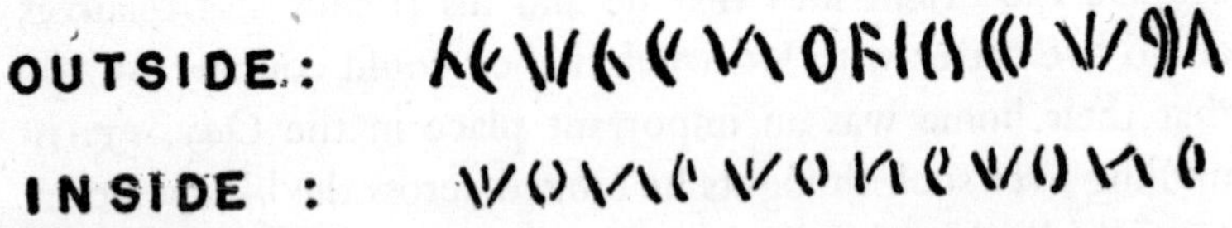

OUTSIDE.: ⫫⫫⫫⫫⫫⫫⫫

INSIDE : ⫫⫫⫫⫫⫫⫫⫫

FIG. 4.   Inscription in unknown, presumably Tartessian, characters, on the outside and inside of a girl's ring, found in 1923 on the site of Tartessos by Prof. Adolf Schulten. On the inside the same word repeats three times; since the characters are unknown this reproduction may be upside down.

tides and a strong surf; it stood on an island at the mouth of the Guadalquivir River—or more exactly between the two mouths. Behind it the great estuary of the Guadalquivir (or Baetis or Tartessis) extended inland almost to Seville. Nowadays the northern mouth of the river has silted up and become dry land, and the bay has turned into a vast malarial marsh, Las Marismas. And the ruins of Tartessos itself have sunk so deep into the mud that Schulten, excavating the site in 1923, found practically no remains but a few pieces of ancient masonry and a small golden ring inscribed with words in an unknown alphabet resembling the Etruscan.

The Phoenicians, arriving at Tartessos around 1000 B.C., found silver so common there that in order to carry away as much as they could in return for olive oil and other wares, they cast their anchor stones in silver.

The Phoenicians soon founded their own colony of Gades (modern Cadiz) about twenty miles southeast of Tartessos. Later they founded Carthage (850 B.C.) which soon rose to be mistress of the western Mediterranean, enforcing an ironclad commercial monopoly not broken until the Punic Wars.

The Greeks first made the acquaintance of Tartessos at first hand about 631 B.C., when a Samian ship under Kolaios, bound for Egypt, was blown far out of its course and ended up at Tartessos—a record detour. The Samians made six talents from their voyage: an enormous sum for the time, equivalent to more than $75,000 in modern money. Next came men of Phokaia in Ionia, who also opened up the Adriatic and Tyrrhenian Seas to Greek commerce and founded Massalia, our Marseilles. The first of these found Tartessos ruled by the benevolent old King Arganthonios ("Silverlocks") though we need not believe with Herodotos that he lived 120 years and reigned eighty of them. For their Tartessian trade the Phokaians used galleys, the swift fifty-oared pentakonter, instead of the tubby merchant ships of the time, because while the galley had less space for cargo it had a better chance of getting away when a Carthaginian galley came crawling over the horizon, like a big centipede chasing a little one, with the intention of making the interlopers walk the plank.

For centuries Tartessos and Gades flourished side by side as trading and mining centers. The Tartessians were rated the most civilized folk in Iberia, with their own literature. Then between 533 and 500 B.C. the Carthaginians reduced Gades to subjection.

And Tartessos disappeared.

Whether Carthage destroyed it or whether the silting up

of the river left it stranded amid the mud flats of the Guadalquivir estuary we do not know. But thereafter no more is
heard of it.

Homer's Scheria looks, however, like Tartessos as much
as it looks like anything—or rather Tartessos with features of
Gades thrown in, like the ship-rock La Galera. But then
Homer, at the opposite end of the Mediterranean, could
hardly have distinguished these two cities, when many later
classical writers confused them.

Odysseus is home at last—but where is "home"? Homer
has described "Ithaka" thus:

> Truly the island is rugged—not fit for the driving of horses
> Still, not utterly poor, though lacking in open expanses
> Corn in amazing abundance it groweth, and also the wine-
> grape
> Ripens, and ever with rain and with freshening dew it is
> moistened
> Good is the isle as a pasture for goats and for kine, and it
> beareth
> Every manner of wood and has watering places that fail not.
> *Odyssey*, XIII, 242ff.

Odysseus himself has told the Phaiakes:

> Ithaka, isle far-seen, is my home; herein is a mountain
> Neriton, waving with woods, conspicuous; islands around it
> Lie full and many and closely adjacent one to the other
> Samos and Dulichion and the woodland heights of Zakynthos
> Lowly does Ithaka lie and is highest out in the ocean
> Far in the western gloom—but the rest t'ward the dawn and
> the sunrise.
> *Odyssey*, IX, 21ff.

A couple of Homer's terms call for explanation: *Zophos*,
"gloom" or "darkness," is here a poetic term meaning, probably, "west," but possibly "north" or even "northwest." Hence
Cotterill translated it "western gloom." And *chthamalē*,

FIG. 5. Sketch map of the Greek islands, with reference to the home of Odysseus.

"low" or "flat," may refer to topography, or it may mean "close to shore"—that is, "low" as seen from a height on the mainland, for so the Greeks spoke of ships as "low" or "high." But since Odysseus also says it is "highest out in the ocean" he must mean "low" in the sense of "flat."

What are the various islands listed by Odysseus?

Off the west coast of Greece, clustered about the entrance to the Gulf of Corinth, lies an archipelago of four large islands and many small ones. Nowadays the four large islands are called (reading from south to north) Zakynthos or Zante; Kephallenia or Cephalonia; Ithake, Thiaki, or Ithaca; and Levkas or Santa Maura. In classical times they were called Zakynthos, Kephallenia, Ithakë, and Leukas or Leukadia respectively. (The forms *Zante, Cephalonia*, etc., are the modern Italian names.) Now Odysseus repeatedly refers to his realm as composed of "Zakynthos, Doulichion, Samos" (or Samë) "and Ithaka," and it would seem no great trick to fit these four names into the four islands in question.

It transpires, however, that Zakynthos is the *only* one we can be sure of. Kephallenia might be either Doulichion (whose description it answers) or Samos (since it has a town of that name) and to confuse matters further Homer speaks of the Kephallenians as subjects of Odysseus but without saying where they live. Conversely Levkas might be either Samos or Doulichion. Ithakë (or to give it its local name Thiaki) despite its name does not very well answer to the description given Alkinoös: It is neither "low" (flat) being a rocky mass of hills rising to 2,645 feet, nor "highest up in the sea towards the gloom" for it lies right in the midst of the group.

In the last century Draheim and Dörpfeld suggested that Levkas was Homer's Ithaka, and the latter (who wanted an excuse for advertising a ruin he had found as the "castle of

Odysseus") was driven to developing a somewhat fantastic line of argument. Others denied this, asserting that Levkas was not an island at all but a peninsula, since it is separated from the mainland only by a shallow ford.

The likeliest solution of the Ithaka puzzle was propounded by a semiprofessional with no reputation to lose: Leutz-Spitta, who asserted that Homer's descriptions of Ithaka would fit, of all places, Corfu, as would long ago have been plain had Corfu not been trying to sell itself as Scheria. It is far out in the western gloom from the rest of the archipelago; it is all wooded mountains, suitable for sheep and cattle but where horses would soon break their necks and legs; it can be seen from afar; it is surrounded by water, but near the Albanian mainland; it has no mighty Scherian river, but it does possess "watering places that fail not." And the plain, two by five miles, was not a plain several thousand years ago but a lake: "not fit for grazing the horses nor driving the chariot."

And so, with Odysseus reunited with his family and the importunate suitors weltering in their gore, Homer takes leave of his hero. There were other legends about his youth and marriage, and several versions of his end. For instance the lost *Telegoneia* told how he set out upon another voyage after his homecoming, in the course of which he was killed in ignorance by Telegonos, his son by Kirkë—this being the first appearance of the durable Sohrab-and-Rustum theme in literature.

But as that takes us out of our chosen field we had better bid farewell to the great adventurer too; and so ends the story of Odysseus—or rather of the modern interpretation of the *Tales*. And whoever or whatever Odysseus "really" was, or wherever he went, the narrative of his adventures is still one of life's major experiences. This fact was recently brought home to a publisher of paper-bound pocket books who reprinted the *Odyssey*, and got a letter from a reader saying please to let him know next time Mr. Homer had a book published because he didn't want to miss it!

CHAPTER III

The Fabulous East

WE ALL KNOW THAT A DESCRIPTION OF ANYTHING IS INFLU-
enced by the knowledge, experience, and attitudes of the
person making the description. Even an honest eyewitness
account of an event varies to some extent with the point of
view. Therefore, since this chapter deals with concepts of
Roman origin, we must try to put ourselves in the place
of a Roman.

A well-read Roman who lived when the Empire was at its
biggest (about 100 A.D.) had a pretty good idea of the earth.
He knew from the Greeks that it was a sphere floating in
space, and from Eratosthenes of Kyrenë about how big it was.
On the other hand his ideas about the proportions of land
and water on the surface of this sphere differed from those of
his teachers, the Greeks, as he showed in using the term *terra
firma*.

To the Greeks of, say, 600 B.C., the earth (or at least its
surface) had been mainly water. Naturally enough, they considered their home country to be more or less in the center
of the inhabited world; and moreover a large proportion of
them lived on islands or on the Peloponnesos which is almost
an island. And while they knew Asia Minor and Egypt, Italy
and Sicily, and had heard of points farther west on the coasts
of Africa and Spain, they were not at all sure whether these
stretches of coast were not parts of islands too. Since the island
was the prevailing geographical feature in the Aegean Sea,

at the very center of their civilization, it seemed that other land masses should be islands too.

To the Roman of the beginning of the second century A.D. things were just the other way round. What the Greeks had called "The Sea" had become *Mare Internum*, the Inner Sea, to them. Although Greece happened to be more or less in the geographical center of the Roman Empire, Greece proper comprised only a small fraction of that empire, and a still smaller fraction of all the land that was known. All the Balkan peninsula was Roman; so were Armenia, Asia Minor, the Crimean Peninsula, Syria, Iraq, Palestine, and parts of Arabia, Egypt, Libya and the rest of the North African coast to the Atlantic coast of Morocco, Spain and Portugal, France, Belgium, most of Holland, England, western and southwestern Germany, and most of Austria and Switzerland. And, of course, Italy and Sicily.

The Roman who contemplated the earth did not make the mistake of thinking that all the *terra firma* was Roman, or even that all of it was yet known. Only in the West had the Empire reached the rim of the land, at the coasts of Iberia, beyond which lay nothing but the waters of the Atlantic—he did not take Plato's Atlantis seriously. Of course if the earth was truly round, as seemed to be the case, you could presumably come to the east coast of Asia by sailing westward far enough. How far this would be our Roman didn't know, but since such a voyage would be impossible anyway with the ships and the seamanship available, he did not bother his head much with such a theoretical question.

Everywhere else the borders of the Empire were land borders. In Germania the frontier, the *Limes*, followed the Rhine, beyond which stretched, unbroken save for patches cleared by the natives, the terrible Hercynian Forest, portrayed in somber colors by Caesar himself: a dark, swampy land, harboring warlike tribes of towering savages, and dangerous beasts—bears, gigantic wild oxen, and birds that made frightening noises—all under a cold, rainy climate that no Roman gentleman, inadequately clad in the skirts and mantles of the Mediterranean, would willingly endure. However, there was evidently more land beyond, as held true for the Danube and the north shore of the Pontus Euxinus, or Black Sea.

Likewise in Africa the indefinite border was land, where the fertile coastal strip gave way to the Saharan wastes. Beyond the Mesopotamian province of the Empire, which we call Iraq, lay the high, arid plateau of Iran, ruled by the powerful Arsacid or Parthian Kingdom, and beyond that India. Once the great Alexander had overthrown the Persian Empire and conquered vast areas there in the East, but even beyond his conquests lay still more land, as the Romans knew from the reports of ships that came to the mouth of the Euphrates River, the easternmost tip of the Empire, for trade.

So our Roman of 100 A.D. knew that much land lay outside his Empire. On the other hand he probably felt that nearly all the *important* land was Roman. In the West was the ocean in which he was not interested; he preferred to travel on good roads, and where the roads ended, the useful land ended too. What lay beyond the Roman outposts in Africa? Desert.

In Arabia? Desert.

North of Armenia? Mountains (the Caucasus) and beyond these, according to reports, more desert. Not the same kind of desert as in Libya but just as useless.

In Germania? The awful Hercynian Forest.

Thus in every direction, when one looked from a hill near Rome, the useful land was Roman, all Roman—except in the East, beyond Iran. The East was large and full of native humanity. It had cities; it produced strange fruit and gold and jewels and works of art; it was the only useful non-Roman land. Logically everything strange and fabulous, everything un-Roman, could be found in the East if it could be found anywhere.

Once, in early Greek times, the extreme West had been the scene of wonder and adventure, for, as the historian Tacitus tartly put it: "the unknown is always taken for the magnificent." (Tacitus, *Agricola*, xxx) The writer Loukianos of Samosata was still treating it as such, though nowadays it was well known and prosaic. However, Lucian the Scoffer was after all making fun of the old stories and did not expect to be believed, as he warned in one of his tales. But in the East —now *there* was the real wonderland. Some of the tales the Greeks brought back from there were probably untrue; however, there were still plenty of wonders of the East that did exist. If the second-century Roman wanted details he had but to go to the library and ask for the work of his compatriot C. Plinius Secundus. Too bad he had to die in that eruption of Vesuvius; luckily, he had completed his great *Natural History* at the time. In it one could read, in the resounding Latin befitting a former commanding officer of Roman cavalry and an admiral of the Roman fleet, about the strange races of the East. . . .

When Gaius Plinius Secundus,* whom we call Pliny the Elder, compiled those pages, he found it hard to believe some of the things he had read. Many of his sources were Greek, and he had a poor opinion of Greek veracity. He did try, therefore, to sort out the facts from the fables, but unfortunately had neither the knowledge nor the critical acumen to do

* Note that the abbreviation for *Gaius* is *C.*, not *G.*—a Roman inconsistency.

so with much success. When his enthusiasm led him to accept some of the wilder stories that his critical judgment doubted, he rationalized his feelings with a bit of oratory that probably served to convince the writer as much as the reader: "Who could ever believe in Negroes unless he had seen them first? Indeed, what is there that does not appear marvelous when it comes to our knowledge for the first time?" (Pliny, *Natural History*, VII, i). Moreover, he added, so great were the differences among human languages that it seemed to him credible that there should be equally great differences in physical form among the races of men.

Having laid this groundwork, he went ahead on the subject of the curious races of men:

"We have already stated that there are certain tribes of the Scythians* and, indeed, many other nations, which feed upon human flesh. This fact itself might, perhaps, appear incredible, did we not recollect that in the very center of the earth, in Italy and Sicily, nations formerly existed with these monstrous propensities, the Cyclopes and the Laestrygones, for example, and that, very recently, on the other side of the Alps, it was the custom to offer human sacrifices . . . and the difference is but small between sacrificing human beings and eating them." (Pliny, *Natural History*, VII, ii.)

To Pliny, cannibalism seems to have been as surprising as dog-headed men and other freaks. In mentioning the Cyclopes and Laestrygones he was quoting the *Odyssey* as a straight source. While one might expect its cannibalistic one-eyed giants to have died out when Sicily became familiar, they did not; with the tenacity of most such myths they simply moved elsewhere. If there were no cannibals in Sicily then there must be cannibals in the East, beyond the *Mare Caspium*.

* East of the Caspian Sea.

And there lived also another "nation, remarkable for having but one eye and that placed in the middle of the forehead," the Arimaspi. Homer's one-eyed people had been moved to the East too, except that they were no longer giants

FIG. 6. A fish-eating Arimaspian, as pictured in an old edition of John de Mandeville's (fictional) travel book.

and presumably no longer cannibals. Pliny got his Arimaspi mainly from the *History* of Herodotos, who said that:

> The regions beyond are known only from the accounts of the Issedonians, by whom the stories are told of the one-eyed race of men and the gold-guarding griffins. These stories are received by the Scythians from the Issedonians and by them passed on to us Greeks: whence it arises that we give the one-eyed race the Scythian name Arimaspi, *arima* being the Scythic word for 'one' and *spu* for 'the eye.'
>
> Herodotos, IV, 27

Herodotos in turn had as one of his sources an old poem, *Arimaspeia,* ascribed to one Aristeas, otherwise unknown.

The poem itself is lost except for six lines quoted in one ancient book, of which the last five read:

> Farther northward [the Issedonians] still have different neighbors,
> Seeming to them, quite numerous are they and fearless in warfare,
> Rich in livestock they are, of sheep and of horse and of cattle;
> Every one of them has but one eye in the well-shaped forehead;
> Shaggy are they of hair, and strongest of all of the mortals.

While "Aristeas" is supposed to have lived in Homer's time and to have wandered far to the East and North with many magical circumstances (for example he is said to have reappeared 340 years after his own death), there is evidence that the poem could not have been written earlier than the sixth century B.C.—the century before Herodotos. Obviously the author of the *Arimaspeia*, whoever he really was, transplanted that bit of Homeric lore to the country beyond the Caspian Sea when these legends had become untenable in their old home.

To get back to Pliny: the great Roman encyclopedist elaborated a bit on Herodotos's remark about gold-guarding griffins. Those one-eyed Arimaspi "are said to carry on a perpetual warfare with the griffins, a kind of monster, with wings, as they are commonly represented, for the gold which they dig out of the mines and which these wild beasts retain and keep watch over with a singular degree of cupidity, while the Arimaspi are equally desirous to get possession of it." (Pliny: *Natural History*, VII, ii.)

The gold-guarding griffins suggest a couple of other legends. The one that comes first to mind is the dragon Fafnir and the Hoard of the Nibelungs. The other theme is the one told by the same Herodotos about the origin of the gold of India. In the Indian deserts, Herodotos reported: "there live among the sand great ants, in size somewhat less than dogs, but bigger than foxes. The Persian king has a number of them, which have been caught by the hunters in the land whereof we are speaking. Those ants make their dwellings underground, and like the Greek ants, which they very much resemble in shape, throw up sandheaps as they burrow. Now the sand which they throw up is full of gold." (Herodotos, *op. cit.*, III, 102)

The men of Paktyika went to the desert of the big ants with camels, making sure that they had both male and female camels with them—"for the females are faster than the males" —and making sure, too, that they would arrive during the hottest part of the day when the ants would be underground, hiding from the heat. The gold-gatherers quickly scooped up the gold-bearing sand and rushed away with the ants in pursuit. As the slower male camels lagged behind, presumably appeasing the ants, the prospectors on the female camels got away.

"Such," said Herodotos, "according to the Persians, is the manner in which the Indians get the greater part of their gold; some is dug out of the earth, but of this the supply is more scanty." Following Herodotos the story of the giant ants entered the stream of European legend and grew with the centuries, until in the Middle Ages European writers were crediting the ants with seven legs and four wings.

One may dismiss the whole story as a fairy tale designed to obscure the origin of the gold that was brought to market. And the tale was no doubt used for that purpose. There may, however, be a tiny grain of truth in the story, some small fact that set the imagination working. For example, the starting point of the tale might be an actual burrowing animal that happened to dig up gold-bearing sands in a river bed, without getting any ideas of personal possession. If that guess (which

FIG. 7. Gold-digging ants. (From Mandeville.)

has been advanced several times) is correct, then Herodotos's gold-mining ant might be the bobac, an Asiatic marmot much like our own prairie dogs.

Likewise, the gold-guarding griffins may have been simply invented by some trader to keep competitors out of a lucrative trading area, just as the Phoenicians endowed the Western Sea with horror tales. Indubitably the griffin story was utilized for this purpose, but there seems to be a special reason for the choice of this particular monster as a commercial scarecrow.

The Issedonians seem to have lived in the southern Ural Mountains, and the Arimaspi and the griffins have to be sought north or northeast of the Issedonians. The gold which the griffins guarded probably came from the Altai Mountains, where modern Siberia, Outer Mongolia, and Sinkiang come together; these mountains were once a rich source of minerals and were mined in very ancient times.

Now it seems that once the Chudi, a tribe related to the modern Finns, had a big loose empire stretching from east of the Volga to the Altai Mountains. While we know little about them, these Chudi did mine their own metallic ores in the centuries before the Christian Era, and buried their dead in elaborately carved stone tombs. People who have examined these tombs say that the griffin is often found among the carvings, which suggests that the griffin was some sort of symbol or totem of the Chudi. If that is so, then the statement that the griffins dug gold from mines and guarded it against their neighbors may have originally been a metaphor like saying that the British Lion guarded the Suez Canal. In such a case the "griffins" are not fabulous monsters at all, but a mine-working people known to their enemies by their favorite symbol.

Fafnir, who guards the Hoard of the Nibelungs, then

becomes only a late adaptation of an older misunderstanding which had by then become universal. Between the time of Herodotos and that in which the Fafnir legend originated, the dragon myth had come into being. (To Pliny "dragons" were still only large snakes.) Thus the transfer was not only from the Altai Mountains to the Rhineland, but also from the Asiatic griffin to the Germanic dragon.

The mention of Pliny brings us back to the ideas of the Romans about the mysterious peoples of the East. In Albania, he said (referring to a Roman province on the west shore of the Caspian Sea, near modern Baku) there lived, according to one Isogonus of Nicaea, "a race of men whose eyes are of sea-green color, and who have white hair from earliest childhood, and these people see better in the night than in the day." A family of albinos? Perhaps.

The next strange race baffles the interpreter. In great valleys in the East lives a savage race with feet turned backwards, though fleet of foot nevertheless. "We learn from Baeton, whose duty it was to take the measurements of the routes of Alexander the Great, that this people cannot breathe in any climate except their own, for which reason it is impossible to take them before any of the neighboring kings; nor could any of them be brought before Alexander himself."

A few pages later we meet another race, living on a mountain in India, also with feet turned backwards and with eight toes on each foot. One may guess that deformities well-known to modern medicine may have given rise to such legends. Cuvier, the French "father of paleontology," who commented on Pliny's *Natural History* a little over a century ago, made the pointed remark that such races are always placed in the mountains where it is harder for travelers to check their existence. Still, something else may have entered here. An authority on Biblical lore, Henderson, once remarked that some natives of the Caucasus believe in a race of demons that assume the shape of men, but which can be recognized by having their feet turned backwards. This is the same type of belief as the Christian legend to the effect that no matter what shape the Devil assumes he can still be recognized by his cloven hoof.

Pliny then gives some space to various races around the Black Sea, some of whom have double pupils in their eyes, and others of whom do not sink in water. These last may be connected with the swimming ordeal in witchcraft trials during the European witch mania of the sixteenth and seventeenth centuries. Some witch-hunters thought that if you bound the suspect and threw him or her into the water, he would sink if innocent and float if guilty. The ancient Babylonians had used a similar system but in reverse: those who had floated had been deemed innocent.

At last Pliny reached India. "It abounds in wonders," he wrote, and went on to tell of the great fierce dogs of India, about the Indian fig tree big enough to shelter a whole troop of cavalry*, about the marvelous health of the Indians who are "subject to no pains, either in the head, the teeth, or the eyes" and about "their philosophers, who are called Gymnosophists, remain in one posture, with their eyes immovably fixed upon the sun, from its rising to its setting, and, during the whole of the day, they are accustomed to stand in the burning sands on one foot, first one and then the other."

So far, except for an exaggerated idea of the Hindus' health, Pliny is fairly accurate. But then mistakes begin to creep in again.

Ktesias, the body physician to Artaxerxes II of Persia, had written a book on India, based upon Persian beliefs about

* The banyan, *Ficus religiosa*, by forming secondary trunks to hold up its branches, produces something like a copse which is really one tree.

India and tales he heard from travelers at court. The original book is now lost, our knowledge of it being derived from quotations, especially an epitome in the *Library* of the Patriarch Photios. Ktesias, while he added a number of facts to Europe's knowledge of India, such as the existence of the myna bird and the bamboo, collected an even more impressive assortment of fictions: a fountain of liquid gold, dog-headed men, and Pygmies a yard high.

Even when Ktesias was describing real things, the exaggerations of his informants and the treacheries of translation grotesquely distorted his accounts. Thus he described the Indian rhinoceros as an animal resembling a wild ass, which description became the basis of the European unicorn legend; and the tiger appears in his work as the *martichoras*, a great red-skinned carnivore with a human face, shooting poisoned darts from its tail as the American porcupine was once thought to do among the uninformed. And those who quoted from Ktesias, by preserving his more startling stories at the expense of the more sober, no doubt made him seem even more credulous than he was.

It is this Ktesias, at any rate, who was the source for what was to follow in Pliny's gigantic compilation: "On many of the mountains there is a tribe of men who have the heads of dogs and clothe themselves with the skins of wild beasts. Instead of speaking, they bark; and, furnished with claws, they live by hunting and catching birds. . . . The number of these people is more than 120 thousand." It hardly needs to be said that this "tribe" is a tribe of monkeys. Moreover the same simple explanation applies to some of the other "montrous races" mentioned later, "people" who walk sometimes erect and sometimes on all fours, "people" who screech instead of speaking, "people" whose bodies are covered with fur.

But then Pliny, following Ktesias, could relate a few real marvels. Ktesias, he said spoke "of another race of men who are known as Monocoli, who have only one leg, but are able to leap with surprising agility. The same people are also called Sciapodae, because they are in the habit of lying on their backs, during the time of the extreme heat, and protect themselves from the sun by the shade of their feet."

Monocoli is Latinized Greek for "one-legs." Just what Ktesias meant to describe, if it was anything in the real world, remains a mystery, though his description intrigued artists for centuries to come. No illuminated medieval manuscript, either of Pliny's book or of one of the many later writers who cribbed from him, fails to show a Sciapod resting comfortably in the shade of his big foot, usually in the center of India though sometimes elsewhere. Even some of the early printed books carried Sciapods. Professor Heinrich Balss suggested that the legend may have been caused by a case of elephantiasis.

The next item on Pliny's list is of considerable ethnological interest: "Eudoxus tells us that in the southern parts of India the men have feet a cubit in length; while those of the women are so remarkably small, that they are called 'sparrow-footed.' " * This Eudoxos, usually called "of Kyzikos" to distinguish him from the Greek astronomer Eudoxos of Knidos, was a navigator and geographer commissioned by Ptolemy to explore the seas south and east of Arabia. He sailed to India for his royal master, though we don't know just how far east he got.

The item itself sounds like a reference to the bound feet or "golden lilies" of Chinese ladies. However, there are diffi-

* Pliny's word *struthopodes* can also be translated "ostrich-footed," depending on whether you assume it to be based on a Greek or a Latin root. The former seems more likely.

FIG. 8. A Sciapode, resting in the shade of his foot. (From Mandeville.)

culties of chronology involved. The custom is usually said to have started at the court of the Emperor Li Hou-chu, about 970 A.D. or roughly 1,200 years after the voyage of Eudoxos. Even that date has been disputed because Marco Polo, the most famous and most reliable source of knowledge of things Chinese of his time (the thirteenth century), failed to mention the "golden lilies." But then, Friar Odoric did mention them only twenty years later, and some Chinese sources claim an earlier origin; so maybe the custom did exist in Eudoxos' time and was revived again later.

After having thrown the riddle of the Struthopodes into our laps, Pliny proceeded to the Astomi, the most charming of all his incredible Indians, located "at the very extremity of India, on the eastern side, near the source of the river Ganges." These Astomi ("no-mouths") were pictured as having no mouths and subsisting by inhaling the smells of fruits and flowers through their nostrils. "But an odor which is a little more powerful than usual easily destroys them."

Even though the Astomi lived at the end of India they were still not the farthest race, for: "beyond those people and at the very extremity of the mountains" were yet others: the Trispithami ("three-spans") and the Pygmies of the same size, about twenty-seven inches high. While they lived in a country of perpetual spring, their lives were not happy because of their dangerous enemies the cranes. But that they went down to the breeding places of the cranes once a year to destroy the eggs and as many young cranes as they could find, there might be no Pygmies left.

These Pygmies terminate what we like to call the "Pliny collection." Pliny's great encyclopedia was preserved in many copies, and late-Roman writers like Julius Solinus and Isidore of Seville used it as a quarry for their own compositions, collections of marvels which preserved Pliny's taller tales while omitting his many sober facts.

More than a thousand years after Pliny's death, interest in geography and related sciences revived, partly as a result of pilgrimages to Jerusalem. Several learned monks compiled encyclopedias of all the knowledge having to do with what we call the natural sciences—just in time to have their knowledge made obsolete by the dawning age of discovery. The greatest of these were three Dominicans: Thomas of Cantimpré (or Thomasius Cantipratensis), Vincent of Beauvais (Vincentius Bellovacensis), and Albrecht von Bollstädt (Albertus Magnus). While the most influential of the three men was Albertus, the most influential of the three books was that of Thomas.

Thomas's work was subdivided into twenty "books"— divisions that we should call chapters. The first of these was titled *Of Man;* the second, *Of the Soul,* while the third—well, that was the one most eagerly read and copied: *Liber de monstruosis hominibus orientis,* or *Book of the Monstrous People of the East.* This was simply the "Pliny collection," amended and elaborated.

While the monks marveled at the "facts" related in the Latin manuscripts by Thomas of Cantimpré and his colleagues as they copied them, the nobles gaped at recitations of a German metrical romance that originated around the middle of the twelfth century and that purported to relate the adventures of one Duke Ernest of Swabia—*Herzog Ernst von Schwaben* as the German title reads. Several versions of this romance exist: in German verse, in German prose, and in Latin verse, the last apparently being an adaptation of the German metrical version and not the original as one might think. Such was the popularity of that romance that it became a part of German folklore, right up to the present. The author may have been one Heinrich of Veldeck, who flourished around 1160 A.D.; the proof is not conclusive, but if not he then the author is quite unknown.

It might be well to state at the start that the Duke Ernest of the poem is a historical character: Duke Ernst II of Swabia, a son of Gisela, the second wife of Emperor Konrad II, who reigned as King of the Germans and Holy Roman Emperor back in the early eleventh century when the Dark Ages were becoming what we call the Middle Ages.

At first this Duke Ernst was on good terms with his foster father, the Emperor, until the latter annexed Burgundy, which Ernst claimed for himself. After rebelling repeatedly and without success he was jailed, and later released on the condition that he delivered his friend Count Wernher von Kyburg to the Emperor as hostage. Instead, Ernst began his rebellion again as soon as he was out of the Emperor's reach, and kept at it thereafter, until about 1030 both Duke Ernst and Count Wernher died fighting the Emperor's soldiers.

Events of this kind were common at the time. Less than a century earlier Liutolf, Duke of Swabia and Bavaria, had risen in revolt against his father, Emperor Otto the Great. However, in that case, after a battle near Regensburg, the rebellion ended with reconciliation (954 A.D.) and Liutolf soon after left for Italy to recover from some illness. Instead, he died there.

In the legend that formed after the rebellion of Duke Ernst, the careers of Ernst and Liutolf are strangely mixed. "Duke Ernest" of the poem is said to have rebelled against Otto, who in his day had long been dead. Duke Ernest and Count Wernher (called "Count Wetzel" in the poem) were supposed to have fought the Emperor near Regensburg, but instead of becoming reconciled to his antagonist the Duke is said to have fled the country with his friend Wetzel and their followers. The actual release from prison in Duke Ernst's case was interpreted as the return from the long journey, bringing with him as a present to the Emperor a great ruby, the largest jewel in the German Emperor's crown.*

While this is what may be called "*bona fide* confusion" on the part of the poet, he seems to have added some points of deliberate simplification. In reality both prototypes, Duke Liutolf and the real Duke Ernst, fought their respective Emperors for political and material reasons in carefully planned revolts. In the poem, however, the reason for the insurrection is the result of an impetuous act of personal revenge—the slaying of the *Pfalzgraf* Heinrich, a vassal and relative of the Emperor. Immediately afterwards Ernest, realizing that the Emperor will not forgive him, flees, but resists for a while at Regensburg, hoping that his mother's influence might bring about a reconciliation.

But the Emperor's men (in the poem, not in history) slowly push Ernest and his friend "Wetzel" out of Germany. Followed by fifty knights they enter Hungary, and Ernest decides to make a pilgrimage to the Holy Grave, trying to combine his escape from the Emperor's wrath with atonement for the killing of Heinrich.

At first they have a pleasant journey through friendly lands. Things only become a little more adventurous when they cross into the land of "the wild Bulgars where it was often necessary to hack one's way with the sword." In time that stage passes too. They enter Greece and near Constantinople, the seat of the mighty Emperor of Byzantium, who wel-

* Konrad II did order his goldsmith to put a ruby into the crown, though whether it was the largest gem in that crown is doubtful.

comes Ernest because he has learned that Ernest is on bad terms with his foe the German Emperor. Therefore the Greek Emperor greets Ernest as a friend and ally. When the Duke finally leaves for the Holy Grave not only is he furnished with a ship, but also several Byzantine war galleys are sent along for protection.

For seven days and nights the voyage proceeds pleasingly, but on the eighth day dense clouds hide the sun and a terrible storm arises. For three days it whirls the fleet through a sea beset with rocks and cliffs on which all the galleys are destroyed. When the storm lifts, Duke Ernest's ship lies alone on the sea, but on the horizon they sight land. Approaching it, the men soon see that it is fruitful and cultivated, with grainfields, vineyards, and orchards. Beyond the tilled fields appears a city with silvery battlements and towers.

They land and walk inland, all in a happy frame of mind save old Count Wetzel. The Count warns them that he's heard of an island like this called Grippia, as large as England but inhabited by villainous folk of monstrous form who kill all visitors with poisoned arrows. Ernest, after listening to his friend's advice, orders the sailors to go back to the ship and hold it in readiness for flight, while he, Wetzel, and the armed knights reconnoiter.

They accordingly march to the stronghold, and entering find large tables set with food and wine, which they consume. Then they hear the sound of an approaching army.

They rush to the tower and realize that Count Wetzel has guessed right: this is Grippia, for the Agrippians themselves are coming nigh. These are people with the heads and necks of birds: the men those of cranes, and the women those of swans. The men all wear red tunics, without armor, and carry each a bow, a knife, and a buckler.

Although Count Wetzel advises a quiet retreat, the Duke

answers with a laugh that his sword should cut nicely through those cranes' necks. When it transpires that a white maiden with the Agrippians is a prisoner, even the cautious Count agrees to battle. The knights rush upon the Agrippians and almost rescue the maiden, but at the last minute an Agrippian stabs her fatally with his beak. Dying, she utters a few words identifying herself as the "Princess of India," and then the knights have to cut their way back to their ship through masses of Agrippians, who almost overwhelm them by weight of numbers. They finally make their ship under cover of the archery fire of the sailors. After they have cast off, the ship's master assures them that the wind has turned fair in the meantime and that they should reach Syria in another three days.

Now, the story of Duke Ernest can easily be divided into a number of successive adventures or sets of adventures. The first set comprises the setting and the political background, and the events leading to the arrival in Constantinople. All this is on safe ground, the listener being familiar with the events and settings. Homer used the same literary device when he began the *Odyssey* with familiar scenes and gradually bore his hearer beyond the horizon of the known world. Ernest's second set of adventures, beginning with the departure from Constantinople, deals with the concept of the Voyage to the Holy Land, familiar from the Crusades. (The first two Crusades, note, had taken place in the time of Henry of Veldeck, though *not* in the time of the historical Dukes Ernst II and Liutolf of Schwaben.)

However, the details now begin to blur and to become fabulous. While Grippia lies in the Mediterranean, but three days' sail from Syria, where did it get its strange crane-headed natives? They don't appear in the Pliny collection. In fact, the only other mention of them outside the Duke Ernest poem and works derived from it is a brief mention in Chapter 175 of the *Gesta Romanorum*, a medieval collection of stories and fables in Latin prose, that "somewhere in Europe there live beautiful people with the neck, head, and bill of the crane." And the *Gesta Romanorum* was probably first compiled over a century after the Duke Ernest romance was written. So, is the crane-folk idea a case of pure imagination, or based upon "facts" of some sort?

When thinking about such questions, remember that the people of those times were not given to careful investigation and reporting. They thought they were being accurate to the point of meticulousness if they mentioned that they had got their information from one "Job the Syrian" or other such worthy, though whether Job was trustworthy as an eyewitness never bothered them. Consequently they reported hearsay as fact, and facts that did not seem to make sense were "adjusted" until they did. This careless and naïve attitude (to our way of thinking) led an early traveler to India to conclude in all seriousness, from seeing the statues of Hindu gods, that a race of many-armed folk must live somewhere in that country.

As an example from four centuries after the composition of the "Duke Ernest" romance, take a strange woodcut printed in 1545 as part of Ryff's German translation of the Latin works of Albertus Magnus. Although the South German artist who made the woodcuts for this edition had never seen many of the beasts described by Albertus in the zoological part of his treatise, he was not daunted by what to us would be a major obstacle. He simply followed the written descriptions: thus when Albertus described an octopus as "a fish in the seas which has eight legs," the artist drew a fish with eight legs—something like a spider with a fish's body!

So, you see, anything could have served as a basis for the Agrippians: a mistaken report, a faulty translation, or a picture seen somewhere by a pilgrim. We strongly suspect that in this case it was a picture. Until somebody offers a better explanation, we are inclined to think that the "island" of Grippia was Egypt (about the right distance from Syria in the story) and that the "Agrippians" were based on pictures of Tehuti or Thoth, the Egyptian ibis-headed god of magic and writing.

Naturally the Agrippians had to be an unfriendly race, or the poet would have been faced with the problem of explaining why, though at no great distance from the known lands, they were not better known.

The third set of adventures then takes place in the "fabulous East," and in order to get his characters there the poet resorts to another device: the myth of the Mountain of Lodestone. Now this Mountain of Lodestone had its own history, which we shall discuss in more detail in the next chapter. It may be mentioned, however, that the poet took his license even with this myth, moving it from the Indian Ocean to the Mediterranean. (Of course one can reflect that the average twelfth-century German was probably not sure whether the Mediterranean Sea and the Indian Ocean were two separate bodies of water or not.)

However, to skip unimportant details, Duke Ernest's ship, instead of sailing straight to Syria as promised, is caught by the Mountain of Lodestone and wrecked, with the result that most of those on board perish. Escape seems impossible until Count Wetzel observes that griffins come to the mountain to pick up and carry off dead bodies. Therefore he and the Duke sew themselves into the hides of steers and are promptly carried a vast distance to be dumped in a griffin's eyrie. Having killed the young griffins who try to devour them, they climb out of the eyrie and find to their great pleasure that two of their most trusted servants have escaped in the same manner. Together they walk until they come to a river which, as they see, disappears into a mountain. After a short discussion they decide to risk the journey through the mountain and fashion a raft to travel on.

When the raft emerges from the darkness they find themselves in a forest. After having moored the raft they continue afoot, and presently come to a cultivated country with cities in the distance. The people seem well dressed and civilized, but when they come near, the travelers discover that the natives have each a single eye in the middle of the forehead . . . They have reached the land of the Arimaspians.

The one-eyed folk prove friendly and curious about the strangers with two eyes, something they had never seen before. The travelers, unable to make themselves understood, are taken first before the local judge and finally to their king.

The rest of this set of adventures is straight medieval romance in a setting of Pliny's monstrous peoples of the East. Duke Ernest and Count Wetzel, after learning the language, are appointed supreme commanders of the Arimaspian army, since the Arimaspians themselves are a peaceful race ignorant of military matters. Their prosperity, however, exposes them to the attacks of their brutish neighbors. First come the Sciapods. After they are beaten off, a tribe with ears so big and tough they serve as arrow-proof cloaks tries to seize the Arimaspian riches. When these, too, are defeated a third foe appears, the giant "Sons of Anak."

FIG. 9. Representation of a headless man, reported to have his eyes near the armpits and a large mouth in the middle of the chest. This legend was localized in two places, India and Africa. The origin is probably a mistaken report about native dancing masks. (From Mandeville.)

Although he beats these also, Duke Ernest is not happy. The king of the Arimaspians won't let his ever-victorious generals go home, though Ernest and Wetzel, despite the friendliness of their hosts, always feel a shudder when scrutinized by one of those single eyes. Finally they are rescued when for the first time in Arimaspian history a ship of two-eyed men lands on the coast.

Wetzel secretly arranges a passage for his master and himself, and they leave three days later. However, the ship soon has to stop for water at the first coast they find. It turns out to be the land of the Pygmies, and while the men are filling their casks at a spring a delegation of the little folk comes from the mountain in which they live in tunnels and offers gold and silver to the tall men if the latter will only help them to fight the cranes who threaten their existence.

The men accede to this request; they set a trap for the cranes, using an army of Pygmies as a decoy, and after having slaughtered many of the birds they return to their ship laden with precious metals. Their next stop is in India.

The remaining adventures of the homeward journey consist mostly of battles with Saladin's hosts, of no special interest.

It is interesting to see how the Pygmies, in the words of the old German poet who composed the romance of Duke Ernest, almost automatically become gnomes. Or to put it more accurately, how the original Pygmies of Homer and Herodotos became assimilated to the earth fairies, the "knockers" or *Kobolde,* of medieval European peasant folklore. It was a general belief among miners that these two-foot beings haunted mines, and if well disposed towards the miner could lead him to rich ore, but if antagonized could cave in his tunnel or suffocate him with gases. Later, in the sixteenth century, when Paracelsus developed his doctrine of the four races of elemental spirits (of earth, air, fire, and water) he adopted the kobolds as earth-elementals, renaming them "gnomes" from the Greek *gnōmōn*, "knower."

The general impression from classical references to the Pygmies, however, is of a poor race living in swamps or forests. Pliny said they lived in huts of mud mixed with feathers and eggshells; Aristotle casually mentioned that they dwelt in caves "like Troglodytes."

However, in the story of Duke Ernest the Pygmies live, not on a mountain, but *in* it. They are not poor, and are vulnerable only because of their small size. They offer gold and silver to possible protectors, and are industrious enough to furnish these friends with well-made weapons of adequate size and number. To the German writer they are not classical "Pygmies" at all, except by name; they are a Far-Eastern variety of the rich and industrious Nibelungs or kobolds of his own mountains.

The real Pygmies are the same five-foot Negrillos described in any modern book on Africa, located in the Ituri forest near the equator. The Egyptians knew about them, as is shown by sculptures on the tombs of Saqqara, dating back to the Fifth Dynasty or about 2900 B.C., and passed on their knowledge to the other nations of the Mediterranean. Aristotle's Pygmies lived far to the south, near the sources of the Nile, while Pliny, following Greek authors, spoke of Pygmies in Africa as well as in the East.

Even Homer referred to them: At the beginning of the third book of the *Iliad* he tells how they live in the far southern land whither the cranes fly when winter drives them from their usual northern abode. Here occurs the oldest surviving literary reference to the never-ending war between the Pygmies and the cranes:

E'en as the clamor of cranes in the heavens ariseth,
When they would flee unspeakable rains and storms of the
    winter,
Clamorous thus while flying afar to the currents of Ocean,
Bearing destruction and doom unto men—to the race of the
    Pygmies;
Battle and ruinous strife they offer to them at dawning.
The Iliad of Homer, III, 3-7

We don't know what fact, if any, formed the basis for the legend of the crane-Pygmy hostilities; cranes and herons can defend their nests with their formidable beaks, but are not normally so foolhardy as to attack a man. Would a crane try to spear a Pygmy who tried to steal its eggs? Perhaps Homer's statement was just a way of emphasizing the Pygmies' small size, for his hearers would have known that cranes would not assault *them*.

At any event the Greek Land of the Pygmies was the dwelling place of the real Congo Pygmies, slightly displaced to the enormous swamps of the Upper Nile, whither the cranes actually do fly in winter.

But then the Pygmies were moved again, to the East, perhaps in part because the African Pygmies do have an eastern counterpart, the Negritos of the Andaman Islands, the Malay Peninsula, Sumatra, New Guinea, and the Philippines. It doesn't matter that the annual visits of the cranes from the North does not apply to these Eastern Pygmies—the cranes had become associated in people's minds with the Pygmies, so when the Pygmies were moved the cranes went along, especially as the African Pygmies had been more or less forgotten in the meantime. (They were rediscovered for modern science as late as 1870.)

Naturally the Pygmies shrank even more in the course of their transplantation. While the Egyptians, who had seen them, knew them to be up to five feet tall, the Greeks who had not knew only that they were "small." In Pliny's time they were "three-spans." When the idea of twenty-seven-inch people in the East had taken a firm root, it degenerated, as often happens, into a plain hoax. Western travelers to the East, full of Pliny, demanded to see two-foot people, alive or dead. When the natives understood what was wanted, they smilingly set to work to supply the demand at a profit to themselves. The story of Homer's Pygmies comes to an anti-climax in the memoirs of Marco Polo, who told what really happened:

> It should be known that what is reported respecting the dried bodies of diminutive human creatures, or pygmies, brought from India, is an idle tale, such men being manufac-tured in [Sumatra] in the following manner. The country produces a species of monkey, of a tolerable size, and having a countenance resembling that of a man. Those persons who make it their business to catch them, shave off the hair, leav-ing it only about the chin, and those other parts where it naturally grows on the human body. They then dry and pre-serve them with camphor and other drugs; and having pre-pared them in such a mode that they have exactly the appear-ance of little men, they put them into wooden boxes, and sell them to trading people, who carry them to all parts of the world. But this is merely an imposition. Neither in India, nor in any other country, however wild, have pygmies been found of a form so diminutive as these exhibit.
>
> *The Book of Ser Marco Polo*, III, xii

CHAPTER IV

The Sea of Sindbad

AT THE TIME OF THE CALIPH HARUN AL-RASHID THERE LIVED in the city of Baghdad, as you know, two men of the same name: Sindibád of the Sea and Sindibád of the Land, or to use their more familiar forms Sindbad the Sailor and Sindbad the Porter. One day, you remember, Sindbad the Porter, a poor man, happened to be near the house of his rich namesake, who invited him in and began to tell him and his other guests the story of his adventurous voyages.

These voyages, a well-loved and well-remembered fragment of everybody's childhood reading, are the real origin of the "fabulous East" as we think of it. Moreover they are easily the most colorful of all the collection of stories called the *Arabian Nights' Entertainments*, or the *Thousand and One Nights*, which contain others almost as familiar: "Aladdin and His Lamp," "Ali Baba and the Forty Thieves," "The Fisherman and the Jinn," and so on.

These stories have become such an integral part of our literature that it is surprising to learn that they were introduced to the West in comparatively recent times, and to realize that in their native land they are not held in anything like the esteem we accord them. One feels that literate Arabs, in conversation, should quote from *Sindbad* as an English-speaker quotes from Shakespeare, a German from Goethe, or a Russian from Pushkin.

Well, they don't.

But, the Westerner will ask, don't they at least esteem them as masterpieces of the storyteller's imagination? The answer is no, and to make it worse they are, strictly speaking, no masterpieces of imagination at all. They are masterpieces of literary larceny.

Before we go into the problem of the origin of Sindbad's adventures, a few words should be said about the book itself.

The *Arabian Nights* or, better, *The Thousand and One Nights*, were first translated into a European language by a French orientalist and archeologist who had a high reputation in his field but who is now remembered chiefly as the first translator of these stories. His name was Antoine Galland, and he published the twelve volumes of the collection over a period of years beginning in 1704.

It so happened that Galland had started with the stories of Sindbad the Sailor, thinking them a unit, before he learned that they were only part of a larger collection. Then he succeeded in obtaining the other stories of the collection by a succession of lucky accidents fantastic enough to have a place in the *Thousand and One Nights* themselves.

Galland's version was a paraphrase rather than an accurate translation or a carefully edited collection of all the tales. In fact, it has been said that Galland produced a good *French* storybook, based more or less remotely on the Arabic. For this very reason the French reading public took to it at once, and soon translations into other European languages followed—all of them from Galland's French, not from the original. The stories also excited the interest of Galland's colleagues, with the result that for nearly two and a half centuries orientalists have hunted manuscripts, checked other

Arabic and Persian literature for cross references and allusions, and tried to pin down the dates of the stories from internal evidence.

The result, while enlightening and interesting in detail, is somewhat meager, because the Muslim world, as we said, did not think much of these stories. Learned Muhammadans regarded them as coffeehouse literature, possibly useful for the entertainment of guests with somewhat depraved tastes . . . in short they had much the attitude of Western musical classicists towards current song hits—especially when the classicist discovers that the latest *How I Want My Baby* is nothing but an adaptation of a theme lifted from Tchaikovsky or Schubert.

Because of this attitude on the part of Muslim scholars, the stories varied greatly through the centuries and were not written down until comparatively late. It seems as if the storytellers had a certain number of stock items and the framework story, and then just used whatever came to hand to fill out the needed number of "nights." The so-called "complete" manuscript, the one translated by Lane, Torrens, Payne, Littmann, and Burton, is of Egyptian origin and was compiled at the end of the eighteenth century. In the Burton translation it fills seventeen large volumes, several of them devoted to notes and variora. Besides the well-known tales mentioned previously there are many others: collections of anecdotes and animal fables, and interminable love-and-swordplay romances much like those composed in medieval Europe by Ariosto and his ilk.

When dates can be established for particular stories they are all pretty late; thus the story of the two wazirs cannot have been written much before 1260 and is probably more recent. And the so-called Hunchback Cycle cannot have been written before 1300 and is probably later too. The deeds attributed to Harun al-Rashid, of going about among his people disguised as a commoner, are properly not those of that cautious and calculating eighth-century Caliph, but those of Baibars, the fearsome thirteenth-century Sultan of Egypt. Some of the stories involve the Crusades—from the Muslim side, of course, and to a reader accustomed to the usual treatment of the theme in Western fiction it is entertaining to read of a Muslim hero overthrowing hordes of "Franks" practically singlehanded. The coarse humor of the stories and the curious effeminacy of some of the heroes are typically Egyptian, not Arab, touches.

The earliest known date at which the collection (but not any specific tale) existed has been established from a remark in the encyclopedia written by Mas'udi, who died about 956 A.D. This distinguished Baghdadi scholar took time out to sneer at fantastic tales "like the books transmitted to us and translated for us from the Persian, Indian, and Greek . . . such as the 'Book of the Thousand *Khurafas*' . . . the people call this book 'A Thousand Nights and a Night.'"

The word *khurafa* means "fantasy" or "canard," and we might say that Mas'udi spoke of the *Book of a Thousand Whoppers*. Thus learned Arabs not only took a dim view of the collection, but even disclaimed Arabic authorship, calling the tales translations. Properly speaking the stories are adaptations, the original plot being furnished with Muslim names, places, and atmosphere with which the listening audience would be already familiar.

Let's follow Sindbad on his voyages.

Their locale is the Indian Ocean and, more particularly, the large islands of the East Indies, or Indonesia (of which Sumatra was usually taken to be a part of the mainland) and the Philippines beyond. The destination of these voyages was clear to the listeners, for not only was Arabian sea trade Indian trade almost by definition, but even the hero's name contained the Arabic word for India, *Sind*.

The First Voyage, like all the others, begins with the minor overland or river trip from Baghdad to Basra, the seaport at the head of the Persian Gulf. Thence Sindbad embarked "with a company of merchants" to sail down the Gulf. They "sailed many days and nights, and we passed from isle to isle and sea to sea and shore to shore, buying and selling and bartering everywhere the ship touched. . . ."*

So far the trip is commonplace; the hearers knew all about these trading voyages down the coast of Fars and beyond, on which the lateen-rigged dhows of the Arab maritime world were constantly setting forth—as they still do. However, by this literary device the author, like those of *The Odyssey* and *Herzog Ernst*, gets his hero away from the known and the normal to far places where the strange and the monstrous are to be expected. Remember that to the hearers of the *Nights* the Near-Eastern world of Cairo, Damascus, and Baghdad was the humdrum world of every day, *not* the land of the exotic and fantastic.

On they went, south and east, under their bellying trapezoidal sails—pretty things and efficient in light breezes, but the Devil's own job to tack with—"till we came to an island as it were a garth of the gardens of Paradise. Here the captain cast anchor and making fast to the shore, put out the landing planks. So all on board landed and made furnaces and lighting fires therein, busied themselves in various ways, some cooking and some washing, whilst other some walked about

* *The Book of the Thousand Nights and a Night* (Burton transl.), VI, p. 5. The other quotations in this chapter are from the same volume.

the island for solace, and the crew fell to eating and drinking and playing and sporting."

After weeks at sea, crowded aboard a little dhow, it would be good to go ashore and stretch and do the things one could not do on the ship.

> I was one of the walkers but, as we were thus engaged, behold the master who was standing on the gunwale cried out to us at the top of his voice, saying, 'Ho there! passengers, run for your lives and hasten back to the ship and leave your gear and save yourselves from destruction, Allah preserve you! For this island whereon ye stand is no true island, but a great fish stationary a-middlemost of the sea, whereon the sand hath settled and trees have sprung up of old time, so that it is become like unto an island; but, when ye lighted fires on it, it felt the heat and moved; and in a moment it will sink with you into the sea and ye will all be drowned.'

The Big Fish mistaken for an island is one of the most ubiquitous adventure tales in sea stories of the Middle Ages. It appears with great regularity in the North (for instance, in the story of the Voyages of St. Brendan, where the Fish is called "the beast Jasconius") where it had the authority of Archbishop Olaus Magnus in back of it. The statements of Olaus even caused the story to get into some of the early books on natural history, though with a question mark attached to it.

The Arab storytellers could likewise point to a scientific book by one of their own people, which had comparably great authority among them. Its author, Zakariyya ibn-Muhammad ibn-Mahmud al-Qazwini, is now chiefly remembered for his remark that the greatness of Allah can be deduced from the fact that he lets the rain fall only on fruitful land and not on the desert where nothing would grow anyway, but he was for a long time the chief authority on things zoological in the Muslim world. He died in 1283, about nine years after the completion of his *Ajayyib al-Makhlukat,* which may be translated as *Wonders of Animate Creation.*

The island-that-turns-out-to-be-a-fish story can be found in the section devoted to the animals of the water. There Qazwini says that the tortoise occurs both as a land beast and a sea beast, and that moreover the sea tortoise (or turtle) grows to enormous size. He then quotes the account of a merchant regarding the size of this creature, and orientalists state that the Sindbad tale is clearly copied from this account, the wording being identical in places.

But where did Qazwini get the tale, or the merchant who told the *khurafa* to him? While there must have been intermediate stages in the development of the myth, now lost, the idea seems ultimately to go back to Pliny's *Natural History,* where in speaking of sea beasts he says: "Largest of all these animals are those found in the Indian seas, among which are the balaenae, four iugera in extent, and the pristis, two hundred cubits long." Two hundred cubits is a shade under 300 feet, while a *iugerum* was a measure of area: a space 240 by 120 feet, or about two-thirds of a modern acre.

Although Pliny says nothing about his sea beasts' being mistaken for islands, the idea still might easily have suggested itself, especially since small islands (like the "Phantom Islands" off the West African coast) often appear and vanish in shallow coastal waters. Sometime between Pliny and Qazwini, evidently, somebody "correlated" the reports of the big monsters of the sea and the disappearing and re-appearing islands which were such a hazard to coastal navigation, apparently finding it easier to believe in drifting sea-monsters than in small sandy islands shifted about by currents between one high tide and the next.

To return to the tale, Sindbad is not among those lucky

enough to reach the ship before the monster disappears beneath the waves.

However, he clings to one of the big wooden tubs that had been used for laundering, and after a day and a night he is cast upon the shore of a large wooded island. A man who identifies himself as a servant of King Mihrján finds him and feeds him. The rescuer tells Sindbad that he and many other servants of this king have brought the royal mares to the island that they may be tethered out to attract the sea horses and thus produce the highly valued hybrids between horses of the land and of the sea.

Afterwards Sindbad is taken to the city of the king and stays there, on the island, for some time. During this time he sees many wonders, a fish 200 cubits long which menaces sailors and fishermen but which can be shunted off by the noise of knocking pieces of wood together, and a fish with a face like an owl. He also sees the island of Kásil, whence the sound of drums echoes all night, and which his hosts believe to be the abode of al-Dajjál, the Muslim Antichrist, who will some day lay waste the earth at the head of an army of 70,000 Jews. Sindbad also meets parties of men from India, and learns of the curious customs of that country.

Finally a trading ship casts anchor in the port of King Mihrján's city—and Sindbad is delighted to find that it is the ship in which he sailed from Basra, with all his property still safe aboard. And on this ship he returns home without further adventures. . . .

The identification of the islands mentioned in this narrative can be established, without too much difficulty, from three Arabic works. One is the already-mentioned marvelbook of Qazwini; the second, the ninth-century *Account of India and China by Two Muhammadan Travelers* which, though infested with some hearsay marvels, seems to be a real travel tale; and the third is the so-called *Rogerian Treatise*.

The last-named (in Arabic, *Al-Rojari*) represents almost the last serious geographical effort of Muslim science. In the twelfth century, the time of the First Crusade, one of the greatest monarchs of Europe was Roger II, the Norman king of Sicily and southern Italy. Besides extending his territorial power he attracted to his court men of genius of all creeds and nations. Among the men of parts with whom he surrounded himself was a Spanish Moor, Abu Abdallah Muhammad ibn-Idrisi (or Edrisi), a kind of Muslim Henry the Navigator. Idrisi and his master conceived the idea of sending out scouts in all directions—north, east, south, and west—to travel for hundreds of miles and then to return to tell what they had seen. When they came back, Idrisi used their information to construct a silver map of the world and to write a geography. This was an exceptionally learned work which is also exceptionally tedious to read. However, whatever the faults of Idrisi's style and method, the treatise is still the best and least fantastic of all the general geographical works of the Arabs that have come down, and therefore is very helpful in identifying places known by Arabic names.

Arabic writers, now, call the island ruled by King Mihrján Ráneh, Ráyyij, Zánij, and various other names. Nevertheless it seems they all meant the same large island: to wit, Borneo, which is bigger than Texas. Al-Qazwini calls it the farthest of the islands of India (a matter of definition, of course) and names the king; Idrisi gives enough details to permit us to identify some of the smaller islands between Borneo and Sumatra.

The 200-cubit fish is already familiar to us from Pliny's *pristis*, taken over by Qazwini, who enlarged it to 300 cubits and added the touch about its being afraid of the noise of knocking pieces of wood together. This allegation suggests the celebrated incident of Nearchos and the whales. When Alexander of Macedon's admiral, Nearchos, was sailing the fleet home from India along the coast of Iran, his men were terrified to see a school of whales (some of them probably longer than the ships) approaching. Nearchos ordered the men to blow their trumpets and make as much racket as possible, whereupon the sea mammals sounded and bothered them no more.

Furthermore both Qazwini and ibn al-Wardi, another zoologist of wonderland, report on the owl-headed fish, said to be a cubit long—perhaps meaning one of the parrot wrasses, a widespread family of tropical fish with beaklike jaws they use to break up coral to get at the polyps living therein.

The mystery of the island of Kásil may have been a natural phenomenon. The first commentator, Hole, suggested that it may have been a small rocky islet where the roaring of the waves among the rocks made a sound like the roll of distant drums. It was but natural that such an island, which probably could not be approached with safety, would become the focal point of local superstitions about demons.

The story of the mares and the sea horses goes back to several sources. The storyteller's direct source, for one, was once more Qazwini, who described a "water horse" and stated that on occasion a mare brought forth a foal of supreme excellence, whose sire was a water horse. Qazwini was really trying to describe the hippopotamus (Greek *hippos*, horse, + *potamos*, river) from its name alone, without ever having seen one or knowing what it looked like. The development of the bulbous three-ton hippo into a "sea horse" parallels the evolution of the porcine Indian rhinoceros into the graceful unicorn of European legend as a result of Ktesias's description of it as a kind of wild ass.

Naturally there are no horse-hippopotamus hybrids, though stories of "rare hybrids" between such unrelated species have been common traveler's tales for many centuries. However, another source of Sindbad's sea-horse story may lie in the fact that in parts of Asia where the Asiatic wild ass* lives, and in Arabia, where the African wild ass is found, men sometimes have picketed mares and female asses in order that the male wild asses shall get mules or asses on them.

Pliny's account, which presumably started the whole fable, can be found in his *Natural History*, reading: "It is well known that in Lusitania [Portugal] in the vicinity of the town of Olisipo [Lisbon] and the river Tagus, the mares, by turning their faces toward the Westwind as it blows, become impregnated by its breezes and that the foals which are conceived in this way are remarkable for their extreme fleetness; but they never live beyond three years." (Pliny, *op. cit.*, VIII, i, xvii.) This, in turn, was a nice trader's tale, based on Phoenician accounts of the incredible fertility of Lusitania and the fleetness of those "sons of the wind," the Lusitanian horses.

Ten centuries after Pliny, when Portugal and Lisbon were too well known, the tale had to be transplanted to the Far East, which then harbored the marvels once characteristic of the West.

The Second Voyage begins like the first. Sindbad and other merchants embark on a new, stout ship and sail until they reach a beautiful island "fair and verdant, in trees abun-

* The onager or kiang, an animal larger and more horselike than the African ass (from whom the domestic donkey descends).

dant, with yellow-ripe fruits luxuriant, and flowers fragrant and birds warbling soft descant; and streams crystal and radiant; but no sign of man showed to the descrier, no not a blower of the fire."

Falling asleep in the soft breeze, Sindbad is left behind when the ship sails, since nobody notices his absence. When he awakens he wanders about and finally climbs a tree to see better. And in the distance he espies a large white object. When he climbs down and walks towards the thing, and

> behold, it was a huge white dome rising high in the air and of vast compass. I walked all around it, but found no door thereto, nor could I muster strength or nimbleness by reason of its exceeding smoothness and slipperiness. So I marked the spot where I stood and went round about the dome to measure its circumference which I found fifty good paces. And as I stood, casting about how to gain an entrance, the day being near its fall and the sun being near its horizon, behold, the sun was suddenly hidden from me and the air became dull and dark. Methought a cloud had come over the sun, but it was the season of summer; so I marvelled at this and lifting my head looked steadfastly at the sky, when I saw that the cloud was none other than an enormous bird, of gigantic girth and inordinately wide of wing which, as it flew through the air, veiled the sun and hid it from the island. . . .
> My wonder redoubled and I remembered a story I had heard aforetime of pilgrims and travellers, how in a certain island dwelleth a huge bird, called the 'Rukh' which feedeth its young on elephants; and I was certified that the dome which caught my sight was none other than a Rukh's egg. As I looked and wondered at the marvelous works of the Almighty, the bird alighted on the dome and brooded over it with its wings covering it and its legs stretched out behind it on the ground, and in this posture it fell asleep, glory be to Him who sleepeth not!

But the monstrous bird, terrifying though it be, will provide Sindbad with means of escape from the island. "I arose and, unwinding my turban from my head, doubled it and twisted it into a rope, with which I girt my middle and bound my waist fast to the legs of the Rukh, saying to myself, 'Peradventure, this bird may carry me to a land of cities and inhabitants, and that will be better than abiding in this desert island.'"

The plan succeeds. At dawn the Rukh wakes up, utters a loud cry, and flies away, carrying the voyager along. After a long flight it descends and finally comes to rest amidst forbidding mountains. Sindbad hastily unties himself and watches how the Rukh picks up an immense serpent and flies away with it seawards.

Looking around, Sindbad finds himself in a huge valley barren of all vegetation and swarming with snakes "that would have made but one gulp of an elephant." After a sleepless night he wanders on, trying to find a way out, when he suddenly sees something fall from above. It turns out to be part of a slaughtered animal, and he remembers the story of the terrible valley whence all diamonds and other precious stones come, and of the stratagem by which merchants obtain these stones:

> . . . they take a sheep and slaughter and skin it and cut it in pieces and cast them down from the mountain-tops into the valley-sole, where the meat being fresh and sticky with blood, some of the gems cleave to it. There they leave it till mid-day, when the eagles and vultures swoop down upon it and carry it in their claws to the mountain-summits, whereupon the merchants come and shout at them and scare them away from the meat. Then they come and, taking the diamonds which they find sticking to it, go their ways with them and leave the meat to the birds and beasts; nor can any come at the diamonds but by this device. . . .

Waiting for another slaughtered animal to be thrown down, Sindbad fills his pockets with gems, and then ties himself to a carcass to be carried to the top of the mountain by a large bird of prey. (Storytellers have always much exaggerated the weight-lifting powers of such birds; hence stories of children being carried off by eagles. A few years ago a series of tests with a healthy tame eagle showed that the bird could just about maintain altitude with two pounds attached to his legs.)

When Sindbad has made his escape by this means, he rewards the merchant whose animal-carcass he has used in this manner. Then he returns with him and others to the coast, to an island abounding in camphor trees. This is the home of the rhinoceros:

> . . . a huge brute, bigger of body than the camel and like it feedeth upon the leaves and twigs of trees. It is a remarkable animal with a great and thick horn, ten cubits long, amiddleward of its head; wherein, when cleft in twain, is the likeness of a man. Voyagers and pilgrims and travellers declare that this beast called 'Karkadan' will carry off a great elephant on its horn and graze about the island and the seacoast therewith and take no heed of it, till the elephant dieth and its fat, melting in the sun, runneth down into the rhinoceros's eyes and blindeth him, so that he lieth down on the shore. Then comes the bird Rukh and carrieth off both the rhinoceros and that which is on its horn to feed its young withal.

Judging from the presence of the rhinoceros, the island might well be Sumatra or Java. What has happened to the rhinoceros in this tale makes a somewhat complex story.

As regards the "likeness of a man" in its horn, the facts are obvious. Rhinoceros horns, like other horns, were thought to "harbor enmity" against poison. Therefore, naturally, beakers were made of horns so that their owners should be protected, and some of these vessels were artistically carved. Carved rhinoceros-horn beakers, some of which still exist, were deemed especially valuable, and some Arab who saw one took these carvings to be a natural formation of the horn.

The other features are a stew of meat from many books. The "enmity" between elephant and rhinoceros had been reported by Pliny, who told how the rhino prepared for battle by sharpening its horn against a rock. Such tales of hostilities among beasts belong to a large family of *khurafas* that have existed in all cultures at all ages, and which in the modern West we call "nature faking."

This type of writing is luckily scarcer now than a generation ago, when Kipling, Curwood, Burroughs, and many less-known writers described packs of wolves chasing muzhiks across the Siberian snows, snakes avenging their slain mates, gorillas kidnaping African women, and various beasts talking, rearing human children, sacrificing themselves for their young, and obeying the Ten Commandments or the Law of the Jungle or some such elaborate code, none of which happens in real life. One of the authors, for instance, recalls in his boyhood reading in an early edition of the *Book of Knowledge* a statement that the sawfish attacked whales; actually this fish, a sluggish bottom-living relative of the skates, uses its saw merely to dig out of the mud the marine worms on which it feeds, and wouldn't think of bothering a whale.

The idea of such irrational enmities among life forms goes back, not to any careful observation of animals in their natural state, but to medieval and ancient beliefs to the effect that all natural things were connected with all others by occult sympathies and antipathies. Medieval books of magic, for instance, consisted largely of interminable lists of such relationships: the planet Jupiter hates Mars and loves the sun; the olive tree loves the myrtle and hates harlots; elephants hate hogs; and so on *ad nauseam*.

The rhinoceros-elephant antipathy belongs to this class of beliefs, and has continued to be repeated in books down to quite modern times, without ever citing actual cases. In a normal wild state duels of this sort, among animals of different species, are almost unknown. In obedience to their instincts the animals try to eat without being eaten. Carnivores attack herbivores to eat them, preferring species that can be overcome without risk to the eater, while they usually ignore or avoid other carnivores and herbivores too big for them. Herbivores flee carnivores big enough to menace them, and among some species the males fight each other for the females, but herbivores usually ignore herbivores of other species.

As for the size attributed to the rhinoceros, Pliny had said that "the two animals are of equal length, but the legs of the rhinoceros are much shorter," which only slightly exaggerates the size of the Indian rhinoceros, the biggest of the three Asiatic species. Evidently the increase in size took place elsewhere.

Perhaps a translator failed to copy Pliny's sentence about the animals' sizes, and a reader got the impression that an animal that attacked an elephant had to be larger than its victim. And then there was the Talmudic tale about the unicorn destined to be saved from the Flood, but so large that it failed to fit into the Ark. Therefore it had to swim all the 150 days the waters prevailed upon the earth, now and then resting the tip of its horn on the stern of the Ark. Where the Talmud got that story will probably remain a mystery, but it seems likely that the Arabs got it from their cousins the Jews. One could believe that a beast so huge might not notice the weight of an elephant impaled on its horn, until the elephant's melting fat blinded it and the Rukh got both. A powerful illustration of *tertius gaudens* (as Pliny would have said): "The third is pleased."

We hardly have to tell you that the *direct* sources used by Sindbad's creator were again Idrisi and Qazwini, especially the latter. Both mention the figures of men in the horn of the rhinoceros, and Qazwini reports a rescue from an uninhabited island by a bird as a fact—not the Rukh, but a large bird that became friendly with the man and as a supernatural reward for his virtue carried him to shore, as the dolphin did with the legendary Greek bard Arion when the sailors gave him the Jonah treatment.

As for the Valley of the Diamonds in the Far East, Qazwini has that too. His treatment shows Northern mythological influence. The serpents of this valley, he says, were so venomous that their mere glance was fatal. Therefore the hero Iskander (that is, Alexander the Great) foiled them by throwing mirrors into the valley, in which the snakes stared themselves to death. The mirror was the only weapon with which to combat the terrible basilisk (so venomous that its breath killed), for if a horseman speared it the poison would travel up the spear and kill both man and horse. Pliny, who told this story about the basilisk (as something "formerly a general belief") did not know the story of Alexander and the mirrors, which appeared in some of the pseudo-Aristotelian writings about Alexander that came out in Europe about the time of Qazwini's birth.

While Qazwini emphasizes the venomousness of the serpents, the creator of Sindbad enlarges them to enormous size; later they shrink to normal size again. Marco Polo related the tamer version in the nineteenth chapter of his book, cautiously designating it as hearsay:

"Messer Marco was told that in the summer, when the heat is excessive and there is no rain, [the diamond collectors] ascend the mountains with great fatigue, as well as with considerable danger from the number of snakes with which they are infested. Near the summit, it is said, there are deep valleys, full of caverns and surrounded by precipices, amongst which the diamonds are found; and here are many eagles and white storks, attracted by the snakes on which they feed. . . ." The rest of Marco's story is the same as that of the Sindbad tales.

The whole thing seems to be a development of the older tales of gold-digging giant ants and gold-guarding griffins discussed in our third chapter, and the story was no doubt put to the practical use of making diamond prospecting seem so dangerous as to frighten off competitors.

Far in the East, most writers of that time were agreed, lay the island or islands of the satyrs. Now, the original satyrs were snub-nosed, horse-tailed supernaturals of the Greek imagination, whose main characteristic, as you can see from pictures on Greek vases, was a constant state of frantic lust. They were connected with the goat-legged Arcadian fertility-god Pan, with whom they were sometimes confused and whose form they were sometimes given in later times.

While we don't know just how the original satyr myth originated, references to satyrs in historic times usually can be accounted for by stories of apes and monkeys brought back by travelers to Greece, which possessed no such animals. At first, for instance, it might have been the hamadryas baboon, which the ancient Egyptians tamed; later, as we shall see when we come to the legends of the Atlantic, it may have been the chimpanzee.

However, in the times of which we are now speaking, there is little doubt that the satyr was the proboscis monkey of Borneo, *Semnopithecus nasicus*, an animal quite grotesque enough in looks and behavior to qualify as a satyr. And it is to this "island of the satyrs" that Sindbad is led on his Third Voyage.

The story starts with almost the same words as those of the First Voyage, with a company of merchants sailing from Basra and trading busily at every stop.

When they are far from home, however, a strong wind drives them to "the Mountain of the Zughb, a hairy folk like apes" who board the ship, drive the men off, and sail away with the vessel.

The castaways wander about disconsolately until they find a large house, where they rest till sunset. Then they feel the earth shake, and a vast giant draws near, "tall and big of bulk, as he were a great date-tree, with eyes like coals of fire and eye-teeth like boar's tusks and a vast gape like the mouth of a well. Moreover, he had long loose lips like a camel's, hanging down upon his breast, and ears like two Jarms falling over his shoulder-blades and the nails of his hands were like the claws of a lion."*

What follows is simply the Sindbadian version of the story of Polyphemos the Kyklops in the *Odyssey*. The giant eats one merchant for each meal until the men, recovering from their horror, blind him in his sleep and flee on rafts. The giant, together with a female of his kind, casts rocks at the rafts until all the men but Sinbad and two others are slain. Then a huge serpent devours the two others, but Sindbad foils it by tying to himself pieces of wood sticking out in all directions so that the supersnake can't swallow this spiky morsel.

Sindbad then is picked up by a passing ship, which takes him to "an island, called Al-Saláhitah, which aboundeth in sandal-wood" and where he recovers the gear he had with him on the Second Voyage after he proves his identity, and

---

* An earlier version is said to give the giant a single median eye. A *Jarm* is a kind of triangular barge; another version says "like two mortars."

returns home prosperously as he had done on the previous voyages.

The story is an obvious adaptation of Odysseus' adventure in the land of the Kyklopes, which corresponded in a vague way with Sicily at a time when the Greeks had only begun to hear rumors of Italy and Sicily to the west, but had not yet come to know these lands at first hand. Arab geographers, however, knew Sicily much too well to attribute such monstrosities to it; therefore they removed them to the Far East.

So much for the Third Voyage, except for the identity of Al-Saláhitah, which also appears in Arabic literature as Al-Seláhit and Al-Kaláhsitah. Idrisi placed it near Java and told of a constantly active volcano, which would bear the same relation to the giant with his fiery eyes and stone-throwing ability at Mount Aetna in Sicily does to Polyphemos. Qazwini (who wrote the name as "Al-Salámit") knew of the sandalwood and a boiling lake, whence Lane, the first English translator of the *Nights*, inferred that it might be the island of Sumbawa, east of Java.

If that is right, there might be a more tangible reason for the man-eating serpent than just the general knowledge that the East harbored large snakes. The next larger island east of Sumbawa is Flores, and between Sumbawa and Flores lies little Komodo, the home of *Varanus komodensis:* the giant monitor lizard of which twelve-foot specimens have been collected. The Komodo monitor (which also occurs, though rarely, on neighboring islands) has been reported as reaching a length of twenty feet and as being a man-eater if given the chance.*

* A fifty-foot lizard closely related to the Komodo monitor lived in Australia during the Pleistocene Period. This was a true lizard, not a dinosaur, all of which became extinct 60,000,000 years earlier.

While these Malay yarns are thought to be exaggerations, we can still be sure that the Komodo monitor is a dangerous antagonist even if the specimens in our museums are the largest that ever were. And if the natives tell such stories now, they probably told them in times of yore, so that Arab merchants may well have carried such accounts of the dangerous "serpents" of the Far East back to Basra and Baghdad as genuine fact.

The Fourth Voyage follows the familiar pattern. When Sindbad's ship is wrecked by a storm, he and some of the other merchants cling to planks and are finally cast ashore on an island where naked natives seize them and bring them before their king. The captives are fed a food that stupefies them so that they can be conveniently fattened for eating. By refusing this food Sindbad keeps his reason and escapes from the kingdom of the Ghuls—or ghouls, as we should write it. He walks seven days and seven nights until he reaches another and more civilized kingdom.* There he endears himself to the king by introducing the saddle and acquires wealth, rank, and honor. To keep such a useful man in his kingdom the king commands him to marry a beautiful heiress. This he does and settles down in perfect happiness.

However, the custom of the country is that when any married person dies, his or her spouse is buried alive too in the great common burial pit outside the city, with a pitcher of water and seven biscuits by way of provisions. Then Sindbad's wife dies, and despite his struggles and protests he is given the same treatment.

* In Semitic literature "seven" is often a figure of speech meaning "many."

With the rather unscrupulous practicality of the Egyptian hero, Sindbad keeps alive by murdering other unfortunates lowered into the pit after him and taking their provisions. Finally he notices that wild animals enter the pit to eat the bodies of the dead. Following them he finds another way out, and after stripping the dead of their jewels he signals a passing ship and is brought home.

Some authors have sought the cannibal island in the Andamans, in the Bay of Bengal, especially since Marco Polo said that the inhabitants of those islands eat anybody not of their tribe. But this seems to be just an accidental similarity, and Lane was probably right when he picked Sumatra as the locale of this tale. Qazwini (always the direct source of the storyteller) places the cannibal feasts on the island of Saksár—either Sumatra or Zanzibar—but without the stupefying drug, which is probably an echo of Odysseus' adventure with the Lotus-Eaters.

The escape from the burial pit was perhaps suggested by the Greek tale of Aristomenes who was taken prisoner by the Spartans and thrown into a pit with fifty of his men. Although all the others died of the fall, Aristomenes survived and found his way out by following a fox he heard gnawing on a corpse.

"Sir John Mandeville" took over these Sindbad tales with gusto and reported both incidents as items of fact, saying: "in the Yle of Calanak 3if a man that is maryed dye, men buryen his wif with him alle quyk" and in Lamaray (Sumatra?) "thei eaten more gladly mannes flesche than any other flesche" and adding what is probably a touch of his own: "Thidre gon marchauntes, and bryngen with hem children, to selle to hem of the contree, and thei by3en hem: and 3if thei ben fatte, thei eten hem anon: and 3if thei ben lene,

thei feden hem, tille thei ben fatte, and thanne thei eten
hem."*

The Fifth Voyage implies Sindbad's waxing wealth by
making him owner of the ship in which he sails. After the
usual prelude of routine trading the men arrive at a desolate
island where they see a great white dome, the egg of our old
friend the Rukh.

Although Sindbad knows what it is, the others in their
ignorance break open the egg with stones and cut up the
Rukh chick they find within. The Rukh, returning in due
course and finding what has happened, calls up its mate, and
both bomb the fleeing ship with boulders so that Sindbad
finds himself adrift on a plank again. Once more he is cast
up on the shore of a tropical isle and next day, after resting,
he finds a man sitting on the bank of a stream. The man indicates by gestures that he wishes to be carried across. Sindbad
takes him upon his shoulders, carries him over, and asks him
to get down.

> But he would not get off my back and wound his legs
> about my neck. I looked at them and seeing that they were
> like a buffalo's hide for blackness and roughness, was af-
> frighted and would have cast him off; but he clung to me and
> gripped my neck with his legs, till I was well-nigh choked,
> the world grew black in my sight and I fell senseless to the
> ground like one dead.

The Old Man of the Sea (*Shaykh al-Bahr*, literally
"Chief of the Shore") keeps his seat, however, and when
Sindbad comes to forces him by kicks and scissoring to serve
as his slave and steed. Finally Sindbad finds a patch of pump-

* In reading this passage ignore the letter "3," which is the Old English
yogh, sometimes printed as "z" or "y." It had the sound variously of
y (as in *yet*), of the German *ch*, and of the Spanish *g*.

kins. He squeezes grapes into a dry pumpkin and waits for the juice to turn to wine. While his objective is to forget his own troubles, the Old Man demands a share too, and is promptly intoxicated so that Sindbad can throw him off and kill him.

The commentators agree that the Old Man is a portrait of the orangutan, the great red tree-ape of Indonesia. The Malays regard him as a man—in fact his name means "forest man."* Lane, while translating the *Nights*, found other Arabic stories, older than the Sindbad cycle, in which the Old Man is described as having "slender and pliant legs." This fits the orang, too, for along with its tremendous arms this beast possesses comparatively small legs that can be twisted into positions impossible for any man except a professional yogi.

And Burton suggested that another element of the story might have been inspired by a custom once found in parts of Africa where the tsetse fly made the rearing of burden-beasts impossible. There chiefs and kings, lacking horses, donkeys, and suchlike, rode piggy-back on stalwart slaves.

And now, how about the Rukh, or Roc, which has played such an important part in two of Sindbad's Voyages?

The history of the Rukh legend is a little hazier. The Sindbad stories and other Arabic sources place the Rukh's home far beyond the horizon of the known world, somewhere out in the blue sea where the sand of the beaches is gold dust and the pebbles are precious stones, where the air is heavy with the perfume of spice-bearing plants and fantastic blossoms.

Marco Polo assigned the island of Madagascar to the Rukh: "The people of the island report that at certain seasons of the year, an extraordinary kind of bird, which they

* The common misspelling "orang-utang" means "man in debt!"

call a rukh, makes its appearance from the southern region. In form it is said to resemble the eagle, but it is incomparably greater in size; being so large and strong as to seize an elephant with its talons, and to lift it into the air, in order to drop it to the ground and in this way to kill it. When dead, the bird feasts upon the carcass."

So far, straight Sindbad; but then comes more definite information: "Persons who have seen this bird assert that when the wings are spread they measure sixteen paces in extent, from point to point; and that the feathers are eight paces in length and thick in proportion."

Polo then anticipated some obvious questions by dictating: "Messer Polo, conceiving that these creatures might be griffins, such as are represented in paintings, half birds and half lions, particularly questioned those who reported their having seen them as to this point; but they maintained that their shape was altogether that of birds, or, as it might be said, of the eagle."

And then Polo produced another clue by telling that the Great Khan, hearing of the Rukh, determined to find out something more conclusive and sent envoys to Madagascar under a political pretext, with instructions to ask about the Rukh. When these messengers returned "they brought with them, so I have heard, a feather of the rukh, postively affirmed to have measured ninety spans, and the quill part to have been two palms in circumference."

We now have two urgent questions: First (assuming Marco told the truth about the Madagascan expedition) what was the Rukh's feather; second, why Madagascar?

As for the first question, the messengers probably brought back a frond from the *Raphia* palm of Madagascar, whose fronds reach unusual size and do look like enormous feathers when dried.

The answer to the second question is: the elephant-bird, *Aepyornis ingens*, a flightless bird belonging to the ratite group that includes the ostrich, the rhea, the emu, and the extinct moas of New Zealand. Like the moas, *Aepyornis* was still alive in historic times; around the middle of the seventeenth century a Frenchman named Gaston de Flacourt wrote that they could still be found in the interior of Madagascar.

Even if de Flacourt was mistaken, the elephant-bird was certainly still alive when Qazwini wrote his *Wonders of Animate Creation* on which the author of Sindbad drew so heavily. Now, the elephant-bird was not so big as the Rukh; you may imagine it as an emulike bird about as tall as an ostrich, but much more massive, weighing up to a thousand pounds. It is, in fact, the heaviest bird ever known to have lived, though surpassed in stature by the moas. But its most distinctive attribute was not so much its size as the size of the eggs it laid, which are the biggest eggs any naturalist ever heard of. While they were not fifty paces in circumference, like those of Sindbad's Rukh, they had a capacity of 2 1/2 gallons, or 6 times that of an ostrich egg and 150 times that of a chicken's egg. They are still found in Madagascar; in fact, the first scientific inquiries about *Aepyornis* were caused by halves of such eggs used as buckets by the natives.

There were, then, adequate reasons for locating the Rukh in Madagascar: the combination of *Aepyornis* eggs and *Raphia*-palm fronds.

Quite nice, says the gentleman from Scotland Yard, but what about that little matter of flying off with elephants and rhinoceroi in its talons? I thought *Aepyornis* was a bird of the ostrich type and hence unable to fly.

Well, nobody quite knows the answer to that one. Several peoples have immemorial myths about birds of continental size; like the thunderbird of the North American

Indians, who flies about with a lake on his back, and when he banks for a turn the lake spills and makes a rainstorm. In the case of the Rukh, the likeliest source seems to be the Simurgh, the "all-knowing bird of ages" who in Iranian legend lives in Qaf and has thrice seen the world destroyed.

Of course in the real world flying organisms are limited by the square-cube law to about the size of the present-day condors. That is, when you double the dimensions of a bird, you increase the area and hence the weight-lifting power of its wings by four times, but you multiply its weight by eight. Hence somewhere between twenty and thirty pounds you reach the point where muscle tissue is simply not efficient enough to get the living flying machine off the ground.

However, people like Qazwini and the creators of Sindbad and the Simurgh knew nothing of the square-cube law, and if they felt like imagining a flying bird of dinosaurian dimensions, who was to stop them?

Once the British naturalist Richard Lydekker made an ingenious guess about Sindbad's Rukh. He said the story concerns two animals, an eagle-shaped bird and an elephant, the former carrying the latter. And if a bird large enough to carry an elephant is impossible, how about an elephant small enough to be carried by a big bird? Back in the Pleistocene there had lived in Malta an interesting fauna that included a hippopotamus less than six feet long; the Maltese elephant, *Elephas melitensis*, standing three feet at the shoulder when grown; and the Maltese vulture, *Gyps melitensis*, with the twelve-foot wingspread of the modern condor.

Here, said Lydekker, we have a very large bird cohabiting with a very small elephant. And even if the bird could not carry a full-grown elephant, couldn't it lift a half-grown calf? Conclusion: people might have seen such a bird carrying such an elephant, and later, when only the present large elephants were known, have enlarged the bird of the story in proportion.

A nice guess, but it breaks down on three counts. First, Malta's unusual island fauna ceased to exist at least 5,000 years ago and probably much more. Second, if as seems likely the Rukh is derived from the Persian Simurgh, Iran is a long way from Malta. And finally, as was pointed out earlier, the maximum payload of any flying bird is now known to be a mere two or three pounds. Hence an eagle or condor can carry off a small chicken or rabbit, but larger prey must be devoured on the spot. And even a new-born Maltese elephant would be too much of a load for an effective take-off.

To go on with Sindbad we have to change the subject and speak of Duke Ernest of Swabia again. You remember that he and his men escaped from Grippia after a desperate battle and hoisted sail for Syria. However, the next land they sighted was not the Lebanese coast, but a sinister-looking black mountain. The ship's master, terrified, implores everybody to row with all his might, for that bleak island on the horizon is the dreaded Mountain of Lodestone. Row as they can, its magnetic attraction draws them closer and closer.

The Duke's party know what to expect. Such is the power of the mountain that if the ship be not well-found it will tear out the bolts and all other iron parts, which will fly toward the mountain like arrows from bows. Even if the ship be so solidly built that the mountain cannot break it apart at a distance, it will still be drawn as a whole to the mountain and wrecked on the beach, and all those who survive the surf will be caught by the griffins which fly to the mountain to find food for their young.

When their ship strikes, old Count Wetzel bethinks him of the trick of sewing themselves into the hides of freshly killed steers, to be picked up by the griffins and carried to the mountain through which a river flows. When they entrust themselves to their raft and drift into the mountain, they sit in total darkness for a long time until they begin to see light ahead.

It looks like a ruddy sunset, though the time of day is wrong for sunrise or sunset either. The swirling waters then bring them to the mountain of carbuncle, the most precious of precious stones, around which the underground river winds its way. In passing Duke Ernest strikes at the mountain with his sword, and a piece as large as a man's fist breaks off and falls on the raft. Now they have light, and soon daylight begins to glimmer far ahead. They are nearing the exit from the tunnel into a green valley. . . .

Let's compare this with Sindbad's Sixth Voyage, the last of his adventure-filled journeys. (Some editions like Burton's include a seventh voyage, but this is of only mediocre interest. Sindbad is wrecked as usual, finds his way to a city of magicians who periodically transform themselves into birds, and finally returns home bringing another wife.)

In the Sixth Voyage, however, after the usual preliminaries

> . . . the ship struck the mountain and broke up, and all and everything aboard her were plunged into the sea. Some of the merchants were drowned and others made shift to reach the shore and save themselves upon the mountain; I amongst the number, and when we got ashore, we found a great island, or rather peninsula whose base was strewn with wreckage of crafts and goods and gear cast up by the sea from broken ships whose passengers had been drowned; and the quantity confounded compt and calculation. So I climbed the cliffs into the inward of the isle and walked on inland, till I came to a stream of sweet water, that welled up at the nearest foot of the mountains and disappeared in the earth under the range of hills on the opposite side. But all the other passengers went

over the mountains to the inner tracts; and, dispersing hither and thither, were confounded at what they saw and became like madmen at the sight of the wealth and treasures wherewith the shores were strewn. As for me I looked into the bed of the stream aforesaid and saw therein great plenty of rubies, and great royal pearls and all kinds of jewels and precious stones which were as gravel in the bed of the rivulets that ran through the fields, and the sands sparkled and glittered with gems and precious ores. . . .

This mineral wealth, however, does not save the company of survivors from dying of starvation one by one until only the indestructible Sindbad is left. He, feeling his end near, digs his grave, in which he will lie down and die when his time comes. However, he then looks at the river and says to himself: "By God, needs must this stream have an end as well as a beginning; ergo an issue somewhere, and belike its course may lead to some inhabited place. . . ."

No sooner said than done. Sindbad builds a raft and embarks upon the river, which presently plunges into a mountain. For a long time he drifts in darkness, the roof of the tunnel being sometimes so low that he must lie down to clear it.

"And in such condition my course continued down the channel which now grew wider and then straiter still, sore aweary by reason of the darkness which could be felt, I fell asleep, as I lay prone on the raft, and I slept knowing not an the time were long or short."

At last Sindbad emerges from the tunnel and finds himself on the island of Serendib (Ceylon) surrounded by natives one of whom speaks his language.

This last incident looks as though it were modeled on the Homecoming of Odysseus in the *Odyssey*: the hero is carried to a familiar place while asleep, and on awakening finds that his trials are over.

Well, who stole from whom this time? Probably the

author of *Sindbad* borrowed (through intermediaries) from the older *Duke Ernest*, for while Sindbad's mountain is not specifically described as magnetic, his voyage by raft on the subterranean river shows a highly probable connection between the tales, the author of *Sindbad* having naturally shifted his locale from the Mediterranean to the Indian Ocean for reasons of fictional expediency. Moreover Qazwini says nothing about the Mountain of Lodestone, one of the leading geographical bugbears of medieval literature.

The dreadful mountain crept into literature for the first time in the *Geography* of Claudius Ptolemy, the second-century Egyptian geographer. He stated that in the Far East, near the Island of Satyrs, lay an island mountain of lodestone which destroyed all ships that passed near it by drawing out the nails that held them together. It has been suggested that the story was invented to explain the fact that so many ships and boats in the Indian Ocean are built without nails, by sewing planks together or fastening them with wooden pegs. The real reason for such shipbuilding methods is, of course, simply that the vessels are built in countries so poor in mineral wealth that the shipwrights cannot afford to use iron.

Aside from Claude Ptolemy, the only other early source of the magnetic-mountain story is a rather feeble Chinese one. In the eleventh century one So Sung quoted "from an older book" the passage: "Near the promontories and peninsula of the Changhai [the sea of Cochin China] there are shallow places and lodestones in such numbers that the large foreign vessels, which have their bottoms sheathed with iron, are attracted by them when they come near and never are able to pass these numerous places." We may if we like rationalize this statement to an assertion that there were straits among the hundreds of Indonesian islands too shallow for deep-draft ships, which is no doubt true. Wherever this story originated—as a version of Ptolemy's magnetic-mountain tale carried east by Arab traders, or otherwise—the Ptolemaic version still remains the main source.

The Magnetic Mountain also plays a part in the European Virgil-legend cycle, which originated just about the time the suppositious Heinrich of Veldeck was writing *Herzog Ernst*. These medieval legends transformed the gentle poet of Mantua into a mighty wizard who built Naples on a foundation of eggs and who kidnaped the daughter of the Sultan of Egypt by riding across the Mediterranean on a bridge of "immobile air" which he created by means of his spells. He also made a brazen talismanic fly which kept all flies out of Naples, a bronze archer which kept Vesuvius in check by threatening it with a drawn bow, medicinal baths to cure all diseases, an aqueduct to take wine from Naples to Rome, and many other wonders.

Virgil got started on his magical career (to condense the many versions into one) by sailing to the Magnetic Mountain where he found, guarded by sirens, griffins, and crocodiles, a grimoire (magical textbook) that had been written by Zabulon, a Jewish magician of 1200 B.C. A devil whom Virgil found imprisoned in a bottle agreed to teach Virgil to read the book if Virgil would let him out; Virgil did so, and then when he had learned what he needed to know he beguiled the demon back into the bottle, exactly like the fisherman and the jinn in the *Arabian Nights!*

The Mountain of Lodestone appears full grown in Idrisi, who says: "The author of the Book of Wonders reports that no ship held together by iron nails can pass near the mountain Murukeyyin without being attracted and held so fast that it cannot leave again." About the location of this mountain Idrisi was hazy, though it might have been on the east coast of Africa.

Then, fifty years before Qazwini wrote, the princely savant Abu al-Fida* gave a watered-down and matter-of-fact description of the same phenomenon. The mountain Kherani, he wrote, is well known to all travelers because of its size and the way it juts out into the sea. "Among the memorable things about this mountain are . . . an iron mine well inland on its back, and a place where lodestone is found on the part surrounded by the sea."

In other words, the terrible Mountain of Lodestone has resolved itself into a mountain containing a rich and workable deposit of iron ores, including magnetite, Fe_3O_4.

However, the Magnetic Mountain did make one more comeback. In Qazwini's time the magnetic compass was slowly coming into use, until in the days of Columbus all mariners and geographers were perfectly familiar with it.

But still nobody knew why it pointed north—or south, for that matter.

And in 1508 Johannes Ruysch published a map of the world that tried to answer that question. The map showed the Arctic Ocean spangled with islands, and in the midst of them, close to the pole, one more island whose nature is indicated by the captions, which read, translated:

Here begins the amber sea
Here the nautical compass is no longer steady
And ships, built with iron, cannot return . . .
Under the Arctic pole there is a rock of
Magnet-stone, 33 German miles† in circumference
Surrounded by the amber sea.

The Mountain of Lodestone to explain the behavior of the magnetic needle! But thereafter the "magic mountain" disappeared for all time.

---

* Or Abulfeda; systems of transliterating Arabic vary widely.
† About 150 modern miles.

CHAPTER V

The Land of Prester John

AROUND THE YEAR 1165, THE THREE MOST POWERFUL RULERS of Christendom, Pope Alexander III, Emperor Manuel Komnenos of Byzantium and Emperor Frederick Barbarossa of Germany, each received a long and still mysterious letter. What evidence can be traced indicates that the three letters, written in Latin, read more or less alike. Nothing is known about the person or persons who delivered them, but the letters purported to come from the East. The originals are lost and not even copies of the letters to the Pope and to Frederick Barbarossa have been found. However, the letter received by Emperor Manuel was copied and became known, whereupon it was recopied so that over a hundred old manuscript copies are known to scholars.

The letter to Emperor Manuel began with a formal salutation:

> Iohannes, Presbyter by the Omnipotence of God and the Power of Our Lord Jesus Christ, King of Kings, Ruler of Rulers, hopes for the well-being of his friend Emanuel, Prince of Constantinople and wishes that the Grace of God be with him in the future.

Then it went on to tell about the person and the power of its writer in a manner which must have sounded stilted and exaggerated even then:

I, the Presbyter Iohannes, the lord of lords, surpass all those living under the sky in virtue, wealth and power. Seventy-two kings pay tribute to Us, Our Magnificence rules in the three Indias and Our lands extend until the Far India where the body of the Holy Apostle Thomas has been laid to rest. Seventy-two provinces, only a few of which belong to Christians, are in Our servitude.

Our land is the home and the dwelling of elephants, dromedaries, camels, *Meta collinarum* (?), *Cametennus* (?), *Tinserete* (?), panthers, forest donkeys, white and red lions, white bears, white *Meruli* (?), mute griffins, tigers, lamias, hyaenas, wild horses, wild asses, wild oxen, and wild people, horned people, one-eyed people, people with eyes in front and in back, centaurs, fauns, satyrs, pygmies, giants forty ells tall, cyclops and their women who are of the same kind, the bird known as phenix, and almost all other kinds of animals under the heavens.

This, of course, is the list not of the animals actually occurring in Asia, but the list of those wonders which according to the beliefs of the time could be found in Asia. It jibes not with reality, but with the wonders of the Pliny Collection and the digests of contemporary beliefs preserved in the Herzog Ernst romance and the adventures of Sindbad of the Sea. After enumerating the natural wonders of India the letter proceeded to the marvels of the court.

Every day Our table is set for 30,000 people, not counting unexpected arrivals, and none of them leaves without a present from Our treasurers, it may be horses, it may be other things. Our table is made of the rarest emerald and supported on four pillars of amethyst. Every month We are waited on at table by seven kings in succession; sixty-two dukes and two hundred and sixty-five counts do various kinds of work. Every day twelve archbishops are seated to Our right and twenty bishops on Our left at Our Own table, also the patriarch of St. Thomas and the Protopapa and Archipapa of Susa where the throne of Our glory and the Imperial Palace are located . . .

Our palace is founded on gems and gems are its walls, held together by the best and purest gold serving for mortar. Its roof is fashioned from the clearest sapphire stones, with occasional topazes in various places. The gate is made of the clearest crystal bound with gold. It opens to the East, is 130 ells tall, and opens and closes by itself when Our Supremacy enters the palace. . . . In one direction Our realm extends four months' journey, how far Our superiority extends in the opposite direction is known to nobody. . . .*

That this letter was not genuine and had been written by somebody who knew more about India from contemporary books than from personal experience (if any) has been obvious and clear to every literate person for the last 400 years. But nobody who thought about it during these four centuries has been able to advance even a theory of what the unknown forger wanted to accomplish by writing it. If he had gone to the court of Manuel Komnenos or Frederick Barbarossa, pretending to be the ambassador of Iohannes the Presbyter—or Prester John, as we say—he might have hoped for valuable presents. But nothing like this took place and the motive is unknown—provided, of course, that there was a clear-cut motive. Fairly recently, in 1931, the historian Leonardo Olschki, writing in the German *Historische Zeitschrift*, suggested that the "Letter of Prester John" may have been a political pamphlet, intended to show the rulers of the West how prosperous a permanently peaceful realm could grow. This idea is not completely impossible, but sounds feeble, weak and far-fetched.

In short, the letter is a puzzle.

* The full text of the letter (which gets boring very quickly) can be found in the book by Gustav Oppert: *Der Presbyter Johannes in Sage und Geschichte* (Berlin, 1864), Latin original on pages 167-179, German translation on pages 26-50.

It seems to have puzzled its original recipients too. True, India was traditionally the land of wonders and the Christian rulers of the West, struggling against Islam, could hope for nothing better than a large and powerful empire with a Christian overlord in the East. However, they seem to have felt that such a large rich country should be known to them even without a direct communication from its ruler. There were some vague rumors about it, but no more than that. Both Manuel Komnenos and Frederick Barbarossa seem not to have replied at all.

Only the Pope, after considerable hesitation, finally did send a reply. This letter "given at the Rialto in Venice, the 27th day of September [1177]" was probably dictated because skepticism should not be permitted to grow into neglect of duty. And *if* there was a Christian king in the East it was duty to reply. But skepticism made the reply a diplomatic masterpiece.*

It also began with a formal salutation which lacks the name of the addressee: "Bishop Alexander, the servant of the servants of God, extends to the dearest son in Christ, the famous and high king of the Indians, the holy priest, his greetings and apostolic benediction." After this salutation the letter stated in about a thousand words that the Pope is the head of the church and is always willing to teach and accept converts. Virtually the only positive statement in the letter (aside from the assertion that the Pope is the Pope) is a guarded offer: "after consideration of the duties of our office and after careful weighing of your wishes and plans, Magister Philippus would be sent" to teach the Presbyter the Catholic doctrine. This would be done the more willingly the sooner messengers bearing sealed replies would be received and "the less you brag about your wealth and power."

* Printed in *Annales Ecclesiastici*, XIX, Lucca 1746, p. 45of.

And that ended the "correspondence" between Prester John and the church.

If this forged letter, of unknown origin and mysterious intent, were the only piece of writing relating to Prester John and his kingdom, one could treat it more as a literary than as a historical matter. But Prester John, sometimes without being so named, crops up in serious historical chronicles too. The most famous of them is that of Otto, Bishop of Freising, who reported that he once met the Bishop of Gabula in Syria. That bishop told him about a ruler "beyond Persia and Armenia in the uttermost East." He called him *rex et sacerdos* (king and priest) and said that the priest-king and all his subjects were Christians, if Nestorians. This king won a victory over two brothers who were the kings of Persia and of Media. He could not make contact with the Christians of the West because his armies could not cross the river Tigris by boat and waited for several years for the river to freeze. When that did not happen, they returned to their homeland.

The priest-king of the extreme East is mentioned three times in the *Chronicle* of the monk Alberich, written around 1250. The first entry, for the year 1145, tells the same story as Otto of Freising. The second entry, for the year 1165, states that the Pope and the emperors Manuel and Frederick received the letter from Prester John of which quotes are given. The third, for the year 1170, tells of the Pope's reply and the mission of Bishop Philippus. Alberich was mistaken about the year of the event to which his third entry refers and did not really add anything to the story. But he helped to spread it.

Just at about that time a number of Westerners actually traveled to the Far East and would have come across Prester

John's domain had there been one to come across. None of them actually reported the existence of such a kingdom, but every one of them heard stories which he reported back. No two of the tales are alike, and in tenor they rank from somewhat awed reporting to casual debunking. The earliest of the actual travelers who later reported on Prester John was Friar John of Pian de Carpini, a Franciscan monk who made the journey during the years 1245-1247. He reached the East just in time to witness the coronation of Kuyuk Khan, the son of Ogotay Khan who was the son of the mighty Jenghiz Khan. The friar reported that Jenghiz sent his son Ogotay against the Indians, adding that "these Indians are the black Saracens which are also called Ethiopians." If you take these names too literally you get a picture of violently confused geography, but all that seems to have been meant was that those "Indians" were darker of skin than the Mongols. However, Ogotay's men were beaten back by the new weapons of the Christian king called Prester John. The vivid if somewhat confused description sounds like "Greek fire"—an incendiary, not an explosive—which made the Mongols recoil in a rout. "Neither did we hear that they ever returned."

The next reporter was a French monk, Friar William of Rubruck, who made the journey in 1253-1255 as an envoy of the king of France. His report, which he both wrote down himself and told by word of mouth to Roger Bacon, sounds entirely different. He tells that he traveled over highlands in the middle of Asia and that in a plain country within those mountains "there lived a Nestorian shepherd, being a mighty governor over the people called Naimans, which were Christians, following the sect of Nestorius."

After the death of Con Khan, Friar William continued, that shepherd made himself ruler of the kingdom. "They called him King John, reporting ten times more of him than was true. For this is the way of the Nestorians who come from those parts." But Friar William had something else to tell. Three weeks' journey from John dwelt his brother Unc, also a ruler, lord over "a village called Caracarum" inhabited by Nestorian Christians. But Unc was not a Christian. When the Mongols appointed Jenghiz Khan to be their chieftain, Jenghiz attacked Unc and won. Unc fled to Cathay, but his daughter was captured and became the wife of one of Jenghiz's sons.

When Marco Polo journeyed to the Far East (during the years 1271-1295) these bits of information about tribal wars in Asia had coagulated into a more complete story; at least Marco Polo delivered a more complete account of what he had heard, in the chapters 46 to 50 inclusive of his book. His story differs from that of Friar William in quite a number of respects.

Unc Khan and Prester John are the same man, ruling a vast territory. The Tartars* who lived there paid him tribute and Prester John used them for constabulary service whenever there was a rebellion in one of the provinces of his realm. Not only did the Tartars serve well in this capacity; the practice also helped to check their ever-growing numbers, of which Prester John was afraid. Finally the Tartars realized the hidden purpose behind the constant calls upon them and rallied together, electing their own king, Jenghiz Khan. Jenghiz Khan, when firmly established as lord of the Tartars, asked for Prester John's daughter in marriage. He was refused and both rulers collected their armies for a decisive battle. Before battle was joined, the magicians performed a ceremony. They

* Properly *Tatar* (a Persian word) but medieval Europeans used the form *Tartar* as a result of confusion with *Tartaros*, the classical Greek Hell.

split a green reed lengthwise, wrote on one the name of Jenghiz Khan and on the other that of Prester John and placed the pieces on the ground. While they said their incantations, the pieces approached each other and the one with Jenghiz's name placed itself on top of the other. The Tartars then attacked, certain of victory, and routed Prester John's army. Prester John himself was killed and Jenghiz married his daughter.

After Marco Polo's story there are only casual mentions of Prester John's domain in travel reports, like that of Friar Odoric of Porteneau, another Franciscan monk who left for China in 1318 and returned six years later.

But then a magnificent liar took over, the "English knight" Sir John de Mandeville. If you take what he said on trust he was born at St. Albans in England and had to flee his native country because he had killed a man in a duel in 1322. Remorse made him go to the Holy Land, whence he proceeded on a voyage to the East, lasting all told thirty-four years. Then he went to Liège to consult the famous doctor Jean de Bourgogne and gave him the manuscript of his travel journal. This was in 1355 and the doctor circulated the journal of the English knight. His friends and neighbors had no trouble reading it because it happened to be written in French, not in English and not even in Latin, which would have been the most logical language for a travel diary of that time.

On his deathbed, in November 1371, Doctor Jean de Bourgogne suddenly admitted that he was John de Mandeville himself! Historians who later had to struggle with the explanation of the incredibly successful book of John de Mandeville are convinced that this deathbed admission was true, in the sense that Jean de Bourgogne had written the book. They are also agreed that Bourgogne-Mandeville did live for years at least in the Near East and Constantinople, and that he probably went on a pilgrimage to Jerusalem. But everything which geographically belongs east of the Jordan river was plainly borrowed, filched, stolen, or plagiarized with astounding distortions and exaggerations. The victimized pieces of literature were Carpini's report, Odoric's journal (verbatim), Marco Polo's book, and, of course, classical authors like Pliny and Ptolemy.

The major distinction between John de Mandeville and people like Carpini or Marco Polo was that those travelers had merely reported what they had heard about Prester John. But John de Mandeville had been *there*. He had seen all the marvels of Asia; they were just as described in various books, only more marvelous. There is the isle of Silo with its two-headed geese and white lions; the isle of Pathen where the snails are so big that their shells could be used as houses; the land of Pantoroze with its gravely sea "that is of sand and gravaile and no drop of water, and ebbeth and floweth with right great waves as another sea doth," and the isle in the river Renemar with its feathered men. And, of course, dog-headed men, headless men, one-eyed men, Pygmies, giants, satyrs, gold-mining ants, and all the rest.

And he had been in Prester John's kingdom; he knew about the horned men in the deserts. He knew more of Prester John's armed might than anybody had described before: "Emperour Prestre John, whan he gothe in to Battayle, azenst ony other Lord, he hathe no Baneres born before him: but he hathe 3 Crosses of Gold, fyn, grete and hye, fulle of precious stones: and every of the Crosses ben sett in a Chariot, fulle richely arrayed. And for to kepen every Cros, ben ordeyned 10,000 men of Armes, and mo than 100,000 men on Fote, in maner as men wolde kepe a Stondard in oure Countree. . . ."* and so on and so forth, for pages and pages.

* Quoting from the earliest printed version.

Thus John de Mandeville revived and perpetuated the dying legend of the kingdom of Prester John. And Mandeville was imitated in turn by other writers. The general impression was that Prester John did exist in the East—it was too pleasing an idea to drop just for lack of confirmation. That lack of evidence merely indicated that people had failed to look for it in the right place. After all, in the year 1480 so much more was known about geography than in 1280 or even in 1380. Prester John's kingdom was in the East, of course, somebody in Portugal reasoned around that time. But there were more lands in the East than just Asia, these others had just been confused for lack of geographical knowledge. The land of Prester John might be, and probably was, in Africa.

Consequently King John II of Portugal (ruled 1481-1495) sent a mission to Prester John in eastern Africa. The names of the two men who comprised that mission are on record: Petrus Covillanius and Alphonsus Paiva. (In Portuguese, Pero de Covilhão and Affonso de Payva.) Their instructions were to go to Egypt and to proceed east, staying on African soil, until Prester John was found. Just to make certain that his attempt should not be frustrated because of the religion of his envoys, King John II dispatched a second mission a month or so later, consisting of two Jews of proven linguistic ability.

Petrus Covillanius, in due time, arrived in Abyssinia. He saw that these people were dark skinned, that they had a ruler who traced himself back to King David of the Bible, that the ruler was a Christian, that the country was mountainous and stretched no one knew how far. He reported that he had, at last, succeeded in finding Prester John, and that he was the Emperor of Abyssinia, or Ethiopia as we now call it. When some years later an envoy of the Emperor of Abyssinia arrived at the court of the successor of John II in Lisbon, everybody was convinced. Geographers inscribed the region of Abyssinia on their maps with the words *Regnum Presbyteri Johannis* and historians like Joseph Scaliger tried to account for the reports of Carpini and Marco Polo by surmising that the domain of the Emperor of Abyssinia had once extended across Asia to China and that this part of the domain had been lost to Jenghiz Khan.

Strangely enough, the very Portuguese who had started the myth that Prester John's realm was Abyssinia demolished it later, especially the historian Balthasar Tellezius and the patriarch of the Roman Catholic Church in Abyssinia, Alphonsus Mendesius. By the year 1800 it was certain that the identification had been a mistake.

Then what was the original kingdom of Prester John? What had been the fact, or the event, from which the myth had grown?

Let's recall the main facts of the story. It centered around some place in Asia, farther away from Europe than Persia, but no so far as China. It told about a large territory—large from the contemporary European point of view used to small dukedoms and baronies—and a Christian ruler who also was the archpriest. It told of countless subjects, not all of them Christians.

The problem is either to find a historical figure with these general attributes, or, at least, a land which satisfies the general requirements.

It was a Catholic author who, some twenty-five years ago* advanced a hypothesis which is convincing because of its simplicity. He wrote:

* John C. Rowe in *The Catholic World*, August 1926. The Father Stockmann mentioned in the article is the Rev. Alois Stockmann, S.J., of Frankfort-on-the-Main, Germany, who contributed the long article on Prester John in the *Catholic Encyclopedia*.

The writer of this article has long entertained the opinion that, if Prester John were not an absolute myth, Tibet may have been his country; and he has just made the discovery that an ancient map—the oldest on which America is mentioned, discovered by Joseph Fischer and dated 1507, places the Presbyter's country in Asia (Province of Thebet; Tibet) in the following words: "This is the land of the good King and lord, known as Prester John, lord of all Eastern and Southern India, lord of all the kings of India, in whose mountains are found all kinds of precious stones."

[Obviously the Portuguese identification of Prester John with the Negus of Abyssinia had not yet found general acceptance in 1507.]

Father Stockmann mentions this map. In Tibet we have all the reasonable alleged attributes—the priest-king, or Dalai-Lama, whose sovereignty is only checked by the authority of China; a perfectly organized hierarchy; a well-built, strongly fortified, and populous capital, Lhasa, containing many magnificent convents, with thousands of monks. . . . The only thing not in accordance with the idea of Prester John is that the priests, monks and people are and were Buddhists and not Christians. But travellers might very easily confuse the national religion with that of Christianity. Tibet was conquered and ravaged by Ghingis Khan . . .

If Rowe's hypothesis were accepted the famous letter may have been an attempt by a Christian (probably Nestorian) monk to describe Lhasa and the Dalai Lama under the mistaken assumption that he was a Christian. Since the monk probably was not too well versed in the language of the country, that should not be considered an insurmountable obstacle.

The main reason why Rowe's guess at Tibet as the prototype of the land of Prester John and at the Dalai Lama as the prototype of the priest-king himself may be thought a mistake, in spite of its reasonableness, is that historians have succeeded in finding a real Christian king in Inner Asia at just the right time.

During the twelfth century a comparatively unimportant people, the Kerait or Karakhitai (*kara* is a Turko-Tatar word meaning "black"; the term therefore means literally "black Chinese") of northern China suddenly formed a large empire. Having been forced out of northern China by the Chinese, they first settled in the area of Lake Balkhash, north of the Tien-Shan. Just as in the case of Jenghiz Khan of the Mongols, who came not quite a century later, these "black Chinese"—Carpini's "black Saracens also called Ethiopians" —produced a great leader from amongst their midst. Their chieftain Yeliutashi, who in Chinese chronicles appears under the name of Ye-lü-ta-shi, conquered Turkestan about 1130 and then assembled an army to move against his Mohammedan neighbors.

The decisive battle of this war was fought September 8 and 9, 1141 A.D., near Katvan in the vicinity of Samarkand. It is reported to have been an enormous engagement for its time, with 300,000 men in Yeliutashi's army and similar numbers in the army of the enemy. It allegedly resulted in 100,000 casualties and a victory for Yeliutashi. But if the number of casualties reported is only approximately correct the army of Yeliutashi must have been seriously weakened too, which fact explains why he did not go on with his conquests after his victory. Yeliutashi himself died two or three years after that battle; his empire split after his death into a western and eastern half and was destroyed by the Mongols in 1203.

Yeliutashi is a far better prototype for Prester John than the Dalai Lama. He was a mighty warrior (which the priest-king of Lhasa is not) and he commanded an enormous army. And he was a Christian! It does not seem to be known whether he belonged to any sect, but since a number of his warlike subjects were Nestorians it is likely that Yeliutashi was too.

Yeliutashi, Christian king in Asia and belligerent enemy of an Islamic nation, ruled for about eighteen years, from 1126 until 1143 or 1144. By the time the famous letter arrived in Europe he was dead and his realm, which had been a really big empire for only two years, was shattered. By the time the first Christian missionaries and envoys to the Far East traveled across it, even the remains had been ground up by the Mongols. All that these travelers could do was to listen to less than half-understood stories, garbled bits of information related by "the other side" and further disfigured by linguistic difficulties. But when these travelers returned home and told what little they had learned, they reinforced the legend, which had meanwhile been established by that mysterious letter.

CHAPTER VI

The Mislaid Tribes

FOR SEVERAL CENTURIES THERE EXISTED A PARALLEL TO THE great Christian kingdom of Prester John of the East, namely the Jewish kingdom of the Ten Lost Tribes. Just as Prester John's kingdom was shuffled around in the course of time and the legend attached itself to several historical facts, so the Jewish kingdom of the East was not a clear-cut case. There were several "kingdoms" which might have served as starting points although it is exceedingly doubtful whether any one of them comprised the Ten Lost Tribes or even just one or two of them.

But what started out as a purely historical problem—and, at times, as a hope for Jews living elsewhere—later degenerated into one of the wildest sleeveless errands in the story of strange quests. Just as Atlantis has been "found" all over the globe, with the exception of Australia, so virtually all the peoples on earth have at one time or another been "identified" with the Lost Tribes by somebody, again with the exception of the Australian aborigines.

To begin the story at the beginning we have to inquire how these Ten Tribes ever got lost in the first place. The story is simple enough and is told in one of the historical books of the Old Testament. When King Solomon died the Israelites sent a delegation to his son Rehoboam, asking him to rule them less harshly than his father had. Rehoboam, an arrogant youth, replied tactlessly: "My father hath chastised you with whips, but I will chastise you with scorpions." *

This answer was all that was needed to set off a revolt against the house of David that had been smoldering for a long time and had been kept under cover mainly by hopes for a change after Solomon's death. Rehoboam kept his hold over the two southernmost tribes, Judah and Benjamin, but the other ten (Reuben, Gad, Zebulon, Simeon, Dan, Asher, Joseph, Levi, Naphthali and Issachar) made their rebellion stick. They set up their own kingdom, which they called Israel (formerly the name of the united kingdom) or, sometimes, Ephraim. Rehoboam's shrunken kingdom came to be called "Judah" after one of the two tribes comprising it.

For the next two centuries these two kingdoms fought each other and the other little Syriac states with the desultory ferocity characteristic of people on that level of culture, completely ignoring the great Assyrian thundercloud rising in the East. Then, in 734 B.C. King Tiglath-Pileser III overran the northern provinces of Israel and carried off many of the people to Assyria.

Twenty years later the terrible Assyrians, the Nazis of their day, came back under Shalmaneser (Akkadian, *Ulula Shulmanu-asharid*) IV and besieged Samaria, the capital of Israel, for three years. Although Shalmaneser died during the siege, his death did not save the city, for one of his generals seized the throne and continued the operation. This general took the name of Sargon, after a king of Babylonia who had lived 2000 years earlier, and from whom the second Sargon claimed descent. In due course Samaria fell. After the usual horrors of an ancient sack, Sargon II dictated a

* 1 *Kings* xii, 11. "Scorpions" does not refer to the poisonous invertebrates of that name, but to whips with metal knobs or points.

report of his victory to be inscribed on clay tablets and filed away in the national archives. It began:

> The city of Samaria I besieged, I took. I carried away 27,290 of the people that dwelt therein; 50 chariots from them I took and the others their share I caused to take.
>
> L. W. King, *First Steps in Assyrian*, p. 47

And the deportees? Their feelings are not recorded. However, years later a historian among the Hebrews of Judah took note of the event, writing:

> In the ninth year of Hoshea the king of Assyria took Samaria, and carried Israel away into Assyria, and placed them in Halah and in Habor by the river of Gozan, and in the cities of the Medes. [That is, along both banks of the Tigris river, at the other end of his huge empire.] So was Israel carried away out of their own land to Assyria unto this day.
>
> *2 Kings* xvii, 6, 23

This is absolutely the last authentic word on the fate of the Ten. While there are a few later references to them in Hebrew literature, these are matters of conjecture, not of fact; thereafter Biblical history deals exclusively with the kingdom of Judah.

Fifty years later Assyria had fallen to a combination of her former victims, even as the Hebrew prophets had foretold:

> Woe to the bloody city! Because thou hast spoiled many nations, all the remnant of the people shall spoil thee; because of men's blood, and for the violence of the land, of the city, and of all that dwell therein. Thy shepherds slumber, O king of Assyria: thy nobles shall dwell in the dust: thy people is scattered upon the mountains, and no man gathereth them.
>
> *Nahum* iii, 1, 18; *Habakkuk* ii, 8

But another power had arisen with the Assyrian downfall: the Chaldean or Neo-Babylonian empire. And Nebuchadrezzar* II of Babylonia did the same thing to Judah that Sargon had done to Israel: conquered the country and deported a large part of the people to Babylonia. However, under the milder Babylonian rule these deportees did not "disappear" as had their predecessors. They flourished, and after the Persian conquest of Babylonia many of them returned to Palestine.

But what, then, did become of the Ten Tribes of the Sargonid deportation? Of course many peoples have disappeared: Where now are the Scythians, the Galatians, or the Huns? Nevertheless it seemed to many, as it still does to some, incredible that such resourceful and proud people, to whom God had made such glowing promises in the book of *Genesis*, should simply vanish off the face of the earth.

Later Jewish writers occasionally referred to the Lost Ten; thus in the first century A. D. Flavius Josephus, the warrior-historian, casually stated that "the ten tribes are beyond the Euphrates till now, and are an immense multitude." † During their wars with the Romans, Josephus said, the Jews of Palestine kept hoping for help from their brethren across the Euphrates, but none ever came. However, Josephus's remark does not show any firsthand knowledge of the Lost Ten beyond what he could read in *2 Kings*.

Then in the apocryphal *2 Esdras*, or *Apocalypse of Ezra* (written in Greek about 100 A.D.) an angel shows Ezra visions of a crowd of people, explaining:

> Those are the ten tribes, which were carried away out of their own land in the time of Osea the king, whom Shalmanasar the king of Assyria led away captive, and he carried them over the waters, and so they came into another land. But they took this counsel among themselves, that they would . . . go forth into a further country, where never mankind

* Or *Nebuchadnezzar;* Akkadian, *Nabu-kudurri-ushur.*
† Josephus, *Antiquities of the Jews*, X, v, 2.

dwelt. . . . For through that country there was a great way to go, namely, a year and a half: and the same region is called Arsareth.

2 Esdras, xiii

However, *Esdras* is not to be taken seriously as shedding light on the fate of the Ten, for it is an apocalyptic vision that does not even pretend to be history. What is Arsareth? Ararat, or a corruption of the Hebrew *'erets 'akhereth*, "another land"? Nobody knows. Moreover, if they went to an uninhabited country eighteen months' journey away, how could Ezra have found out about them?

The matter might have dropped there, but for the circumstance that the Romans destroyed Jerusalem and scattered the Jews of Palestine, and that two heretical offshoots of Judaism, Christianity and Islam, waxed great and became the dominant religions of Europe and the Middle East. Presently hostility among Christians, Muslims, and Jews was whipped up by their respective priesthoods. Being the fewest, the Jews suffered the most in this strife, and soon began to wish that there were a powerful Jewish state somewhere to which they could go for refuge, or which could at least give them some protection. The wish was father to the thought, with the result that by the seventh century rumors circulated about a mighty Jewish kingdom in the East.

For quite some time there actually was something that could be called an Asiatic Jewish kingdom. The Turkish Khazars built an empire north of the Caucasus, with advanced ideas about commerce and religious tolerance, which flourished for several centuries. In about 740 A.D. Jewish missionaries converted Bulan, the Khakan of the Khazars, to Judaism and in time most of his people followed suit. Although the Russians overthrew the Khazar empire in the tenth century the memory of their enlightened rule lingered for a long time.

This originally Turkish empire happened to fall into one of the few and short periods when there were Jewish missionaries. Ever since the time of the original kingdom of Judah there have been two currents of thought in Judaism, one nationalist and one universalist. The nationalists, in former days, took the "God's Chosen People" theory seriously and held that nobody could or should be admitted into their ranks. The universalists leaned toward the idea that the religion made the Jew and that Judaism was the proper world religion to be propagated by proselyting. The nationalists were probably in the majority at any given time, but from time to time the universalists formed considerable minorities which engaged in missionary efforts whether the nationalists liked it or not. They did make large numbers of converts too and not always just by preaching and argument; some of the post-Exilic Jewish kings like Hyrcanus converted thousands of their neighbors at the point of the sword.

In such cases the nationalists had one weapon left. They scorned recent converts as *Ersatz* Jews and the recent converts, in turn, resorted to the faking of genealogies going back to Israel and Adam. This explains why, among the little groups of Judaists scattered about in Asia and Africa, many stoutly claim to be the only true and authentic Jews, even though they are racially identical with the Tartars, Chinese or Ethiopians among whom they live.

The hunt for the Lost Ten Tribes got started in earnest in the ninth century, when one Eldad ben Mahli appeared in Kairawan, Tunisia, announcing that he was from a Jewish kingdom in Ethiopia, comprising four of the Ten Tribes. They lived, he said, on the banks of the river Sambation, a waterless torrent of gravel which for piety stopped flowing on the Sabbath. The local rabbis behaved very much like the Christian Church dignitaries when they were confronted with the stories of the glories of Prester John's kingdom; they were very polite and listened carefully, but they were also most noncommittal.

The story of the Eastern kingdom of the Jews gained more impetus at the time of the Crusades, when nerves were on edge with prophecies of the End of the World and the Coming of Antichrist. Persecution of the Jews in Europe became unusually vicious and many Jews set out to escape from persecution by finding the Jewish kingdom in the East. Their hopes were strengthened by stories like those of Benjamin of Tudela, a Spanish-Jewish traveler who appeared in Germany with an account of the Jewish communities of the Near East. There were such communities but Benjamin of Tudela greatly exaggerated their size and wealth. He also told of the Lost Tribes which were stated to live together either in Iran or beyond.

The next "ambassador" from the Lost Tribes came some five centuries after Benjamin of Tudela. He was David Reubeni, who announced in 1524 that his brother was king of the tribe of Reuben, somewhere in Asia, and wanted an alliance with the Christian kings against the Muslims. Although for a time David impressed the Pope and the king of Portugal, they at length became doubtful of his credentials, and he was burned by the Inquisition. The sad part of this story is that David may not even have been a faker; there was a Jewish colony in India which might just possibly have sent him to Europe.

When the Jewish Empire was not found in Asia, the search for the Lost Tribes continued elsewhere. The discovery of the Americas started a new wave of speculation about the fate of the Ten, which by this time had become a cult like the lost continent of Atlantis, the esoteric meaning of the pyramids, and the prophecies of Nostradamus. People who met the American aborigines for the first time, having no special knowledge of anthropology and linguistics, jumped to conclusions that the natives were either speaking Welsh and so must be descended from the half-legendary Welsh hero Madoc ap Owen Gwynnedd and his band, who were supposed to have sailed away into the Atlantic; or else that they were practicing Hebrew religious rites and were therefore the Lost Ten Tribes.

This last theory was floated by Diego de Landa, the "discoverer" of the Mayan "alphabet." According to his *Relación* (Tozer ed. pp. 16f, 169) the Mayas had a tradition "that this land was occupied by a race of people, who came from the East and whom God had delivered by opening twelve paths through the sea. If this were true, it necessarily follows that all the inhabitants of the Indes are descendants of the Jews."

De Landa's suggestion was taken up by a Spanish-Jewish adventurer, Aaron Levi (or Antonio de Montezinos), who told the learned rabbi Manasseh ben Israel of Amsterdam a fascinating tale of his adventures in the New World, which included a visit to a society of Jewish Indians in Peru. These were the Tribe of Reuben.

Manasseh wrote the tale up as *The Hope of Israel*, and entered into correspondence with some Puritan divines in England. These embraced the Jewish-Indian theory and brought it to the attention of Oliver Cromwell, who invited Manasseh to England. As a result of the friendship between himself and Manasseh, Cromwell tried to get the Jews readmitted to England, though he was able to effect this on a small scale only. It was even seriously suggested that the Indians should migrate back to Palestine, but fortunately for the peace of the world they showed no disposition to do so.

The Jewish-Indian theory had a good 200-years' run.

The last prominent Amerind-Israelite was Lord Kingsborough, who a century ago spent his fortune of £50,000 publishing *The Antiquities of Mexico*, a monumental work in nine huge volumes, any one of which takes a strong man to lift. These books contain reproductions of the Aztec picture writings and works of art, and voluminous notes arguing the Jewish-Indian theory. Kingsborough included a treatise that one James Adair had written a century before while a trader among the Chickasaws and Choctaws. Adair feebly argued that the Indians must be Jews because they had tribal organization, belief in the Great Spirit, decimal numerals, and things like that which most human beings possess. Poor Kingsborough's obsession finally landed him in Dublin's debtors' prison, where he perished.

Those who were not satisfied with this identification of the Ten Tribes continued to find them elsewhere. Odlum identified them with the Japanese, Tyler with the Zulus, others with the Masai or the Malays. Joseph Smith's *Book of Mormon* makes the American Indians descendants of a party of Jews who emigrated from Jerusalem in the reign of Zedekiah, though these were not the Ten. The most original theory was that of Capt. J. C. Symmes, an American hero of the War of 1812, and his son: these asserted that the earth was hollow with a hole at the top and the Ten Tribes inside. (We shall hear more of Captain Symmes later.)

Confusion was aggravated by the fact that many people have claimed, on very doubtful grounds, to be the descendants of the Lost Ten Tribes or of other Old-Testament characters. The Karaite Jews of Russia, racially and linguistically Tatars, claimed to be the Ten; so did the Mountain Jews of Daghestan, a tribe of stalwart Caucasian highlanders; so did the Nestorian Christians of Kurdistan. While the Muslim Yosufzais of Afghanistan claim descent from Saul's father Kish, some Moroccan Jews and Muslims say their ancestors were Philistines driven from Palestine by the Israelites.

Groups practicing Judaism (in varying degrees of purity) are found among the Falashas of Ethiopia, the Negroes of Portuguese West Africa and Madagascar, and the Chinese of Kaifeng, all with elaborate and unreliable tales of how they got there. It is evident from these people's appearance that whoever the original colonists or missionaries were, their physical type has long since vanished through intermarriage with the local people.

Some American Negro cults, even, have taken up the theme; W. S. Crowdy, who founded the Church of God and Saints of Christ in 1896, said the Negroes were the Lost Ten Tribes, while, conversely, the Commandment Keepers, Holy Church of the Living God, regard the Negroes as the authentic Tribe of Judah, the Whites being the Lost Ten.

During the nineteenth century, however, all other Ten Tribist theories were driven into the shade by the wonderful British-Israel or Anglo-Israel movement, which has been responsible for more printed matter, meetings, lectures, and general bustle than all the other Ten Tribists put together.

The notion that the Ten Tribes were the people of the British Isles was first suggested by John Saddler in 1649, but did not really take hold until the coming of Richard Brothers (1757-1824). Brothers was a Newfoundlander who settled in London, having tried a naval officer's career, marriage, and vegetarianism all with indifferent success. In 1794 he caused to be posted on the walls of London a proclamation reading:

TO GEORGE III

The Lord God commands me to say to you, George III, that, immediately upon my being revealed in London to the Hebrews as their prince and to all nations as their Governor, your Crown must be delivered up to me.

Richard Brothers, *Nephew of God*

This proclamation was merely the first snowflake of a blizzard of books and pamphlets which Brothers continued to issue until his death. Brothers proclaimed himself not only a "Nephew of God" (a relationship to puzzle the acutest theologian) but the divinely appointed prophet and descendant of David who was to rule the world. He prophesied the violent deaths of the kings of France and Sweden; the fulfillment of this prophecy gained him a great occult reputation in short order. He also prophesied the imminent overthrow of the Russian, Turkish, and German empires. The government, already nervous about their own king and alarmed by Brothers's demand that George abdicate in Brothers's favor as the first step towards his world rulership, locked Brothers up as a criminal lunatic.

Brothers, however, had acquired an influential follower in the person of the distinguished orientalist and Member of Parliament Nathaniel B. Halhed, to whom Brothers had promised the post of viceroy of India when he became king. Halhed, therefore, got Brothers out of jail—to his own undoing, for his speech in Parliament on Brothers's behalf made him so unpopular that he had to resign his seat.

Brothers spent the rest of his life in private insane asylums or living with and on his disciples. The failure of the Russian and other empires to collapse damaged his credit. His followers dwindled, and his favorite disciple left him for the prophetess Joanna Southcote.

After Brothers's death (of tuberculosis), his followers Hine, Finlayson, and Wilson published British-Israelite books a little more coherent than those of Brothers. Wilson's book converted the Scotch astronomer Charles Piazzi Smyth. Smyth was a good astronomer but a religious fanatic who had also been converted to the fantastic idea of John Taylor, a London publisher, that the Great Pyramid of Gizeh was not after all the tomb of the Fourth-Dynasty Egyptian king Khufu or Cheops, but instead had been built by Noah and his descendants under divine guidance, and incorporated in its dimensions such cosmic wisdom as the value of pi, the ratio of the circumference to the diameter of a circle.

Smyth, like a good pseudo-scientist, first published a book on the Great Pyramid and then went to Egypt to confirm the theories set forth therein. He spent three months at the Pyramid, measuring it with a multitude of specially built instruments and the aid of a gang of temperamental Arabs. By making his measurements with incredible inaccuracy and converting them into imaginary units like his "pyramid inch," Smyth found "proof" that the architect of Khufu's Folly knew the exact length of the year, the latitude of the pyramid itself, the size and shape of the earth and its orbit, and its history, in advance, for the next few thousand years up to the Second Coming of Christ (or some equally revolutionary event) which Smyth predicted for 1882.

The British-Israelites eagerly adopted these vagaries, and neither the failure of the Second Coming to materialize, nor the discovery by the Egyptologist Petrie that Smyth's measurements had been nearly all wrong, dampened their enthusiasm for the Great Pyramid Prophecy. David Davidson substituted Petrie's measurements for Smyth's, juggled the figures some more, and came up with a new body of cosmic wisdom according to which a great war would begin in 1928 and the Coming in 1936. Now of course these events have been cast ahead into the future again, the cult mind being proof alike against the arguments of fact and the lessons of experience.

British-Israelism also took root in America, and reached its climax in the 1880's. Queen Victoria and Mary Baker Eddy expressed interest in the theory. At its maximum the movement was estimated to have two million adherents, although, judging from the volume of publication, the cult began to decline in the 1890's and is now much smaller, notwithstanding some revival after World War I. It still supports publication of an occasional book (repeating the arguments of Totten and other nineteenth-century British-Israelites) and several periodicals such as the *America-Israel Message*, and is organized into associations like the British-Israel World Federation and the Anglo-Ephraim Association.

While most British-Israelites are moderately friendly towards the Jews, the doctrine has been exploited by some anti-Semites. French anti-Semites embrace the theory because it gives them a pretext for hating the English as well as the Jews. Anglo-American anti-Semites argue that the Jews are not Israelites at all, but impostors, and that the Anglo-Saxons are the true and only Israelites and therefore God's Chosen People.

In outline the British-Israelite theory reads as follows: The Ten Tribes were packed off to Media by Shalmaneser. (Actually they were deported by Sargon II, but because *2 Kings* mentions Shalmaneser only, most British-Israelites assume that the "king of Assyria" of *2 Kings* xvii, 6 is the same fellow.) There they remained until 650 B.C., when they revolted and fled. In the short space of 22 years they dropped their Semitic language for an Indo-Iranian speech, adopted pants, multiplied their numbers many times over, and became the Scythians!

As if that transformation weren't sufficiently startling, they set out to the northwest, over the Caucasus and around the Black Sea, till they came to Germany. Somewhere along the march they not only changed their language again, but their appearance as well, becoming blond blue-eyed Nordics. For such accomplished migrants this was easy, or else God helped out with a miracle. They now called themselves "Saxons," meaning "Isaac's sons" (never mind the fact that the Hebrew words for "son" are not the least like "son"). They also forgot their history and religion, but despite all these changes they remained pure-blooded Israelites. At length they invaded England and fathered the British peoples of today. Some liberal-minded British-Israelites allow that they also became Goths (from Gad), Danes (from Dan), or Jutes (from Judah), or any other European people you care to mention.

As if this were not enough, British-Israelites also derive the Irish from Israel, thus: *Jeremiah* xliii tells how, after the Babylonians had conquered Judah, Johanan fled to Egypt, taking a number of Jews including the prophet Jeremiah and the daughters of King Zedekiah. They settled in the Delta, where Jeremiah wrote a book prophesying the restoration of Israel and the destruction of all other nations. Thereafter nothing authentic is heard of him.

Now, in early Irish legends there are accounts of the arrival in Ireland of colonists from Spain and other places. One such party is said to have brought a stone, the Lia-Fail, supposed (by a late Christian addition to the myth) to have been the stone Jacob used as a pillow. There was also in Scotland a real Stone of Scone on which the kings were crowned. This might be the Lia-Fail but for geological reasons probably isn't; and anyway the rival Lia-Fail at Tara has at least as good a title to authenticity. Edward I of England had the

Stone of Scone removed in 1296 and had it built into the base of the English Coronation Chair, where, after a short and spectacular absence in 1951, it still is.

On the slender basis of the lines in *Jeremiah* which tell that he went *to* Egypt the British-Israelites have built the yarn that Jeremiah *left* Egypt, taking with him Zedekiah's daughter Tamar Tephi and Jacob's stone, which had been miraculously preserved ever since the patriarch slept on it. He sailed to Ireland, where an Irishman married Tamar Tephi and begat the Keltic "race." Of course, there is no authentic Irish history before the fourth century A.D., there is nothing about Jewish immigrants in Irish legend, and nothing in the Bible about Tamar Tephi, Ireland, or Jeremiah's departure from Egypt. No matter; it makes a good yarn.

It is a kind of trade-mark of the British-Israelite arguments that they make a great point of the alleged distinction between the terms "Jew" and "Israelite," asserting that the former refers only to the tribe or kingdom of Judah and its descendants, and the latter only to the Ten-Tribe kingdom of Israel and its descendants. Thus, they say, Abraham was not a Jew, Jesus and his disciples were not Jews but Benjaminites, and so on.

However, words mean what the people using them intend them to mean. "Jew" (Hebrew *yehudi*) originally meant one of a tribe whose members traced their descent from a legendary Judah. Later it meant a subject of the Kingdom of Judah, and, after the destruction of that kingdom, an adherent of the Judaic religion, or the worship of Yahveh.

On the other hand "Israelite" was first a general term for a member of the Twelve Tribes, all of whom were supposed to be descended from Israel; then a subject of the Kingdom of Israel; and finally, like "Jew," any professed Yahvist.

Of the 3,000 years of authentic Hebrew history, only during the first three centuries was there any distinction between "Jew" and "Israelite"; though now that the sovereign state of Israel has been revived in Palestine a distinction has again come into being. The Hebrew prophets, the Christian apostles, and Josephus, however, use "Jew," "Israel," "Zion," "Jerusalem," and "the Circumcision" as interchangeable terms.

Having, as they suppose, established a special meaning for "Israel," the British-Israelites point to the Old-Testament prophesies that promise a glorious future for Israel, as that they shall be an island nation (*Isaiah* xlix, 12), they shall be as the sand for multitude (*Genesis* xvii, 4), they shall be ruled by a king of the house of David (*Jeremiah* xxxiii, 17), they shall be the chief of the nations (*Deuteronomy* xxviii, 1-14), undefeated (*2 Samuel* vii, 10), a sea power (Psalm lxxxix, 25) and so on. Since Britain (or to more lenient minds, the English-speaking peoples) are supposed to answer this flattering description, Britain (or the English-speaking peoples) must be Israel.

There is something subtly wrong with some of these quotations, for example the verse from Isaiah says nothing about islands; Jeremiah's prophecy of a never-failing Davidic monarchy was ruined by the fall of Zedekiah. On the other hand England has had her share of defeats, and so forth.

As if the British-Israelites felt that these arguments do not constitute a sufficiently strong case they try to bolster their general idea by (A) showing that the English language is "derived" from Hebrew and (B) finding "Hebrew" place names along the supposed line of travel. In both cases their ignorance of linguistics is appalling and the method consists essentially in hunting for words which have roughly the same meaning in both English and Hebrew and which also sound somewhat alike. Of course, since there is a limit to the number of sounds the human vocal apparatus can produce, the same meaning and the same approximate sound can come together by pure chance. For example the French word for "ten" is *dix* and the Hottentot word for the same number is *disi*.

A real relationship between two languages can be established by looking at *all* the words in certain categories like numerals (English: one, two, three, French: *un, deux, trois*, German: *eins, zwei, drei*) or family relationships (English/German: father-*Vater*, son-*Sohn*, daughter-*Tochter*) or parts of the body.

By such tests you'd find what linguists have known for a long time, namely that the western European languages are related to each other, forming (with still others) the Indo-European languages. Yiddish belongs to that group because of the historical fact that at various times in the past many German-speaking Jews settled in eastern Europe. But Hebrew, which the Lost Ten spoke, belongs to the Semitic languages, related to Arabic, Assyro-Babylonian and others.

As for the "Hebrew" place names, the reader is informed that the names of the rivers Don, Dnieper, Dniester and Danube were all named after the tribe of Dan. By that method you can also prove that the American Indians are neither originally Asiatics (as ethnologists say) nor Welshmen nor Israelites (as some cultists aver) but Greeks. You can derive the Croatan Indians from Crotona, the Mandans from Mantineia, the Chilkats from Chalkis, the Kiowas from Chios, and the Aleuts from Eleusis!

All of which has not yet answered the question of what did become of the Ten Tribes.

The answer is simple when we consider what a tribe is. It is an association of people much like a club or a firm, with the difference that all the members of the family belong to it and that you don't join it but are born into it. Such an association is not a hereditary trait like haemophilia (although family resemblances because of direct relationship may show strongly) nor is it a race. Nor are the Jews as a whole a "race," they are simply men of the white race and when they lived in Palestine they belonged to the same type as the other people of that region. That is, they were a mixture of the Mediterranean type, found most commonly in Italy and Arabia, and the Armenoid type, found most commonly in Turkey, Iraq, and Iran. The Mediterraneans are slender and long-headed; the Armenoids muscular, broad-headed, hairy, and big-nosed. Otherwise both types are rather short and dark. Ever since the dawn of history this mixed type has prevailed in Palestine and adjacent regions, so that the average modern Christian or Muslim Syrian, for example, looks more "Jewish" than the average modern European or American Jew.

The original Israelites, according to the latest historical researches, seem to have been Arabs who rode out of the desert and conquered the Hebrews whom they found living in Palestine. The Hebrews and their conquerors worshipped assorted jinns, bull-gods, snake-gods, and fertility-goddesses. The Israelite ruling class either brought with them, or took over from the Hebrews, the storm-god Yahveh, and Yahvism gradually became the dominant religion of the Hebrew-Israelite states.

By the time of Solomon the original tribes had been in Palestine for several centuries, intermarrying with each other and with the Hebrews. And Solomon himself deliberately broke down tribal distinctions by ignoring tribal boundaries when he divided his kingdom into counties. During the exile these distinctions disappeared for good. Consider, in addition, that Sargon did not deport the whole population of an area, but essentially the militant aristocracy which might cause him trouble later if left where they were. Moreover other kings deported Jews too; Psamtik the First of Egypt for example kidnaped thousands of them. These kidnaped Jews were settled in the countries of their kidnapers as garrison colonies, for they were highly valued as soldiers because of their fighting qualities.

And at least some of these Jewish garrison colonists were universalists, and made converts. By the time of Pliny there were millions of Yahvists in southwest Asia and North Africa. Some were converts, some were the offspring of Jews and of converts and some were actually of Palestinian descent. Many of these were subsequently converted to Christianity or Islam (whichever happened to be dominant in a given area) but many stayed Yahvists and Jews. Trying to find the Ten Tribes now would be like searching for the Twenty Tribes of the early Roman Republic in modern Italy.

For a tribe to disappear under stress of war and migrations is the most natural thing in the world. Where are now the "tribes" of the Hittites, the Etruscans or the Goths? The mystery is not that ten of the twelve tribes disappeared but that the other two managed to survive as a distinct cultural group despite so many adversities.

CHAPTER VII

The Great Dream

THE GEOGRAPHER OSKAR PESCHEL ONCE SAID THAT, IN EXPLORING, the Spaniards went as far as there was gold, the Portuguese as far as spices occurred, and the Russians as far as they found furs.

Like all *bon mots* this observation is both true and false. Or rather, it is true as far as it goes, but it oversimplifies things. For not only did Phoenicians, Greeks, Arabs, Irish, Vikings and others go exploring before Spaniards, Portuguese, and Russians, but also they went without any such clear-cut economic aims. There were quests for new lands to settle, new nations to trade with, and new groups of unbelievers to convert.

But throughout most of the history of exploration runs one continuous theme: the search for a gigantic continent, a continent which, it was thought, might easily be the largest of all. Not only was it deemed gigantic in size, but also it embodied all the hopes and wishes of men. Literary lights of all nations thought about it and sang its praise.

However, the long coastline of that dream continent remained dreamlike. Whenever somebody thought he had reached it, it dissolved like a vision, receding into the misty distance like the King of Elfland's domain.

This fabulous continent was called *Terra australis incognita*, the Unknown Southland. Its existence was sometimes feared, oftener hoped for, but always taken for granted.

The origin of this long-lived myth can be traced to several factors. One is the simple fact that our particular culture, in a broad sense, originated on the shores of the landlocked Mediterranean Sea with its many islands and peninsulas. Therefore, when men imagined the world on a large scale, they thought of it as a large-scale Mediterranean, that is, as a group of islands (the known continents) surrounded by the all-encircling Outer Continent of Pindar, Plato, and Plutarch. Looking at it in another way, you might say that Terra Australis was a psychological recurrence of the northern shore of Africa.

A second factor was the belief of philosophers of the Pythagorean school of thought that the gods had built the universe along lines of artistic symmetry. Now, according to the calculations of the Alexandrine astronomers, the three "continents" (Europe, Asia, and Africa) known to them formed a land mass that occupied less than a quarter of the globe. Therefore it seemed natural to these philosophers of whom we have been speaking that there should be other land masses besides the group they were familiar with, to balance the latter. In fact Krates of Mallos in the second century B.C. worked out a scheme in which there were four such land masses, one occupying each quarter of the globe.

The theory of Krates was popularized long after his own time by two fifth-century Romans, Macrobius and Capella—like most Latin authors of their time, tedious and turgid writers whose sole virtue is their preservation of fragments of the writings of older thinkers that would otherwise have been altogether lost. The Carthaginian Capella gave (though he probably did not invent) names for the three other supposititious land masses that balanced the one we know. The people of the continent to the south of the known land (that is, in the southern half of the Eastern Hemisphere) he called *antoikoi*, "opposite ones." Those in the northern half of the Western

Hemisphere were antipodes, "opposite-footed ones"; while those in the southern half of the Western Hemisphere, who were really opposite to the known *oikoumēnē*, were the *Antichthōnes*, "those of the opposite world." (Actually it would have been more logical to call these the *antipodes*, since their feet would in fact point in the direction opposite to those of the known world.)

The name *Antichthōn*, the "counterearth," was borrowed originally from the Pythagoreans, who used it to designate the imaginary planet they had invented to bring the number of the movable heavenly bodies up to the mystic ten, for which they professed a lofty veneration.

Long after this Pythagorean whimsy had been forgotten, people applied the name *Antichthōn* to the supposed Unknown Southland. And the medieval writer Godfrey of Viterbo asserted that the golden orb of the Holy Roman Emperor, which he held in his hand on occasions of state, with its two circumferential bands crossing at right angles, symbolized the Kratean theory of the four continents.

A third source of the Southland myth seems to have been the mistake of Hipparchos and Claudius Ptolemy about the shape of the Indian Ocean, which was discussed in Chapter II. If as Hipparchos thought the Indian Ocean was a landlocked sea, it must have a southern shore. And, in fact, travelers had reported such a shore somewhere in the sea south of India. They said it was a great land—how big, they didn't quite know yet—and fabulously fertile, with inhabitants of exemplary honesty and democratic ways. And they called this land Taprobanë. Might not Taprobanë, Hipparchos wondered, be a northern cape of the Southern Continent?

Actually this coast was that of the island of Ceylon, whose size and wealth and virtue of whose people the early travelers had much exaggerated.

Then, three centuries after Hipparchos, our old acquaintance Claudius Ptolemy promulgated Hipparchos's ideas on the Indian Ocean, with modifications. True, he showed Ceylon as an island, though much bigger than it really is, for by this time Roman ships had sailed the Indian Ocean, and Taprobanë had been circumnavigated. The coast of the Unknown Southland had receded for the first time.

However, Ptolemy much exaggerated the sizes of Africa and Asia, and moreover he adopted the idea that the Indian Ocean was a second and larger Mediterranean. He simply caused Asia to curve south at its eastern end (where the Malay Peninsula exists in fact) and Africa to curve east at its southern end until they met and inclosed the Indian Ocean. The African east coast is shown as trending east at about the latitude of Zanzibar, where, as you can see from the map, the continent does bulge out eastward a bit. In reality the coast soon turns south and then southwest again, but Ptolemy's map made it extend on eastward, forming the thousands of miles of east-west coast of Terra Australis.

Moreover he made the west coast of Africa trend *west* at about the same latitude as that at which the east coast bent east. In other words, Africa became just a big northerly peninsula of Terra Australis! Evidently the Atlantic, too, was taken to be a lake inclosed by land, like the Indian Ocean, only bigger.

The most amazing thing about this map is not the daring (to put it mildly) with which the learned Egyptian filled in unknown territory with solid masses of land; it was his preference for theory over facts. For he must have known about the report that seven centuries before his time a party had rounded Africa.

The facts were these: Back at the beginning of the sixth century B.C., before Egypt had become a prey first to the

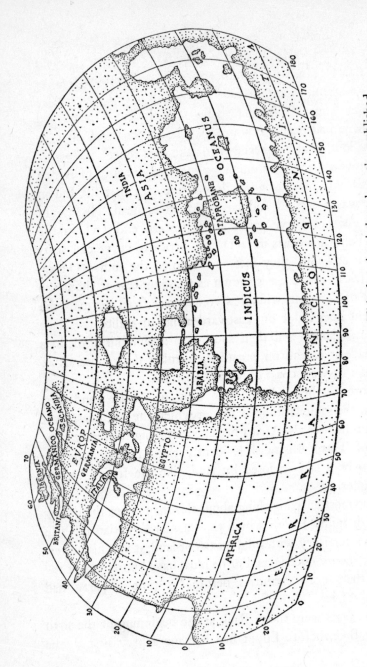

FIG. 10. The World Map of Ptolemaeus. This drawing is based on the published version of 1478. Since the original was quite large, the map had to be considerably simplified to be legible.

Persians and then to the Macedonians, King Niku II (whom the Greeks called "Nekos" or "Necho") pondered the fact that his country bordered on two seas, the Red and the Mediterranean. Unfortunately they were not connected. However, perhaps that could be remedied, so he ordered his men to start digging a canal—not, like the modern Suez Canal, directly from one sea to the other, but from the Nile to the Red Sea, since his small ships could row up the Nile for quite a way.

For some reason the work was not completed. (Later Darius I of Persia worked on it for a while, but desisted when somebody told him, mistakenly, that the Red Sea was higher than Egypt and would flood the country if allowed to flow into the canal. Ptolemy II finally completed it, and it functioned for several centuries before careless rulers let it fill up with sand.)

However, Pharaoh Niku or his advisers thought of something else. He commissioned a group of Phoenicians to sail down the east coast of Africa, round the southern end of the continent, if possible, and then sail up the west coast and return through the Pillars of Herakles to the Mediterranean and finally to Egypt.

Says Herodotos:

> The Phoenicians took their departure from Egypt by way of the Red Sea, and so sailed into the southern Ocean. When autumn came, they went ashore, wherever they might happen to be, and having sown a tract of land with corn, waited until the grain was fit to cut. Having reaped it, they again set sail; and thus it came to pass that two whole years went by, and it was not till the third year that they doubled the Pillars of Herakles, and made good their voyage home. On their return, they declared—I for my part do not believe them, but perhaps others may—that in sailing round Libya [Africa] they had the sun upon their right hand. In this way was the extent of Libya first discovered.
>
> Herodotos, *History*, IV, 42

This story was disregarded all through antiquity, mostly because Herodotos, who reported it, doubted it himself. However, the very reason that Herodotos doubted it—the statement that the sailors saw the sun to northward when they were sailing along the southern coasts of Africa—is the precise reason that forces us to believe it. For in the days of Niku and Herodotos the theory that the earth was round had probably not even been suggested, let alone become generally known among educated men. Pharaoh Niku's Phoenicians, therefore, would not have known that as they went south the sun's path would seem to cross the heavens farther and farther north.

But Hipparchos and Ptolemy, who knew perfectly well that the earth was round, rejected this report of a trip around Africa in the years 596-594 B.C., almost exactly 2,000 years before the trip that is cited in standard geographies as the first successful journey of that kind. They also rejected the statement of an old *periplous* (book of sailing directions) that the Indian Ocean and the Atlantic Ocean meet south of Africa, and of the geographer Athenagoras (fourth century B.C.) that all the oceans were one. Perhaps they thought these statements based upon the report of the voyage of Niku's men —as indeed they may have been.

The next to try the circumnavigation was the young Iranian noble Sataspes, and at about the same time (early fifth century B.C.) a certain Magos appeared at the court of the Tyrant of Syracuse, Gelon, claiming that he had accomplished this feat; but nothing more is known of him.

The next effort—and the last for many centuries—was that of the intrepid Eudoxos of Kyzikos, the same whom Pliny quoted about the "sparrow-footed" women of India. Eudoxos seems to have led a career of adventure that would be a natural for writers of low-cut historical novels.

Eudoxos arrived at the court of Alexandria in the reign of the depraved and bloodthirsty Ptolemy VII—"Ptolemy the Sausage," they called him—who reigned from 146 to 117 B.C., when Ptolemaic Egypt was fast declining as a power. Now, the king's coast guard had found a castaway Indian on the shores of the Red Sea. When the Indian, the sole survivor of his crew, learned enough Greek to make himself understood, he told Ptolemy that he had sailed to the Red Sea directly from India.

He said that this had been an accident—presumably he was aiming for the Persian Gulf, the normal terminus of such a voyage, and was blown out of his course. In any case Ptolemy was delighted, for at that time nobody was sure how far into the Indian Ocean the Arabian Peninsula extended. (Both Darius I of Persia and Alexander of Macedon had made plans for sending fleets around the inhospitable southern shore of Arabia to find out, but nothing had come of these plans.) Now it was evident that the peninsula did not extend so far as to make a direct voyage from the Gulf of Aden to the Persian or the Indian coast impracticable.

So Paunchy Ptolemy sent out a ship loaded with presents and trade goods, to retrace the Indian's route. Eudoxos was the captain and the Indian the pilot. The Kyzikan was highly successful not only on this voyage but also on another on which he was sent by Ptolemy's widow Cleopatra. However, each time he returned with a rich cargo, his royal master would accuse him of stealing royal property and confiscate the entire proceeds of the voyage. (Whether Eudoxos *had* been stealing is something we shall never know.)

In any event Eudoxos tired of this treatment after he had been plucked for the second time and went home to Kyzikos, on the south shore of the little Sea of Marmara. Here, by the use of high-pressure promotional methods, he fitted out an expedition to circumnavigate Africa. He was sure that this could be done, because on his second Indian voyage he had picked up a ship's figurehead on the African coast, and when he got to Alexandria the sea captains there said it was obviously from a ship from Gades in Spain. The inference was that a shipload of the Phoenicians of Gades had set out on Sataspes' track, and had nearly completed their task when they were wrecked.

By the time Eudoxos himself got to Gades, between his ballyhoo and his shrewd trading, his expedition had grown to three ships, one large and two small, equipped with all the latest devices including dancing girls. Alas, after he had sailed down the West African coast a way his big ship ran aground. However, the resourceful Eudoxos succeeded in salvaging most of her timbers and cargo, and with these timbers he built another, smaller, ship in which he returned. Not defeated yet, he drummed up backing in Spain for another voyage, this time using two ships, a merchant sailing ship and a galley. He took with him seeds and agricultural implements so that if need be he could winter and raise a crop on a fertile island (one of the Canaries?) he had seen on his first voyage.

He set out—and that is the last that is known of him. " 'Now I,' says Poseidonios, 'have traced the story of Eudoxos to this point, but what happened afterwards probably the people of Gades and Iberia know.' "* True, Strabo, who tells the tale, doubts the whole thing including the voyages to India. But then Strabo, like Pliny and other ancient writers, would try very hard to sort out fact from fancy and end up believing a lot of things that weren't so and disbelieving a number of reports that later turned out to be quite correct.

During the Roman era the great geographical problem seems to have been simply dormant. Rome "owned" the Med-

* Strabo, *Geography*, II, iii, 5.

iterranean, Rome dominated most of Europe, Rome had trade relations with the Far East. And Rome was essentially a land power. Seas, to the Roman mind, seem to have been deemed obstacles rather than highways. And then, of course, there was the widespread Roman attitude that distant things were not worth bothering with unless there was a prospect of property to loot or people to exploit.

Then the political picture changed, and for a time the most important power in the Mediterranean was that of the Arabs, whose outstanding geographer, a thousand years after Claudius Ptolemy, was Idrisi, whom we have already met. Idrisi's world map was essentially an "improved" version of that of Ptolemy, which he knew well and which he had no reason to doubt.

As in Ptolemy's map, the east coast of Africa turns east to become the north coast of the great Southland. In fact the whole East African coast, fairly well known by then, with all its settlements, its real and invented rivers, its actual and fictitious mountains and capes, becomes a part of Terra Australis, bounding the Indian Ocean on the south.

During this period of Arab supremacy in science and politics, it is hard to say just what conception of the world was held by the people of the Christian nations north of the Mediterranean. It is best to say that there were several beliefs, none actually prevailing, and none too definite. Most of those who formed a conception at all (the great majority seem to have been able to do without) accepted the roundness of the earth.

What seems to have been the most acceptable idea of the shape of the earth is represented by the Macrobius map, made during the tenth century. It is circular and divided into the five climatic zones of the classical geographers. Europe, Asia, and Africa—the classical *oikoumēnē*—are crowded into the northern frigid and northern temperate zones, only some southernmost parts of Asia and Africa projecting into the tropical one, most of which was taken up by sea. Everything else, the whole southern temperate and frigid zones, was filled by the Southern Continent. *"Temperata antipodum"* says the caption, adding cautiously: *"nobis incognita"*—"unknown to us."

Then several important events took place.

One was the introduction of the magnetic compass, shortly after 1100 A.D. Many different nations have been credited with the invention of this instrument, from the Finns to the Chinese. All that we know for certain is that between 1100 and 1300 it came into use, rather suddenly, all the way from the North Sea to the Yellow Sea; that during the twelfth century casual references to the compass begin appearing in the books of European and Muslim writers like Alexander Neckam and Idrisi; and that by the thirteenth century the compass is well known, though in a crude form. The former Chinese claims have now been pretty well disproved, leaving the Europeans and Arabs as the chief contenders, with the weight of the evidence favoring the former—and probably the Northern Europeans. We may suspect the Scandinavians, who were not only hardy seafarers but also dwellers in country rich in iron ores including magnetite or lodestone.

Another group of events was the Crusades. While they added but little to geographical knowledge, they did stimulate interest in geography.

And finally there was the return of the Polos from the Far East. Although it was already known that there were large rich countries in the East, still, Marco Polo's stories stimulated curiosity about them, even though his contemporaries were inclined to regard them as *khurafas*.

Just about a century after the return of the Polos, Prince

Henrique of Portugal was born. History calls him Henry the Navigator, although he never made a long voyage himself, and very few short ones. However, he caused others to do so; he founded what we should call a naval academy (at Sagres, at the southwest tip of Portugal); he saw to it that a collection of maps was made and that learned men devoted their time to geography.

As you might surmise, there was a practical purpose behind all this. While the Polos had reached Cathay by traveling overland, they had made much of their return voyage by ship. If the East could be reached directly by ship from Europe everything would suddenly look different. Trade could be carried on directly, without avaricious intermediaries. It was cheaper to dispatch goods by ship than by caravan, other things being equal. And finally, if the Christian nations, especially Portugal, could gain a foothold in the East they could attack the common enemy, Islam, in the rear.

But the question was: could they? If the maps of Ptolemy and Idrisi were right, no, for Africa simply broadened out to the south until it merged with the main mass of Terra Australis. To get from the Atlantic to the Indian Ocean you would still have to cross Africa—either in the north, where the Muhammadans were in the way, or further south through unknown and altogether savage country.

On the other hand, if the Macrobius map was right, the problem was simple, for this map showed a wide belt of tropical sea between the southern coast of Africa and Terra Australis. One should be able to sail easily around Africa into the Indian Ocean.

Another possibility (which may not have been known to Prince Henrique and his captains) was the dramatic account of the African question by Abu al-Fida, who succeeded Idrisi as the leading light of Muslim geography. At the south end of

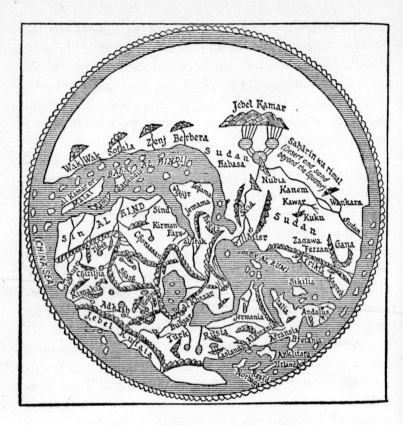

FIG. 11. Idrisi's map of the world.

Africa (he quoted an earlier writer, al-Biruni, as saying) the Atlantic did communicate with the Indian Ocean through a narrow channel between Africa and the Southern Continent. But this channel was full of movable mountains that constantly rose and fell like gigantic pistons. Their motion naturally stirred the water into such a frenzy of turbulence that no ship could pass that way without being broken to bits! Could this be a 2,000-year-old echo of the myth of the Clashing Rocks, between which Jason piloted his Argonauts?

Then, assuming that a waterway was actually open to the East, could one sail through that tropical sea? The older scholars had said an emphatic "no." Aristotle, for instance, averred that the heat of the tropical zone must condense the water into a jelly, so that no ship could pass. Moreover the terrible heat of the sun in these latitudes would first strike dead the captains and crews of the ships and then ignite the ships themselves. Since there was no way of passing the Torrid Zone, mankind could never learn whether the Southern Hemisphere was inhabited or not.

And finally there was the unsettled question of whether a Southland existed at all. Some philosophers, echoing the arguments of Krates and the Pythagoreans, battled for Terra Australis on the ground that the balance of the earth required masses of land in the Southern Hemisphere; it was unthinkable that a globe weighted down "on top" only could maintain its equilibrium. Therefore, Great Lord and dear colleagues . . . And also considering the authority of the great Ptolemaeus . . .

However, not all the "dear colleagues" were convinced. For one thing the newly invented magnetic needle pointed north, obviously attracted either by a particular star in the northern sky, or by the more numerous stars of the northern sky in general. According to the reasoning of the time, the preponderance of northern over southern stars implied more land in the Northern Hemisphere. The only point worth discussing was whether the stars caused the land or vice versa.

(Of course the compass needle points south just as surely as it points north, but since it was early associated in people's minds with the Pole Star—the South Pole of the heavens being invisible from Europe even if there were a star to mark it—Europeans fell into the convention of saying that the needle pointed north.)

If the arguments of these medieval philosophers make you shake your head, those of the theologians are even more breath-taking. They, too, had their own logic.

Among the Holy Fathers, the anti-Southlanders pointed out that Terra Australis could not be reached because of the Torrid Zone. Therefore nobody could ever have preached Christianity to its presumptive heathen natives. But Christ had ordered the Apostles: "Go ye into all the world, and preach the gospel to every creature." Obviously He would not have given such an order unless it could be carried out; and that it had been obeyed was proved by the words of St. Paul: "Yes verily, their sound went into all the earth, and their words unto the ends of the world." (*Mark* xvi, 15; *Romans* x, 18.) Hence there were no peoples who had *not* been reached by the Apostles; hence there were no Southlanders; hence there was no need for this continent; hence it did not exist. Q.E.D.

The other side replied that God had given the earth to man to dwell in. If there was no Southern Continent, most of the earth must be covered with water. But as man cannot live in the sea, it must be a divine command that there be more land than water. However, for the land to exceed the water there must be a large Southern Continent; therefore there was a Southland; therefore it was inhabited by heathens; therefore it was possible to reach this land in order to preach the Gospel to them. . . .

Idrisi's map, fortunately, pointed a way out of this dilemma. Idrisi had done something strange to the Nile. He showed it, true, as emptying into the Mediterranean; but in addition, farther upstream in "Nubia," he caused it to divide and send one long arm all the way across Africa to the Atlantic. That branch was the Gold River, or Rio do Ouro, which helped no end in Portuguese planning. Real rivers don't act that way, but the men of Idrisi's time did not know that. (Nor did they know of the only exception to that rule.)

So, said the Portuguese, if one sailed straight south from Portugal one would, of course, reach Africa. Then one could follow the African coast until the mouth of the Gold River was attained. And then one could sail upstream across Africa. While that still would not get one to the Indian Ocean, one would by-pass the Saracens and reach the land of Prester John, then thought to be Ethiopia. Prester John's kingdom bordered the Indian Ocean on the other side, and since it was a Christian kingdom the Portuguese would have all the help they needed to finish their trip overland and to build a new fleet in the Indian Ocean.

So they started exploring. In 1419 they rediscovered Madeira, and fifteen years later they reached the Canaries, where for many decades Italian, French, and Spanish adventurers had been making life unhappy for the unfortunate Gaunches. The Portuguese observed that, while the climate grew hot, the luxuriant vegetation along the shore was reassuring. Maybe the Torrid Zone would not be so bad as the philosophers claimed. Furthermore, the water, while soupily warm, showed no sign of jelling.

On they went, very carefully, because they were still in the habit of hugging the shore and this habit exposed them to the treacherous Phantom Islands of the West African coast, where powerful coastal currents might fling them onto the shifting sandbanks and where a sandstorm from the interior might cut vision to a few feet.

In 1441 Nuno Tristão reached Cape Blanco (Port Étienne) at 21° N. As the name implies, the cape is made of white sand without vegetation. Was this the beginning of the dreaded Torrid Zone? No, there were people ashore, so conditions must not be too bad. But typically, Dinis Diaz, who reached Africa's westernmost point four years later, christened it Cape Verde ("Green Cape") to reassure others by the name that things grew there. In 1447 they reached Sierra Leone, where Niku's Phoenicians had preceded them 2,000 years previously, going in the opposite direction.

Just before he died in 1460, Prince Henrique was rewarded for his efforts by the report of one Diogo Gomez that a big river, the Niger, did flow from the interior of Africa.

After that, political events interrupted exploration for a while. Then, however, the King of Portugal made an ingenious arrangement with the rich merchant Fernão Gomez to assure the continuance of exploration without risk to his treasury. Gomez was to pay a certain sum to the treasury and obligate himself to push exploration of the African coast by 100 *leguas* (about 335 miles) every year in return for a monopoly of the Guinea Coast trade.

A year after this agreement was signed, Gomez's captains crossed the equator, and a year still later Fernando Po landed on the island that still bears his name. The equator, presumably the hottest place on earth, had been passed, and men still lived!

After a delay of some years the march south was resumed. In 1485 Diogo Cão's ship found the mouth of the Congo. Aboard was a young man from Nuremberg, who was to become one of Portugal's foremost cartographers: Martin Behaim. They sailed upstream a way, wondering whether this was Idrisi's Gold River, but then turned back and sailed south to 16° S, near the present Mossamedes.

The Torrid Zone *could* be passed.

Then Batholomeu Diaz was sent out to find how far Africa extended south. He landed near the present Swakopmund, then pressed on. The coast trended east of south, then farther and farther east. . . . Were they finally nearing the southern end of the continent? Diaz could not follow the coast as far and as closely as he had intended, because a sudden storm blew his ships past a sharp, rocky peninsula which he called *Cabo Tormentoso*, the "Cape of Storms." Ahead, behind, and to starboard there was nothing but water. He did not go on, because his men threatened mutiny and the captain was a bit frightened himself. He returned to Portugal in 1487, announcing that Africa did have a southern end: the Cape of Storms where he had feared being wrecked.

In Portugal they thought differently about this report, not having Diaz's experiences. Africa did have a southern end—the westward projection of Ptolemy did not exist, and even if there was a Terra Australis there might be clear sailing to India between it and Africa. Martin Behaim made a globe that showed things that way: Africa has a long projection eastward from its southern end, but failed to landlock

FIG. 12. The Macrobius map of the world, showing the unattainable Southern Continent.

the Indian Ocean completely. One could thread one's way in between this extension of Africa and the East Indian Islands. If things were like that, everything was fine.

Consequently Diaz's Cape of Storms was renamed the Cape of Good Hope to encourage the sailors. That it was not actually Africa's southernmost point (Cape Agulhas several scores of miles east of it is) was of only academic interest. In 1497, ten years later, Vasco da Gama rounded Africa and sailed to India. On May 20, 1498, he dropped anchor in the harbor of Calicut, on the Malabar Coast, to the consternation of the Muslin merchants who had thought that here, at least, they were safe from the competition of the infidels. . . .

Ptolemy's Terra Australis had at last been expelled from the map.

Or so one might think.

The Terra Australians, however, were by no means silenced. True, Behaim's eastward hook of Africa had to be erased from the map almost as soon as it was drawn, because da Gama had sailed right through it. But all this meant merely that Ptolemy had erred in supposing Africa to be a part of the Southland. If you sailed south from the Cape of Good Hope (something the shore-loving sailors of the time were reluctant to do) you'd find it in due course.

Nobody went searching at once. The Portuguese were more interested in ousting the Arabs from the spice trade than in chasing the Southland, which would not run away. Their pleasure in their new discoveries was partly spoiled by the fact that they had rejected the pleas of a certain Colombo or Colón "whom nobody knew." This Genoese visionary had gone to the king of Spain, and envious Spain had sent him off in three little old ships to discover Asia from the other side.*

The Spaniards, naturally, were elated; they did not need those long trips around Africa, but just a six weeks' sail to the West. It was easily understood that Colón had landed on an unknown land, for there were certainly many unexplored and unnamed islands off Asia's eastern coast.

In 1497 Giovanni Caboto (another Italian unless those are right who call him a Catalan, and who soon Anglicized his name to John Cabot) reached the "mainland of Asia" much farther north. Some geographers began to suspect a new continent. The next year Columbus, in the course of his third voyage, touched the northern coast of South America, around the mouth of the Orinoco.

Then came a report that (three years after Cabot) Captain Pedro Alvares Cabral had found still another land. Having set forth with thirteen ships to follow da Gama's route, he had held off Africa too far to take advantage of the winds and had reached a different land. This he named for the mythical island of Brazil, Brasilia or even Prezilia.

Now, was this new land Terra Australis, or just one more Indian island? With orders to find out whether this land had a southern end Fernando de Magalhães (whom we call Magellan) left Europe in 1519. For a while he was fooled by the estuary of the Rio de la Plata, which is wide enough to look like the arm of the sea. Then he realized his mistake and continued south until he found the strait that bears his name. As he threaded his way through, he saw to the left a forbidding-looking land under a pall of clouds through which the sun seldom shone. At night the shore of this land

* Though an Italian by birth, christened Christoforo Colombo, Columbus first learned to read and write in *Spanish* as a young man in Spain and Portugal. Therefore he always signed his name with the Hispanified form Cristóbal Colón.

was dotted with twinkling fires, so much so that Magellan named this land Tierra del Fuego, "Land of Fire." He did not know that these were the campfires of the primitive Fuegan Indians, trying to keep warm in their lean-tos. Nor did he know how big this land was—whether a mere island or the headland of a continent.

Beyond that strait came open sea—an immense ocean, in fact. Magellan crossed it under great hardships and himself found a violent death in the Philippines, but one of his ships completed the first circumnavigation of the globe.

Brazil, or South America, was not Terra Australis and Magellan had proved it once and for all. . . . Oh, no, Magellan had only proved what another geographer of Nuremberg had prophesied in 1515, four years before Magellan left port. That mathematician, Johannes Schöner, had made a beautiful globe in that year, exhibiting all the latest discoveries. There was Africa with a free tip to the south, showing just how da Gama had sailed around it. There were indications of North America, and there was South America, somewhat small but correct in outline as far as one could tell then. Like Africa it had a free southern tip, but while the sea below Africa was comparatively broad, there was only a narrow channel south of South America. And beyond this channel loomed an enormous Terra Australis, complete with bays and capes, rivers and mountains.

And now Magellan had sailed through this very narrow channel and reported land on his left, exactly as shown by Schöner.

While Magellan, sailing for Spain, had put one corner of Terra Australis on the map, Dom Jorge de Menezes, voyaging for Portugal, provided another. In 1526 a storm had driven him east from Borneo to a coast of the land of a strange black race, big-nosed and bushy-haired, very unlike the Malays of

FIG. 13. World Map of Matthias Quadus, originally published in Cologne in 1608, showing Terra Australis. (Simplified version.)

Adapted from Nordenskiöld's Facsimile Atlas

Borneo. While nothing was done about this discovery then, the land was rediscovered nineteen years later by a Spanish vessel under Captain Inigo Ortiz de Retes, who fought a fierce battle with the long war canoes of these Blacks. He saw high mountains beyond the coast and called the land New Guinea, no doubt because the Papuans reminded him of the Negroes of Africa.

In Europe the name had a different connotation. Since the Guinea coast of Africa was part of a continent, it was assumed that New Guinea was part of a continent—Terra Australis—likewise.

Here we must go back a few decades to discuss business. Just after those first big trips of da Gama for Portugal and Columbus for Spain, the heads of both nations realized that their efforts at long-distance exploration, colonization, and exploitation all over the globe would sooner or later lead to rivalry, disputes, and finally war. Wouldn't it be more Christian to mediate the question of their respective rights before things went that far?

So they went to the Pope, Alexander VI Borgia, who settled these worldly questions as follows: He drew a line around the earth from pole to pole, dividing the earth into Eastern and Western Hemispheres. The line ran down the middle of the Atlantic, leaving all of the Americas to the west of it except part of Greenland and the tip of the eastward bulge of South America. The hemisphere west of this Atlantic line was assigned to Spain, with full rights of conquest, settlement, and trade, while the Eastern Hemisphere, including all of Africa and all of Asia except its eastern tip, went to Portugal. A year later (1494) the Portuguese and Spanish governments agreed in the Treaty of Tordesillas to move the line about ten degrees farther west, which gave Portugal a larger slice of Brazil and explains how that land speaks Portuguese today.

The agreement worked very well, all things considered, until Spain and Portugal came to determine the position of the line of demarcation in the Pacific. Now, while in general the Spaniards were after gold and the Portuguese after spices, the Spaniards had no objection to turning a fast peso in the spice trade too. And the prize, the Spice Islands—the Moluccas—lay right *on* that line.

That is, an objective observer would say they lay on the line; the Portuguese, who were not at all objective, said they lay on their side of the line and produced geographical experts to prove it, while the Spaniards swore it was on theirs and also produced witnesses. As this was in the days before the invention of the marine chronometer, it was hard to measure the longitude of any place very accurately, let alone that of an island on the opposite side of the globe.

But after much bickering the rivals, with more sense than one might expect, came to an agreement. On April 22nd, 1529, the Crown of Portugal paid the Crown of Spain 350,000 gold pieces for a temporary settlement. The Moluccas were to be regarded as west of the meridian of the Treaty of Tordesillas, and hence Portuguese. If later improvements in the science of geography proved that they belonged to Portugal anyway, Spain was to return the money.

The Portuguese were happier with this settlement than the Spaniards. Their spice trade flourished, but a sum of money, even 350,000 pieces of gold, does not last forever. The Spaniards, feeling that they had been had, started looking for more unknown worlds to conquer. Terra Australis, as shown on Schöner's globe, just fitted their bill. Moreover another cartographer, Oronce Fine, had drawn a beautiful map in 1531 with Terra Australis on it. In fact he invented the name; therefore the continent had been called the "Continent of the Antipodes," or *Brasilia inferior*, or most of the time simply *Terra incognita*, "unknown land."

Moreover Fine had influenced another mapmaker, a Flemish gentleman named Gerhard Kremer. Now *kremer* means "merchant," so when he became a savant Gerhard Kremer in due course Latinized his name to Gerardus Mercator.

Mercator put Fine's Terra Australis on his world map of 1538 and later on his famous Chart of the World of 1569, the much-admired masterpiece of cartography for generations. It was the great and infallible authority; therefore if it showed Terra Australis, there must be such a continent, and the inability of seamen to find it was due to their timidity or incompetence.

And it was indeed a wonderful map. Europe, Asia, and Africa are shown with reasonable correctness. South America is too wide in its southern parts, and the Atlantic is speckled with a number of the traditional mythical islands like Brendan's Isle and the rest. But the really beautiful feature was Terra Australis.

Tierra del Fuego is shown as part of the Unknown Southland, and from there the coast of the continent ran east at about the same latitude, passing south of Africa, forming a big gulf south of Ceylon, and then turning north until it almost touches Java and New Guinea. Then it turns southeast and continues across the South Pacific to join Tierra del Fuego again. In addition, Mercator showed another, though much smaller, imaginary continent at the North Pole.

The Mercator chart not only became a standard authority itself; it also influenced countless other maps, such as

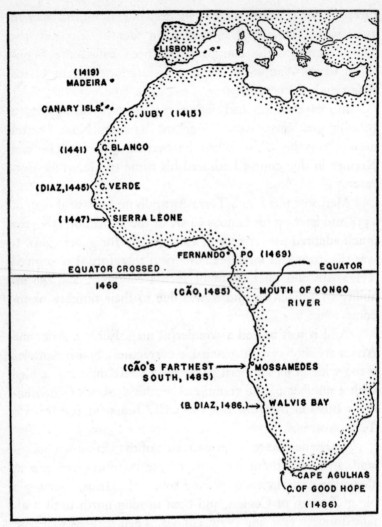

FIG. 14. Outline map of the African west coast, showing the points reached by the various explorers.

those of Thomaso Poracchi, Joannes Myritius, Cornelis de Jonde, and Matthias Quadus—the last dated 1608.

Mercator's friend and colleague Abraham Ortelius in 1570 published an atlas which included a world map that became almost as renowned as Mercator's. This map not only showed imaginary polar continents like those of Mercator; to top off his picture, Ortelius printed a caption at one point on Terra Australis stating that the continent was inhabited by gigantic parrots (*Psittacorum regio . . . ob incredibilem earum avium ibidem magnitudinem*)!

To return now from the strain of mapmaking to the even more strenuous business of finding what the maps portrayed. The Spaniards were, as we said, especially interested in finding new land to take the commercial place of the Moluccas, which they had sold. Accordingly in 1567 the Viceroy of Peru sent forth General Alvaro de Mendaña to "discover certain islands and a continent" in the South Seas. So sure were the Spaniards of finding Mercator's Southern Continent, and finding it moreover inhabited, that they took along a number of priests to begin missionary work from the moment of landing.

While Mendaña failed to find any continent, he did discover "certain islands" which he called the Solomons— whether because their inhabitants practiced circumcision, or because he was thinking of King Solomon's Ophir, we don't know. Despite his fulsome praise of his discovery, he must have been disappointed. In any case he waited nearly thirty years—until 1595—before trying to colonize his islands.

He finally set out with one Pedro Fernandez de Quiros as his chief pilot. When Mendaña died enroute, Quiros succeeded him in command. The result was that the islands were not found at all; Quiros returned to Peru empty handed and thence went to Spain. That he had failed to find "Ophir" was just a minor misfortune, with Terra Australis still waiting for *conquistadores*. He told the Pope how many souls were awaiting salvation on the Southland, and besieged the King of Spain with petitions stressing the riches of the unfound lands. Finally in 1603 the king issued a royal *cedula* sending Quiros on his way with three ships. His second-in-command was a navigator named Luis Vaez de Torres.

After a journey that changed course daily to avoid real and imaginary storms, they reached the islands later called the New Hebrides and found among them a fair-sized island, about as big as our smallest state, and often called Merena. This fact, however, did not faze Señor de Quiros. This "terra australis" was formally annexed to Spain. There was the laying of a cornerstone for the city of New Jerusalem, the formal christening of a middle-sized rivulet as New Jordan, and the saying of three solemn masses with a toast to the king added by Quiros. They christened the island *Austrialia del Espíritu Santo**—"Holy Ghost Land of the South."

Then, anticlimactically, Quiros put to sea in one ship and vanished in the dark of a stormy night in the direction of Spain, leaving Torres with the other two ships. When he got home, Quiros evidently thought that everything had been done except for the proper presentation of his feat. So he sat down and wrote and wrote—from 1607 to 1610 alone he sent fifty long memorials and petitions to the Crown of Spain. He was "convinced" that Espíritu Santo was larger than Europe, richer than Peru at the time of its discovery, and more thickly populated than aboriginal Cuba. Over its plains roamed enormous herds of wild cattle. (There are no native wild cattle in the whole Pacific region east of

---

* "Austrialia" seems to be a pun from "Australis" and "Austria," the latter at that time being the fief of the Spanish King and Emperor.

Celebes, but Quiros was no man to spoil a good story for the sake of a few facts.)

Australia, the real Australia, was still unknown, but it was soon seen for the first time as a result of Quiros's antics. Torres, left behind, waited two weeks and then set out for the nearest Spanish stronghold, the Philippines. In so doing he sailed south of New Guinea through a then unknown strait, and to port he saw what looked like distant islands: the mountains of Cape York, the northern tip of Australia.

The Spaniards, however, believed neither the fabulous accounts of Quiros nor the straightforward report of Torres, which they did not even forward from the Philippines. The British found it in the archives in Manila a century and a half later, and saw to it that at least the strait found by Torres was named after him.

Although the Quiros episode annoyed everybody concerned, it did nothing to damage the reputation of Terra Australis. Things like that had happened before. People had claimed that they had traveled to America and it had turned out to be a hoax; but that had not changed the fact that America existed.

However, the story of Terra Australis then passed from Spanish to Dutch hands. The first connection of the Dutch with Terra Australis was damaging to the great Southland. You remember: One of the main reasons it had been put on Mercator's map was Magellan's description of Tierra del Fuego, which he saw to port while sailing around the south end of South America, in 1520.

Then in 1616 Willem Corneliszoon Schouten and Jakob Le Maire sailed around Tierra del Fuego to the south, discovering the cape which they named after one of their ships, named in turn after the Dutch city of Hoorn, but which

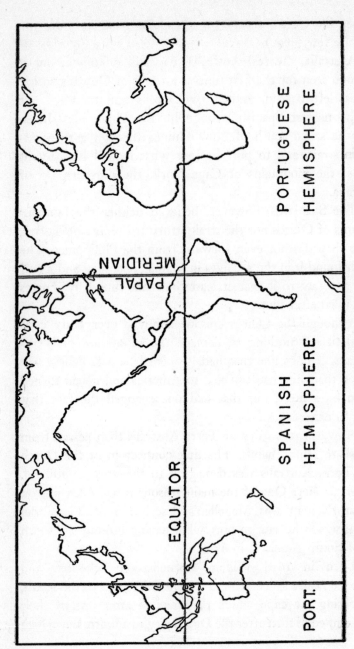

FIG. 15. The papal meridian, dividing the world into a Spanish and a Portuguese hemisphere. (Treaty of Tordesillas, 1494.)

subsequently became corrupted to "Cape Horn." It later became known that Sir Francis Drake, too, had discovered the insular nature of Tierra del Fuego. He had sailed through Magalhães Strait, to be met at the western end of the strait by a storm that scattered his ships and blew Drake far to the southwest. Returning to the entrance, he made another cast to the southeast, finding nothing but Tierra del Fuego and its offshore islands to port, and to starboard nothing but the cold waters of the Antarctic Ocean. Then he returned to the western entrance again and set off up the Chilean coast.

While Schouten knew that the Fuegan Archipelago was just a group of islands, he was uncertain about the easternmost of them, which he called Staatenland. Might it be a cape of Terra Australis? But then in 1643 Hendrick Brouwer found that Staatenland was an island too.

At this point the real southern continent, Australia, begins to seep into the story. Luis Vaez de Torres had sighted it from a distance without realizing what it was. Several sea captains—French, Portuguese, and Dutch—are reported to have seen it in the years after Torres's voyage. But we can never be sure whether these narratives refer to the actual coast of the fifth continent or were cases of wishful thinking colored by Mercator's wonderful map.

From 1600 on, however, there exists a curious touchstone for judging these reports. Terra Australis had by now acquired fairyland attributes, with luxuriant tropical vegetation, beautiful inhabitants, gold an ordinary metal, and diamonds and emeralds just pebbles on the beach.

By contrast, the real Australia was a dreadful disappointment. Its vegetation was not tropical—in fact the continent is mostly one vast flat desert. The coast was generally uninviting, the offshore waters studded with reefs and swarming with sharks, the land completely devoid of gems. And the aborigines were not at all beautiful. In short, the explorers who expressed their disappointment with loud complaints and disparagements were the men who had really set foot on Australia.

By 1642 Australia's west coast was generally known to the Dutch under the name of Nieuw Holland. In that year the governor of the Dutch East Indies, Antoon van Diemen, ordered Abel Janszoon Tasman to sail from Batavia and establish the truth about Terra Australis, especially with reference to the New Holland coast.

Tasman set out on a course calculated to bring him either to the coast of Terra Australis or to whatever open seas lay on the other side of New Holland. After a long voyage he reached an unmistakable southern cape, a southern end of a continent. Tasman called it Vandiemensland in honor of his governor, but later it turned out to be not a part of Australia proper, but the south end of the large island now known—in *his* honor—as Tasmania.

Going on for another thousand miles he saw land again. He looked with amazement at the snow-covered peaks of the "Alps" of the South Island of New Zealand. Then he turned north, sailed through the Tasman Sea between Australia and New Zealand, and returned to the Dutch Indies.

Although Australia had now been rounded, not even Tasman dared delete Terra Australis from the map. The land with high mountains he had seen might, for all anyone knew, stretch all the way to Staatenland near Tierra del Fuego. . . .

During the eighteenth century, however, it slowly became clear that Terra Australis, if it existed at all, must be an antarctic continent. All the coasts still unidentified as islands, and therefore under suspicion of being outposts of Terra Australis, had acquired the same characteristic: No longer did they lie in the tropics, bathed with warm waters and clothed with a dense green cover of vegetation. Instead they were bleak lands rising from the cold whale-swarming waters of the southernmost seas to snow-clad mountains in the background.

A report from a French vessel under Lozier Bouvet pointed to an antarctic Southland: 800 miles south of Cape Town and a little west of it he had found a coast from which a huge glacier seemed to flow into the sea. In the perpetual fog and rain of that zone he had not been able to see much, but he was sure he had found land and named it *Cap de la Circoncision*. He used the term "cape" of course with reference to Terra Australis. Then the antarctic weather kept Bouvet's discovery a puzzle for the whole interval from 1739, the year of discovery, to 1899, when it was rediscovered by the steamer *Valdivia*. Long before that it had become certain that Bouvet had found no continent; the question was whether he had found an island or an oversized iceberg. It turned out to be an island—one large extinct volcano, completely glaciated. Politically, Bouvet Island is one of Norway's few overseas possessions.

Before Bouvet's report had arrived in his homeland, the most versatile French scientist of that period, Count Georges Louis Leclerc de Buffon, had formed a new opinion of Terra Australis, which seems to have expressed the general feeling of the time.

Terra Australis, Buffon wrote, must be a sixth continent, not directly connected with any one of the known five*, and centering in the Antarctic region. It might still be the biggest, as large as Asia (including Europe) and Africa put together. That the Antarctic should be colder than the Arctic, Buffon continued, was a mistake based on the observed fact that the

* Properly speaking, Europe should be considered, not a continent, but a peninsula on the continent of Asia.

Antarctic icebergs were larger than those of the Arctic.

These icebergs, he argued, merely proved the presence of enormous rivers (which could only exist on a large continent) and high mountains on which the moisture to feed those rivers could condense.

And one more thing could be suspected from the evidence. Look at South America. Along the Atlantic parts, first explored, were low-lying lands tenanted by primitive races with no culture and no capacity for abstract thought; no organization and poor technology. But when the Whites penetrated to the Peruvian highlands they found a highly developed system of political organization, religion, culture, and technology.

Well then, the Australian aborigines could be compared to the lowland South American Indians; so why should not the highlands of Terra Australis harbor a rich culture comparable to that of the Andean region?

It was a fascinating idea, and it is almost regrettable that Buffon guessed wrong. His ideas were the last attempt to keep something of the magic of Terra Australis, which had lasted so many centuries. A real Terra Australis would be much more interesting than the vast watery waste of howling winds and mountainous waves that occupies most of the actual site of his suppositious Southland.

While this book of Buffon's was still avidly read in France, an English shipmaster in the British Navy, who had worked his way up from a common merchant seaman (something that took a bit of doing in those days) was surveying the coasts of Newfoundland and Labrador. His remarkable work attracted so much attention that when the Royal Society persuaded the Admiralty to send a ship to the South Seas to make scientific observations, he was chosen captain.

The ship was the *Endeavour* and the captain was Cook,

James Cook. So much has he come to be regarded as the paragon of seamanship that his first name can only be found in reference books nowadays. He is not James Cook, a captain in His Majesty's Navy; he is *the* Captain Cook.

Captain Cook first sailed to Tahiti, since the main objective of the voyage was the observation of a transit of Venus across the sun, and Tahiti was the place to do it. That done, Cook set out to solve the Southland problem—beginning with that mountainous coast east of Australia that Tasman had seen. As it was the only definite thing known about the Southland, Cook began there.

On October 6, 1769, they sighted land: Tasman's northern promontory of Terra Australis without a doubt. But was it a promontory or an island? The thing to do was to try to sail around it. A few months later Cook had rounded North Island of New Zealand and settled that question. But then he found another land south of the first island that called for the same treatment. By the end of March, 1770, that land had been disposed of too; it was New Zealand's South Island. And south of South Island and Stewart Island nothing but open sea.

Cook then returned through Torres Strait, clearing up that old semimystery left over from the Quiros expedition to Holy Ghost Land, and went home. But now, having destroyed the last reliable-looking evidence for Terra Australis, he had become really interested in the problem.

The year 1772 found him on the high seas again, with two vessels, *Discovery* and *Resolution*, for the express purpose of settling the Southland question once and for all. First he cast back and forth across the South Pacific, and north and south, until he had quartered the whole colossal area from New Caledonia (which he discovered) to Easter Island with its enigmatic statues, and from the tropics to the Antarctic Circle. He raised islands a-plenty (in fact one Polynesian cluster is named for him) but no continent.

Still, Terra Australis had been reported from one other point: Bouvet's Circumcision Cape, SSW of Cape Town. Thither sailed the indefatigable captain. Although he missed the island in the rain, his negative report was very positive from the point of view of his objective: *no land*. (He thought Bouvet must have seen an iceberg.)

The only course left was to sail around the earth as far south as weather—or Terra Australis—would permit. Therefore he systematically circled the South Pole between latitudes 55° and 60° S. Time and again he pressed south across the Antarctic Circle, only to have his ships, which were not built for polar work, forced back north by the ice. Occasionally he saw islands; often icebergs, sometimes of fantastic size, for the Antarctic gives birth to bergs a hundred miles across. And once a gigantic ice wall behind which there might or might not be land.

And the result of Cook's great expedition was: The great Southern Continent does not exist! Perhaps there was a much smaller continent around the pole, lying completely within the Antarctic Circle and buried under eternal snow and ice. It is said that Buffon, then an old man, cried when he was told of the results of this expedition, and stated later that any continent that was still possible after Cook's work would hardly be worth finding.

That still left the question of just what did lie behind those terrible ice floes that disputed the passage to the South Polar region. It was now obvious that there was no one great Southern Continent, but three comparatively small ones: South America, Australia, and a possible Antarctica.

By the early years of the nineteenth century it was known that a number of islands were scattered about the seas 500 miles or more south of the southern tip of South America. The South Shetlands and others of these islands were in fact used as bases by sealers and whalers. Then in 1820 Captain Nathaniel Palmer, the twenty-one-year-old captain of the sealing sloop *Hero* of Stonington, Connecticut, ran his little ship south along the west coast of what proved to be a peninsula of Antarctica, called Palmer Land after the man who first sighted it. And so began the process of nibbling away at the Antarctic land mass, which has been carried on since by many discoverers—D'Urville of France, Wilkes of the United States, Ross of Britain, Nordenskiöld of Sweden, de Guerlache of Belgium, and others.

By the early 1900's the explorations of Scott, Amundsen, and others had established the existence of at least some large stretches of high, cold land, hundreds of miles in extent. Evidently Antarctica was no mere archipelago. However, these expeditions also showed that the continent was deeply indented by the Ross Sea on the side towards New Zealand— in fact to within 250 or 300 miles of the pole. Most of this sea, moreover, is filled by that astonishing phenomenon, the Ross Ice Shelf, so that it is hard to tell from the snow-covered surface where the deeply buried coast line ought to run.

And on the opposite side of Antarctica, facing the South Atlantic Ocean, there proved to be another, smaller, indentation occupied by the Weddell Sea. Now, did these two bays extend inland to join in the interior, dividing the supposed continent into two large islands, separated by an ice-choked strait?

Although the Byrd expeditions to the Ross Ice Shelf in the 1930's reduced the possibility of this strait, it was not eliminated altogether until 1947, when the Ronne Antarctic

Research Expedition solved the problem by airplane. On November 21st of that year Finn Ronne (navigator and expedition leader), James Lassiter (pilot) and William Latady (photographer) made a long flight from the Palmer Peninsula south into the interior of Antarctica, and on December 12th another flight southeast from the base of Palmer Land along the Weddell Sea Coast. These flights definitely established that there is land under the ice, and that the Weddell Sea does not extend inland to join the Ross Sea.

So even if Antarctica is the smallest and most useless of the continents, it is at least a continent, and not a group of islands disguised as one by the mask of snow and ice!

So ended the search for Terra Australis, which had begun with Hipparchos in antiquity. It was the end of a long and beautiful dream, the dream of a marvelous continent just outside the explorer's reach. The dream persisted even though the coast of that continent receded again and again, and did not end until it was definitely proved that the grain of truth in it was buried under thousands of feet of ice and snow inside the Antarctic Circle.

CHAPTER VIII

The Western Ocean

PLATO, YOU REMEMBER, HAD FLEETINGLY SPOKEN ABOUT A
continent on the other side of the ocean. If he based this
remark on hearsay originating with Phoenician sources it is
possible that he (being uncertain of the direction) had a
piece of the African shore in mind. More likely, however, this
was just an allusion to the other bank of the older Okeanos.
Although in Plato's time geographers and historians, like Herodotos, had given up the concept of the world-girdling river
and substituted the real Atlantic for the western portion of
the river, the idea still lingered on. Plato's younger contemporary Theopompos enlarged on the thought of "the
other bank" and told that it was inhabited by people called
Meropes, twice as big and twice as long-lived as we are.
Once, he wrote, ten million Meropes set out to invade the
oikoumēnē inside the ocean. But, arriving among the Hyperboreans of the Far North they found nothing worth stealing
and returned home in disgust.

While this was obviously a poetic story with a moral or
two thrown in, remarks about a continent beyond the ocean
began to flare up again a few centuries later, at about the time
of Christ. Some eighty years ago several scholars, having come
across one or the other of these passages by chance, began to

comb the available material diligently, in the hope of finding an undeniable statement which tended to prove that the Americas had been reached in classical times.

At first glance these passages do sound significant. Lucius Annaeus Seneca, a Roman born in Spain, tutor of the young Nero and advisor to the emperor during the early time of his reign, wrote some verses which, translated and condensed, read: "some time in the future there will be centuries . . . when Tethys* [the wife of the sea-god Okeanos] discovers new worlds and Thule will no longer be the most distant of the lands."

Strabo, about one generation earlier than Seneca, indulged in similar speculations: ". . . it may be that in this same temperate zone there are actually two inhabited worlds, or even more, and particularly in the proximity of the parallel through Athens that is drawn across the Atlantic Sea." (Strabo, *Geography*, I, iv, 6.)

The most interesting of these utterances can be found in Plutarch's smaller book *De facie in orbe Lunae* where it says: "An island named Ogygia is far out in the open sea, five days of sea journeying to the west of Britannia. There are three other islands, equidistant from Ogygia and from each other, in the direction of sunset in summer. One of them, the Barbarians claim, was where Kronos was kept prisoner by Zeus. But his normal seat is on the large continent beyond those islands and the sea."

What makes Plutarch's statement especially fascinating is one additional item about that island which was alleged to be the former prison of Kronos: "There they see the sun dip below the horizon on thirty consecutive days for a little less

---

* Though the most authoritative manuscript names Tethys here, other manuscripts name Tiphys, the helmsman of the Argonauts. It makes equally good sense either way. Seneca, *Medea*, 11, 375-379.

than one hour and the darkness of this [short] night is slight and illuminated by the light of the western sky."

Since the direction of the sunset in summer is northwest rather than west the island five days away from "Britannia" might well be Iceland and Plutarch's "Ogygia" (obviously not the same as that of the *Odyssey*) would be the Faeroe Islands. And the land where Kronos normally dwells could only be Greenland, the landfall a sailor would make if he continued from Iceland on the same course he had held sailing from England. Actually this is the route the Vikings followed almost ten centuries later, proceeding, finally, from Greenland to the New England coast.

As in many cases when it comes to the identification of places mentioned by ancient writers, this interpretation fits the geographical facts reasonably well, but not perfectly. It is, therefore, mostly a matter of taste whether one wants to assume that Plutarch had some vague and presumably slightly garbled reports about lands northwest of Great Britain, or whether all this is to be taken as merely an interesting coincidence. The German geographer Eduard Ebner, after a careful study of the problem whether America (or Greenland) had been reached in classical times, summed up his conclusion in the sentence: "The ancients did not discover America, but they invented it."

It must be remarked that this "invention" did bear fruit in the long run: those passages in Strabo and Seneca—plus a number of less important and less definite passages in other classical writing—greatly influenced Columbus in his thinking and contributed to his decision to sail to the west.

In straight contradiction to Ebner's opinion, which is shared by most historians of geography, there are assertions, never too clear and just vague enough to defy attempts at running them down, that Phoenician coins were found on islands in the Atlantic ocean or even on the east coast of the United States. So far one is still justified in stating that there is no convincing evidence that the Phoenicians reached the Western Hemisphere. It may be practical, therefore, to turn the question around and ask: "*Could* they have reached the Western Hemisphere?" And also: "How far did they, to our knowledge, explore the Atlantic?"

The Phoenicians, as has been said in earlier chapters, at one time closed the western Mediterranean and especially the Strait of Gibraltar to all other ships. The Greeks of 800 B.C. (Homer) had some information about the strait itself and about beautiful islands in the ocean. They even had stray bits of information about fine detail, like "Kalypso's sailing directions" in the *Odyssey* and the descriptions by Hesiod (around 770 B.C.) of the swan *Cygnus musicus*, which is a typical bird of the Atlantic shore of western Europe but does not enter the Mediterranean region. And in 660 B.C. Kolaios of Samos actually sailed through the Strait of Gibraltar, although involuntarily. But from 530 B.C. until 206 B.C. the Phoenicians established their version of an Iron Curtain, a curtain of fast ships, manned by men convinced that no mercy could be shown to any interloper.

This interval which made the western Mediterranean forbidden territory is probably responsible for both the name of the Atlantic Ocean and the name of the Atlas mountains in Africa. As regards the name "Atlantic" it was used first by Herodotos, and his word *atlantikos* is an adjective derived from Atlas, whom we have already met in the form of the Titan who upheld the heavens. It was thought later that the ocean had received its name from the Atlas range in Morocco, and Virgil (*Aeneid*, IV, ll. 480 ff.) expressed this clearly in his lines:

Close to the shore of the ocean, not far from the region of
  sunset,
Farthest of all is the Aethiop land, where Atlas the mighty,
Turns on his shoulders the firmament studded with bright
  constellations . . .

Herodotos himself probably thought so too, although he
only knew that there were mountains in the Far West. The
Atlas range did not really become known until Roman times;
the Phoenicians knew of its existence and position but do not
seem to have had a name for it, for the *Periplus* of Hanno,
written around 525 B.C., merely states that the river Lixus
(the Wadi Draa of modern maps) "comes from a high mountain range."

But it is quite certain now that the Moroccan Atlas range
got its name secondhand. It is an extensive range, rugged in
places and rising to a maximum height of 15,000 feet in the
great Tinzár. But most of the peaks are of moderate height
with gradual slopes and with reasonably fertile valleys in between. But the Atlas which upheld the firmament with its
bright constellations had always been described as a single
sky-piercing peak. Pomponius Mela in his *Description of the
World* (III, x) made that quite clear; it was a peak "rearing its
enormous mass, steep and inaccessible by reason of the sharp-
pointed rocks that surround it on all sides; the higher it rises,
the more it diminishes in size; its summit is higher than the
eye can reach: it loses itself in the clouds; also it is fabled
not only to touch with its top the sky and the stars but even
to support them . . ."

Herodotos, Pliny, and Mela all tell of extraordinary races
of people who lived around Mount Atlas, some of them being
duplicates of the freakish folk found in classical descriptions
of the Fabulous East. There were, for instance, the Atarantes,

who ritually cursed the scorching sun every day, and the Atlantes (a different pronunciation of the same name?), who ate no living thing and never dreamed. And:

> The Troglodytes hollow out caverns which are their dwellings; they live on the flesh of snakes, and they have no voice, but only make squeaking noises, being entirely devoid of intercourse by speech. The Garamantes do not practice marriage but live with their women promiscuously. The Augilae worship only the powers of the lower world. The Gamphasantes go naked, do not engage in battle, and hold no intercourse with any foreigner. The Blemmyae are reported to have no heads, their mouth and eyes being attached to their chests. The Satyrs have nothing of ordinary humanity about them except human shape. The form of the Goat-Pans is that which is commonly shown in pictures of them. The Himantopodes ["Strapfoots"] are people with feet like leather thongs, whose nature it is to crawl instead of walking.
>
> Pliny, *Natural History*, V, vii.

Some of these frantic figments can be more or less plausibly explained; thus the Troglodytes may be simply the ancestors of the cave-dwelling Matmata of modern Tunisia. The Garamantes, Gamphasantes, and Augilae were real people whose customs Pliny may or may not be reporting correctly. Satyrs and Goat-Pans we are already familiar with, and the Strapfoots seem to be connected with the Titans, the snake-legged giants of Greek myth who once rebelled against the gods. Atlas himself, you will remember, was a Titan.

The Blemmyae, or Blemmyes, are of course the "men whose heads do grow beneath their shoulders" mentioned by Shakespeare's Othello. The origin of this curious acephalic legend is not known, though some have surmised that perhaps there was a tribe who fought or danced with their heads concealed in some sort of closed helmet or wicker mask, who might have given rise to the tale. In late Roman times the name of the Blemmyae was applied to a warlike Ethiopian tribe living near the shore of the Red Sea in what is now called the Nubian Desert, a good 2,500 miles from the Moroccan Atlas. How the name came to be applied to two peoples, one real and one imaginary, and so far apart, is not known. But, as we shall see, the Blemmyae turned up again later even farther from Morocco—in South America.

Then which was the "real" Atlas which had been forgotten, presumably because Phoenician power politics made it inaccessible to the Greeks?

In 1803 the French scholar Bory de Saint-Vincent suggested, in a book on Atlantis, that the original Mount Atlas had been, not Tinzár in the Atlas range, but the 12,000-foot volcanic peak of Teyde on the island of Tenerife in the Canaries. This idea is not at all implausible, for this great cone rises steeply from the waters of the Atlantic (occupying a large part of the island, in fact) and is crowned by a perpetual cloud of steam. Thus the Pico de Teyde answers the classical descriptions of Atlas much better than does anything in Morocco. And then the derivation of "Atlantic Ocean" becomes obvious: it is the ocean *in* which Mount Atlas is located, the mountain which, to use Homer's words, "knoweth the watery depths of the ocean" because it rises from them.

Now, while the Phoenicians were busily engaged keeping everybody else out of the Atlantic, what did they do themselves to explore it?

Not too much. We know of just two fleets which were sent out, under Admirals Hanno and Himilco. Hanno turned south and explored several hundred miles down the African coast to a small island which he named Kernë—either modern Herné at the mouth of the Rio de Oro, or Arguin at Cape Blanco 200 miles farther south—where he set up a trading post. His people were scared by the sight of the country on fire, not knowing that it was merely the natives burning the grass for pasturage, as they still do. On another island they found:

> . . . savage people, the greater part of whom were women, whose bodies were hairy, and whom our interpreters called *gorillai*. Though we pursued the men, we could not seize any of them; but all fled from us, escaping over precipices, and defending themselves with stones. Three women were however taken; but they attacked their conductors with their teeth and hands, and could not be prevailed on to accompany us. Having killed them, we flayed them, and brought their skins with us to Carthage.
>
> Hanno, *Periplus* (Falconer translation)

Probably the "hairy savages" were chimpanzees, *not* gorillas, shyer animals living much farther south than Hanno went. The true gorilla did not in fact become definitely known to Europeans until a little over a century ago. It was long called by various names—pongo, ingena, African orangutan—until in the 1840's a missionary named Savage, writing from Africa to his scientific friends Wyman in Boston and Owen in London, suggested naming the new ape *gorilla* after the creatures ambiguously described by Hanno.

The other admiral, Himilco, went north to look for the Tin Islands (Cornwall and the Scillies) with which the Tartessians had long been trading. He found them all right, though the round trip took four months. Himilco obviously described his trip later, but we know only a fragment of his description because it was quoted by the Roman Rufus Festus Avienus (in a book which, like far too many others, bears the title *Description of the World*) who understood that the long duration of Himilco's voyage was not due to distance but because:

> Here no breeze drives the ships forward, so dead is the sluggish wind of this idle sea. And then [says Himilco] many

seaweeds grow in the troughs between the waves, which slow the ship like bushes, thus showing that there the sea does not descend to any great depth—in fact that the water barely suffices to cover the bottom. Here the beasts of the sea move slowly hither and thither, and great monsters swim languidly among the sluggishly creeping ships.

To make sure that his readers' flesh crept too, Himilco added that if one kept on one got into regions where "darkness screens the light of day as with a cloak, and always a fog conceals the sea."

The coastal exploration performed by the Phoenicians comprised the distance from Great Britain to about Cape Blanco on the African west coast, nothing that had not been done before. How about the Atlantic islands, particularly the ones off Europe and Africa which we call the Azores, Madeira and the Canary Islands?

It is certain that the Phoenicians reached Madeira—general descriptions of it and its position percolating back to Greece—and that they sailed to the Canaries. As for the Azores there can be some doubt because of the longer distance involved and because of the small sea-keeping capacity of ancient ships. True, several medieval writers tell vague tales of statues on the Azores and other Atlantic islands indicating that men had been there before. And according to a story repeated by Baron von Humboldt early in the nineteenth century, a vase full of coins turned up on Corvo, the westernmost of the Azores, in 1749. Nine of these came into the hands of an antiquarian who pronounced them Phoenician or Carthaginian.

However, there are no such statues in the Azores now, and the coins, if they ever existed, have also disappeared. Perhaps the best guess is that a Phoenician ship may have been blown to the Azores by a storm at some time, perhaps even repeatedly, but that these islands were too far from land for the shore-hugging ships of the time to make them a regular port of call.

The Canaries are something else. The Phoenicians did visit them, finding the domesticable songbirds we know so well. Did they also find people?

About 40 B.C., long after the fall of Carthage, King Juba of Mauretania sent an expedition thither. He later wrote that his men had found huge dogs on one island (whence the name *Canaria*) and huge lizards on another; also ruins of buildings, but made no mention of men. Furthermore, the islands stank from the bodies of monsters washed up upon them.

How much of all this is to be taken seriously? We don't know. Juba, a prolific writer, was also one of the prize liars of antiquity, and we can be reasonably sure that the dogs, lizards, and dead sea monsters are fictitious.

After Juba's expedition nobody is known to have visited the islands for many centuries, though later geographers kept their memory alive. In the twelfth and thirteenth centuries Arab and European navigators began to stop there, one of the first being a small Genoese fleet under Lanciloto Malocello (for whom Lanzarote is named) in 1270. More visitors dropped in, sometimes to hunt the natives for slaves, until in 1402 a French expedition sponsored by the King of Spain conquered the Canaries. After passing through the hands of a long succession of adventurers the archipelago came under direct Spanish rule, as it still is.

The medieval voyagers to the Canaries found the islands tenanted by an interesting race of cave-dwelling stone-age shepherds, the Guanches: a tall athletic folk speaking a dialect of Berber, but displaying in physique and culture a remarkable resemblance to the Crô-Magnon men of western Europe at the end of the Pleistocene ice age. The Guanches went naked or wore goatskins; sat on hillsides playing the flute while they watched their flocks; fished; wrestled; and fought ceremonious duels with sticks and stones. They also danced a dance that the Spaniards took back to Europe where it became a fad under the name of "the Canaries." Although they fought hard against the French and Spanish invaders, their wood and obsidian could do little against steel. The survivors were baptized and mixed with Spanish immigrants, so that they no longer exist as a separate people and are more or less completely Hispanified.

When did the Guanches reach the islands, before or after the visits of the Phoenicians?

There is no way to be sure. Ancient Libyan and Numidic inscriptions show that other visitors from Africa stopped by the islands, but do not say whether this was before the Guanches arrived, or while they were there. Finally, were the Guanches as primitive when they first arrived as they were later: "so grosse and rude, as they knew not the use of fire"? * Or did their culture decline in the islands because they lacked ores and other resources? Some decline there must have been, since they would have needed boats to reach the islands, though after they arrived they lost the shipwright's art. Consequently, there was no communication among the different islands.

In the *Geography* of Abu Abdallah Muhammad ibn-Idrisi of the twelfth century there is a story about eight men, all cousins, who had set out from Lisbon—then a Muslim city —to determine the bounds of the Atlantic. These "deluded folk," as Idrisi called them, sailed west for eleven days, at the end of which they found shallow water covering dangerous reefs, where the light of day shone but feebly. Sailing

* John Pory, introd. to Africanus's *History and Description of Africa* (Hakluyt Soc. ed.) p. 99f.

south they came upon an island inhabited solely by wild sheep, whose meat proved too bitter to eat. Another twelve days south brought them to an inhabited island, where they were seized by tall tan natives. The king interrogated them sharply through an Arabic-speaking interpreter. When he heard their story he laughed and directed the interpreter:

"Tell those fellows that my father once commanded some of his servants to embark on this sea; but after a month of voyaging they had to give up this vain enterprise because they had come to where the light of heaven was altogether lacking." However, he went on, he admired their courage and therefore ordered them sent to the African mainland whence they could find their way home.

Is this the story of real Muslim voyagers who succeeded in reaching the Canaries and were interrogated by a Guanche chief?

Perhaps.

To go back to the Phoenicians: while trips of their vessels to the Azores are still in the realm of possibility, if not provable with the material at hand, Phoenician voyages to the New World are highly unlikely.

There were two types of ship in use in the Mediterranean during the times when the Phoenicians dominated the seas of the West. They were galleys, biremes and triremes, for war and sailing ships for commerce.

It would have been out of the question to try a long ocean voyage with a galley. They were slender ships of low freeboard so that the oars could reach the water, and consequently had to run for shore whenever the sea became at all rough to avoid being swamped. Moreover they were extremely crowded and the rowers had no place to sleep aboard ship.

Galleys therefore had to come to shore every night* to disembark the crew, except in emergencies.

Furthermore, on a transatlantic voyage the galley would have to carry food and water for the journey. With a crew of, say, 125 to 150 men, the majority of them performing backbreaking labor, they would consume 1,500 to 2,000 pounds of food and water a day. Since with the best luck it would take about fifty days to cross, you can see that there would be no room for the necessary supplies.

Then how about a sailing ship? These were tubby little craft with high sterns to take following seas and, like the galleys, a single mast for one square sail and a pair of quarter-rudders or steering oars, one on each side of the stern. With such a rig tacking against the wind is impossible; the square sail, the single mast, and the quarter-rudders are all unsuited to the purpose. The classical merchant-skipper simply sat in port until the wind blew the way he wanted to go.

If you knew all about the wind belts of the Atlantic, and knew where you were going, and had a nice fair wind all the way, with neither gales, calms, nor adverse winds, and clear weather so that you could steer by the sun and stars, you could just possibly cross the Atlantic in such a ship and return. You would have to do what Columbus did: drop down the African coast to the Canaries, whence the northeast trade winds and the Equatorial Current will bear you west to the Antilles; then work north to about the latitude of Baltimore

* Or every morning; during the warm season both Greek and Phoenician galleys seemed to have traveled frequently by night. This not only made the rowers perform better, it also helped them, even if they carried no sail at all, that the wind at evening stands out to the sea and blows toward the land in the morning. Finally, without instruments orientation by the stars at night is easier and more reliable than navigation by the sun during the day. The *Odyssey* refers to night voyages in seven different places.

and sail east on the prevailing westerlies and the Gulf Stream to the Azores and the Iberian coast.

But our poor Punic mariner doesn't know about the winds and currents of the Atlantic; that information transpired only after long and arduous investigations by Prince Henrique's captains and other navigators, and Columbus shrewdly studied up on these phenomena before starting out. He doesn't know that there is land on the far side of the ocean and is unlikely to throw away his life on the remote chance that there may be, certainly not in the cockleshell craft that he has available. He is unlikely to find favorable wind and weather all the way, for even in the zones of prevailing winds the wind does not always blow in the right direction, and the first overcast will leave him hopelessly lost and sailing in useless circles.

The technical advances that made a transatlantic voyage a practical proposition were strung out over many centuries after Plato. In Hellenistic and Roman times geographers worked out the theory of latitude and longitude and learned how to use the Pole Star not merely to give direction but also to tell how far north you are. In Roman times merchant ships added a small square foresail, but to make the ship easier to handle when running free, not to enable it to sail against the wind. For the latter one needed either a fore-and-aft sail or a ship with masts at either end to control the ship's direction.

These improvements came in due course. The triangular lateen sail spread around the Mediterranean in the ninth century, perhaps from Egypt or from somewhere in the Indian Ocean. In the twelfth, two- and three-masted ships appeared, as did the all-important magnetic compass. The central rudder followed in the thirteenth. During the fifteenth there evolved the type of ship Columbus used: three masts, square sails on the fore and main to give a good spread of canvas, and a lateen sail on the mizzen to hold the ship's head into the wind when sailing close-hauled.

So men began crossing oceans just about as soon as they had a practical machine for doing so. True, the Vikings had reached America in open row-galleys with a single square sail, not much different from classical ships, but they did so by the northern route in short jumps of a few hundred miles each. And there is no evidence at all that the Phoenicians ever ventured into those cold waters.

Nor is there any evidence that they knew about the Sargasso Sea as has been asserted later by some imaginative authors. That assertion was based on two passages in classical literature which say nothing of the sort if you take the trouble to look up the original sources.

One of them is in a geographical book falsely attributed to that Skylax of Karyanda who around 500 B.C. had explored the Indus River for Darius I of Persia. Pseudo-Skylax reported in his *Periplous* (112): "The stretches of sea beyond Kernë are not further navigable because of the mud and sea-weed; the seaweed is one hand's breadth in width and at the tip is sharp enough to prick." This evidently refers to the African coast, moreover the description of the seaweed itself does not match anything known to botany, especially not the sargasso weed.

The other passage can be found in the writing of the Greek philosopher and scientist Theophrastos, a disciple of Aristotle and his successor as the head of the Peripatetic School. The statement in question, probably written around 300 B.C., can be found in the work usually quoted under its Latin title *Historia plantarum* and reads: "Outside of the Pillars of Herakles seaweed of astonishing size can be found, it is said, having a greater width than the palm of the hand.

This seaweed is carried from the outer into the inner sea by currents."

Both these passages refer to accumulations of seaweed which can be found off both the Portuguese and the African coasts. The real Sargasso Sea did not and could not have become known until there were ships which could cross the Atlantic *and return*.

Let us imagine ourselves a few hundred miles east of Bermuda in the open ocean. Although the average map shows nothing here but the pale blue that indicates the sea, we are in the middle of a distinct part of the Atlantic Ocean, an area almost the size of the United States. That whole area is slowly turning; it is, in fact, a gigantic eddy between the Gulf Stream to the north and the Equatorial Current to the south. We are in the middle of the nursery of most of the flying fish in the whole Atlantic Ocean, and above the lower level nursery of all the eels in the world.

We are in the Sargasso Sea.

This is a name which is as certain to evoke a mental picture as the name of Atlantis. But while the one conjures visions of gold and splendor and beauty, the other has the connotation of desolation and decay. Here, under the hot rays of an almost vertical sun, ships of all ages slowly rot in the slimy but unbreakable grip of an endless floating continent of seaweed, sometimes heaving with the terrible life of enormous crabs and gigantic cuttlefish. Nothing caught there can escape again, unless it can fly like the birds that come over from less terrifying islands to hunt for dead fish. Here the old dragon-ships of the Vikings lie alongside Arab baghalas and Spanish galleons; here time loses its meaning where there is nothing but silence and haze and heat and the stench of rotting seaweed. It is a place which, as someone said, will forever baffle the best explorers of the land and of the sea, because it is neither. . . .

The age of the helicopter, far from being baffled by such a place, would be delighted to explore this museum of old ships. Unfortunately the island of ships does not exist and the real Sargasso Sea, while of great scientific interest, has no terror about it.

The Sargasso Sea of fiction and the Sargasso Sea of fact have really nothing to do with each other except that both concern seaweed. While the factual Sargasso Sea became known slowly, arousing little interest outside scientific circles, the romantic Sargasso Sea sprang into bloom all at once within the last century.

Columbus was the first navigator to see the Sargasso Sea and to tell of its existence. At first his men had been cheered by the sight, thinking that the weeds meant land soon; then they became nervous lest the ships run on to the shoals from which they supposed the weeds to be growing.

Therefore they lashed a cannon ball to the end of a rope by way of a plumb line and lowered it 200 fathoms without striking the bottom (which was actually more than a mile down). They also hauled up a sample of the strange growth and noticed a queer-looking little crustacean scuttling about it, still called the Columbus crab. Thereafter they took the vegetation for granted and noted its presence in the log every day by three words: *Vieron muchas yerbas*—"they saw many weeds." No horror; the weed did not even impede the progress of the blunt-nosed *navios* of the little squadron.

Thereafter practicing sailors paid little attention to the weeds of the Sargasso Sea. What they did pay attention to was the fact that it lay in the horse latitudes with their frequent and prolonged calms. Prudent skippers stayed away from such places, not wishing to be forced to the desperate expedient of lowering the ship's boats over the side and towing the ship over the glassy sea by oar-power.

Science paid the sea hardly more attention during the three centuries following Columbus. The weed was described in botanical works under the name *Sargassum bacciferum*, and the "little grapes" to which it owed its name, first thought to be berries or seeds, were recognized as swim bladders such as are possessed by many seaweeds of the family *Fucaceae*, the wracks. Since the weed was thought to originate in the Gulf of Mexico it was called "gulfweed."

Columbus and after him the great Alexander von Humboldt thought that the weeds were merely torn off from their normal places of growth and had floated out to sea. Baron Alexander von Humboldt, the widely traveled brother of the equally traveled Wilhelm von Humboldt, has been called the last scientist who was (or for that matter could be) master of the whole field of the natural sciences. His main interest lay in geography and exploration, which included the Sargasso Sea. This he described as the largest and most remarkable aggregation of plants belonging all to one species on earth. The reason the weed collected there, he went on, was simply because this was the one quiet, currentless area of the Atlantic.

As the American naval officer Matthew F. Maury later explained it, if you drop splinters, soapsuds, or other flotsam into a basin of water and set the water swirling, the flotsam will immediately collect in the center. Maury, whose brilliant naval career ended when he joined the Confederates in the Civil War, wrote the first worthwhile textbook on oceanography: *The Physical Geography of the Ocean.* One of Maury's works was preparing a chart of the ocean bottom from the United States to England to prove that a transatlantic submarine cable could be laid. The problems connected with the

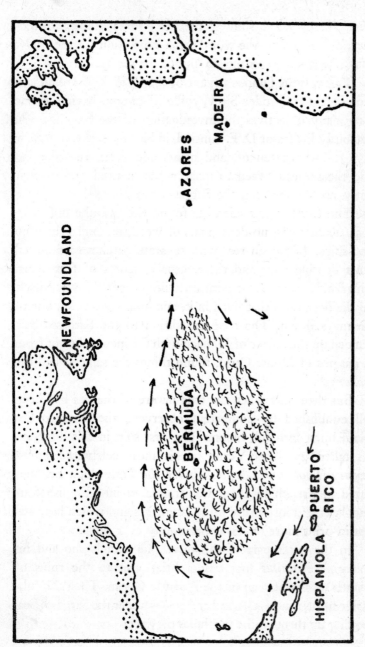

FIG. 16. Sketch map of the area of the Sargasso Sea at its maximum extent.

laying of this cable showed the need for a special oceanographic expedition—the world's first expedition for the study, not of the lands across the sea, but of the sea itself.

This was the famous voyage of the *Challenger* from England, 1872-1876, under Sir Wyville Thomson, having as one of its many objectives the investigation of the Sargasso Sea. Previously Professor D. F. Amsted, in his *Physical Geography* (1860), had written of land plants and even trees floating amid the sargasso weed to make a vast matted carpet—evidently not having seen the Sargasso Sea himself.

The *Challenger's* scientists found things quite different; no shoals or reefs; no dense mats of weed; no land plants; no dead ships. Just open sea, with separate patches of seaweed plants floating here and there, usually scores of feet apart. Remarkably clear water with little life except the weed itself and the organisms that lived in it, and an oozy bottom one to two miles down. The next expedition to the Sargasso Sea, financed by the Prince of Monaco with the income he got from the casinos of Monte Carlo, found things the same as had the *Challenger*.

But then, just when the true nature of the Sea had been well established by competent observers, the Sargasso Sea legend burst into full bloom. The first step in this direction was taken by Jules Verne in his most celebrated novel, *Twenty Thousand Leagues Under the Sea*, which first appeared in French in 1869, was translated into English four years later and into many other languages and which has been kept in print more or less continuously ever since.

In the latter part of this novel, Captain Nemo and his submarine *Nautilus* first pay a brief visit to the ruins of Atlantis on the bottom of the Atlantic Ocean. Then the submarine heads southwestward and passes under the Sargasso Sea. Looking up through the portholes they see:

Above us floated objects of divers origins, jammed in amongst these brownish weeds: tree trunks torn from the Andes or the Rockies and floated down by the Amazon or the Mississippi; and many wrecks—the remains of keels and bottoms, and battered planks so weighted down with shells and barnacles that they could no longer rise again to the surface of the ocean.*

This is practically a paraphrase of Amsted's account with derelict ships added to the tree trunks. The next blossom on this bush of legend was an article in the British magazine *Chambers's Journal* for May, 1897, which told of dense masses of weed holding "keels or skeletons of ruined ships, so covered with barnacles, shells and weeds that the original outline is entirely lost to view; and here and there a derelict ship, transformed from a floating terror of the deep into a mystery out of reach of men in a museum of unexpected enigma." †

Verne over again in slightly purpler prose. Why hadn't this strange place been properly explored? Because a sailing ship would not be able to force her way through the floating carpet, while a steamer would foul her screws and be immobilized.

These hyperbolic accounts by Verne and *Chambers's Journal* are the source of all the stories of the romantic-literary Sargasso Sea; for not only is the concept not found in earlier literature (save for Amsted's hint) but in the many stories of *voyages imaginaires* published during the preceding centuries, which included journeys inside the earth, to the moon, and to the Unknown Southland, the Sargasso Sea is never so much as mentioned. Once the fictional Sargasso Sea had been set afloat, however, writers lost no time in exploiting it. The

---

* Jules Verne, *Vingt Milles Lieues Sous les Mers,* 32d (French) ed., II, ch. xi, p. 170.
† Myron Gordon, *Sargasso Sea Merry-Go-Round,* in *The Scientific Monthly,* Dec. 1941, pp. 542-549.

very next year, in 1898, appeared one of the best of these yarns: Thomas Janvier's *In the Sargasso Sea.*

Herein, the young hero, Roger Stetworth, signs on a small ship for Africa. Learning that the ship is actually on her way to do some slave running, he quarrels with the captain and is knocked on the head and thrown over the side. Rescued by a passing liner he is still in his bunk recovering from his experience when the liner is caught in a hurricane and abandoned. The derelict, partly flooded forward, drifts into the Sargasso Sea where:

> Far away, under the red mist, across the red gleaming weed and against a sunset sky of bloody red, I seemed to see a vast ruinous congregation of wrecks so far extending that it was as though all the wrecked ships of the world were lying huddled there in a miserable desolate company.
>
> (p. 93.)

Roger explores this fantastic world, finding dead men at their posts on abandoned warships, skeletons of slaves still in their shackles, and two other fellow castaways, one dead and the other dying of wounds they dealt each other when they went mad from the monotony.

Eventually Roger finds a steam launch, aboard a larger ship, and with terrific toil he succeeds in reconditioning and launching the smaller vessel. He rigs up a saw sliding in guides at the bow, and for a frightful month saws his way through the weed-continent at three miles a day:

> I had to stand like a machine there, endlessly hauling the saw up and endlessly thrusting it down. Behind me my little engine plugged and snorted; over the bows below me, was the soft crunching sound of the weeds opening as the boat thrust her nose into it, and on each side of me was the soft hissing, rustling of the weeds against the boat's sides.
>
> (pp. 280/1.)

At last he reaches open sea, a passing ship, and safety. The novel is well written and gripping despite the fact that for most of it the only characters onstage are Roger and a ship's cat, left behind like him when his first liner was abandoned.

FIG. 17. The Sargassum Fish *Pterophryne*. Grown specimen measures from 4 to 6 inches. They are an example of perfect camouflage and also a zoological riddle since only females are known.

Although more accounts of the real Sargasso Sea, such as Bullen's *Cruise of the Cachalot*, continued to appear, the literary Sea went right on flourishing. *The Boats of the Glen Carig*, by the English writer William Hope Hodgson, takes the two lifeboats of a foundered eighteenth-century ship first to an island of man-eating trees, then through a hurricane, and then to another island on the edge of an endless floating weed-continent. The sailors, skirting along the edge of the weeds, see rotting old ships in the weed, wherein lurk enormous crabs and gigantic octopodes that reach long arms up to the decks for food. They find one ship near the edge of the weed with signs of life and try to reach it, first with a large crossbow, then by flying a kite across its deck, all the while fighting off hordes of horrible squid-men who squilch ashore to assail them. The line carried by the kite is used to pull a heavier line, and so on until they belay a hawser to the ship and pull it out of the weed. Then both sets of survivors, those of the *Glen Carig* and those of the other ship, refit the ship and return to England.

The story is in the form of a narrative by one of the survivors of the *Glen Carig*, in stiff eighteen-century prose virtually without dialogue, but nevertheless informed with a wonderful feeling of desperate suspense and brooding horror:

> Then, it would be near halfway through my time of watching, there came to me out of the immensity of weed that lay to leeward, a far distant sound that grew upon my ear, rising and rising into a fearsome screaming and shrieking, and then dying away into the distance in queer sobs, and so at last to a note below that of the wind's. At this, as might be supposed, I was somewhat shaken in myself to hear so dread a voice coming out of all that desolation . . .*

Meanwhile the records of *Pilot Charts*, following 157 derelicts over twenty-three years, proved that wrecks that drifted into the Sargasso Sea drifted out again just as easily.

Still the romantic Sea died hard. It appeared in a story by Justus Miles Forman in *Collier's* in 1911, and a dozen or

* W. H. Hodgson, *The House on the Borderland and Other Novels*, Sauk City: Arkham House, 1946, p. 67.

so years later in the novel *The Island of Lost Ships*. The latter, which was made into a silent movie in the 1920's, narrated the adventures of a young electrician's mate on the floating island, where a bully lorded it over a few dozen castaways of various nationalities and the children born to them there, until the hero repaired the radio set of a modern derelict and called seaplanes to help. (In the movie, they got away in a submarine.) The author, a careful man, indicated that there would be no more such events because a change in the currents was beginning to disperse the weed and the ships.

So much for the romantic-literary Sargasso Sea. The real Sea, however, had and still has mysteries enough.

About a hundred years ago the botanist Meyen contradicted Columbus and Humboldt about the origin of *Sargassum:* "Some navigators believe that [the weeds] are driven together by the Gulf Stream, and that the same species of sargassum plentifully occurs in the Mexican Sea; this is, however, perfectly erroneous. . . . I for my part have examined many thousands of specimens, and venture to affirm that they never have been attached to any solid body. Freely floating in the water, they have developed their young germs, and sent forth from all sides roots and leaves, both of the same nature."

To support this theory—that the weed was a pelagic perennial that lived its entire life cycle floating in the middle of the ocean—it was pointed out that specimens from the Sargasso Sea had no holdfasts, and did not even develop any when put in a tank. Furthermore, the weed was inhabited by strange animal life of its own, quite unlike that found along the shore: crabs, octopodes and squids, fishes, sea slugs, and other creatures, mostly camouflaged with ragged appendages and brown stripes to look like the weed. The sargassum fish,

Pterophryne (or *Histrio*), a ragged little creature that climbs about the weed with handlike fins, is a typical example.

In 1909, Dr. Winge of the Danish Oceanographic Expedition asserted that sargasso weed is in fact a pelagic perennial plant of unusual habits. Its method of reproduction is such that it has yet to be named. It does not generate by seeds, budding, runners, fission, or anything else. The 10,000,000 tons of sargasso weed which float in the Atlantic reproduce simply by staying alive—each plant grows at one end and decays at the other. This, however, is not yet the whole story. The latest investigations show that the weed of the Sea consists almost entirely of two species, not one: *Sargassum natans* and *S. fluitans*, which do occur along the Atlantic coast from Cape Cod to the Orinoco, along with many others of the 150-odd species of the genus. On their native soil these weeds reproduce sexually like other seaweeds. When torn away by storms, however, they tangle into large masses, sometimes big enough to foul the propeller of a motorboat.

Then as the Gulf Stream carries these weeds out into the Atlantic, their mode of life changes. They continue to grow vigorously at the ends while decaying, dying, falling off, and sinking at the "roots." The holdfasts by which they clutched the rocks are the first elements to go, which is why Winge found none on plants from the Sargasso Sea proper. Also the process results in the separation of single plants into two or more, as the branches grow while the trunk decays. Hence the largest mats of weed are found, not in the Sargasso Sea proper, but around the shores of the West Indian Islands, before they have been broken up by the natural forces of decay and wave action.

Then *is* the weed of the Sea proper the same as that which floats out from the Atlantic coast on the Gulf Stream? We don't know yet for sure. Beebe believes that, while there is some reinforcement of the weed of the Sea by the Gulf Stream, the weed once arrived in the Sea can live for many years, perhaps indefinitely. So, in a way, perhaps both Columbus and Meyen were right. Moreover Beebe suspects that a seasonal factor controls the amount of weed in the Sea, wherefore at some times of the year it is much thicker than at others. And it is possible that from time to time the vagaries of winds and currents concentrate the weed in some parts of the Sea and scatter it in others, thus accounting for the widely divergent reports on the density of the weed.

But the weed itself is just one of many biological mysteries of the Sargasso Sea. It has been mentioned that there are crabs, sea slugs and fishes which are camouflaged specifically for the sargasso weed. They don't exist anywhere else. How long does it take for organisms to evolve such specific camouflage? In other words, for how long has the Sargasso Sea been in existence? No answer, so far. Why do the tiny crablike animals, of the kind of those daphnia which form the staple diet of aquarium fish, have enormous eyes? That would make sense if they lived in deep or in muddy water. But they live at the surface, in water which is as clear as water can be. And why is there a salt-water insect scuttling from weed clump to weed clump? Water insects are no rarity, but they are all fresh-water insects. The water strider of the Sargasso Sea, *Halobates*, is the only exception to the rule, living a thousand miles from the nearest land and laying its eggs on floating bird feathers which will not sink under, as seaweed may.

Going into detail one might ask about the sex life of the fish *Pterophryne*. It does lay eggs, but so far every one of the thousands caught has been a female. Where are the males and how do they look? And how did the eels ever acquire the extraordinary habit of spawning in (or rather under) the Sargasso Sea, the mature eels then dying off while the embryos, after hatching, swim little by little as they grow to the coasts of Europe and of North America, ascending rivers to grow up in fresh water, finally returning to the deeps of the Atlantic when spawning time has come?

The Sargasso Sea failed to offer a museum of ancient ships. Nor did it provide a source of rich treasure for the man who succeeded in overcoming its alleged impenetrability. But to the biologist it offers a museum of natural curiosities and an almost unlimited field for work and study.

CHAPTER IX

Golden Men and Amazons

"AND THE SPANIARDS," AS PESCHEL SAID, "WENT AS FAR AS there was gold."

We all know how they fell upon the civilized societies of the Americas: the Aztec Empire in Mexico, the Mayan tribes of Yucatán, and the empire of the Quechua kings or Incas in Peru, Ecuador, Chile and Bolivia. We all know how they destroyed them by violence and treachery and set up Spanish vice-royalties and captaincy-generals on the ruins. When not robbing and massacring the natives they fought, betrayed and murdered one another with a cheerful cruelty, a debonair perfidy and an uninhibited villainy hard to match from the history of any age or nation, and left Latin America a tradition of naked rapacity in public affairs which has burdened and retarded these lands ever since.

One of the few satisfactions one gets in reading of the exploits of these indomitable scoundrels is that few of them lived long to enjoy their ill-gotten gains. Nearly all perished by the same violent deaths that they had inflicted upon so many others.

By 1535, having conquered Mexico and Peru and stolen all the gold and other movable wealth that those places afforded, the *conquistadores* began looking around for more victims. In Yucatán the Montejos were engaged in their long-drawn-out conquest of the Mayas, and who could tell what other gold-crusted empires still spangled the vastnesses of the new lands? After all, of the immense area of the Americas, the conquerors had so far explored only a tiny fraction, and already they had seized so much gold as to cause a serious disruption of the European economy by inflation. At that rate, when they really got to know the new lands . . .

It was a plausible guess, a reasonable surmise, but it happened to be entirely wrong. The Aztec, Mayan, and Andean (Inca) cultures were the only ones in the two continents with a standard of civilization comparable to, say, that of the Egyptians of the First Dynasty.

All the other native peoples dwelt on simpler levels, either in the Stone Age or just passing into the Age of Copper. Their largest settlements were villages, their largest political units a confederacy of tribes, their greatest wealth a meager scattering of golden ornaments. The great golden loot of Mexico and Peru was the result, not of the Indians' exploitation of excessively rich sources of gold, but of the fact that they had been accumulating the stuff little by little for many centuries, and, since they used it not as money but for personal adornment and religious objects, it lasted a long time.

In cleaning up the last organized resistance of the Incas, one of the Spanish generals, Sebastián de Belalcázar (or Benalcázar), pursued the army of the Peruvian Apu (lord) Rumiñavi north from Lima to Quito, where the Indians were finally defeated and dispersed. In Quito an Indian told Belalcázar an enticing tale. Far to the north, he said, lived a tribe so rich that they observed the following custom: When the old chief died, the tribe elected a new one and installed him with an elaborate ceremony. The whole male population paraded out to near-by Lake Guatavitá.

In front walked wailing men, nude, their bodies painted with red ochre, the sign of deep mourning among the Muysca. Groups followed, the men richly adorned with gold and emeralds, their heads adorned with feathers, and braves clothed in jaguars' skins. The greater number of them went uttering joyful shouts, others blew on horns, pipes, and conches. *Xeques*, or priests, were in the company too, in long black robes adorned with white crosses, and tall black caps. The rear of the procession was composed of the nobles of the tribe and the chief priests, bearing the newly elected chieftain, or uzaque, upon a barrow hung with discs of gold. His naked body was anointed with resinous gums, and covered all over with gold-dust. This was the gilded man, *el hombre dorado*, whose fame had reached to the seacoast. Arrived at the shore, the gilded chief and his companions stepped upon a *balsa* and proceeded upon it to the middle of the lake. There the chief plunged into the water and washed off his metallic covering, while the assembled company, with shouts and the sound of instruments, threw in the gold and the jewels they had brought with them. The offerings completed, the chief returned to the shore and to the village of Guatavitá. The festival closed with dancing and feasting.*

Obviously people who could afford to throw away their gold so nonchalantly must be fabulously rich. Belalcázar chose a band of eager gold-seekers and clanked over the Andes for nearly 500 miles (the straight-line distance, that is) to the northeast until they came out upon the plateau of Cundinamarca—to find that others had arrived before them.

The extreme northern coast of South America, now Colombia, was then, as New Granada, under a Spanish governor, Pedro Fernandez de Lugo, with headquarters at Santa

* A. F. Bandelier, *The Gilded Man (El Dorado)*, p. 14f. A *balsa* is a raft made of the amazingly light balsa-wood.

Marta. This Lugo had planned an expedition up the Magdalena River to the highlands to the south. He had set in motion a force in two parties, one by land under his lieutenant Gonzalo Jiménez de Quesada, the other in a flotilla of river boats under his own command. They started in 1536, but the boats proved unriverworthy, so Lugo returned home leaving the land force to its own devices.

This party forced its way through dense flooded forests up the Magdalena, enduring frightful hardships and saved from utter destruction only by Quesada's able leadership. One source of trouble was the fact that, though the Magdalena Valley had been inhabited by Indians who would have had food to be bought or stolen, another *conquistador*, Ambrosius Dalfinger, the German governor of Venezuela farther east, had been there seven years before, and all the Indians who had not been massacred or carried off as slaves on this occasion had fled the region.

Now how did Venezuela get a German governor? That question takes us back to Europe for a brief look at the tangled politics of that age.

In 1535 the throne of Spain was occupied by the long-bearded Charles of Habsburg, grandson of that King Ferdinand who had sent Columbus on his way. Charles was also Holy Roman Emperor, King of Castile, Aragon, Navarre, Granada, Sardinia, Sicily, Naples, and Bohemia; Archduke of Austria and Styria, Duke of Württemberg and Silesia, Margrave of Moravia, Count of Burgundy, et cetera, et cetera. We know him simply as Emperor Charles V—a well-meaning mediocrity on whom the complexities of dynastic cross-pollenation had conferred at least nominal sovereignty over the greatest domain in Europe west of Russia from the time of Charlemagne to that of Napoleon.

In trying to shore up his crazy-quilt empire against the

hostility of the French and Turks without and the Pope and Lutherans within, Charles had borrowed money from the Welsers, a banking family of the Bavarian town of Augsburg. In return, as security, he had given the Welsers a feudal fief of Venezuela. So now the colony was ruled by Germans sent out by the Welsers, though most of the non-Indian population was still Spanish.

But to return to Quesada and his expedition: When the party seemed hopelessly lost, a scouting force brought word of a plateau where they had seen sedentary Indians cultivating fields. And thus at the beginning of 1537 Quesada's force—the surviving one-fifth of the original eight hundred—reached the plateau of Cundinamarca.

The plateau was inhabited by the Muysca Indians, a tribe of the Chibcha group who called their domain Bacatá or Bogotá and their chief village Muequeta. Quesada beat them in a series of brisk battles, took their capital, and near-by founded the city of Santa Fé de Bogotá, the capital of modern Colombia. From this headquarters Quesada gradually subdued the country round, extracting from it nearly a quarter-million pesos' worth of gold; a mere fraction of the loot of Peru, but still respectable plunder.

Then came Belalcázar from the south, and hardly had he arrived when a third party appeared: a force captained by one of the Welsers' Germans, Nikolaus Federmann from Venezuela. Dalfinger had died a violent death several years previously and his successor, Georg von Speyer, had set out to explore the southern plains of Venezuela. Federmann was supposed to have joined him with reinforcements, but with the faithlessness of the true *conquistador* he headed west on the track of the late Dalfinger. Thus he too came to Cundinamarca with a little over a hundred out of his original 400. They presented a startling contrast: Belalcázar's men from Peru, who had had a comparatively easy time, in scarlet and gleaming steel; Quesada's from Colombia in native fabrics which they had stolen from the Indians to replace their own tatters; Federmann's from Venezuela, fresh out of the jungle, in the skins of wild animals.

The three parties, all of about the same size, stood off from one another, fingering swords and muskets. The priests with them, however, persuaded the three captains to go back to Spain to ask the king-emperor to settle their arguments, while Quesada's even more rapacious brother Hernán (or Fernán) Perez de Quesada remained as commander of the whole united force.

Of the three who went back—Belalcázar, Quesada, and Federmann—the first was the only one to receive any reward at the time, and he got merely the governorship of Popayán on the western slopes of the Andes about halfway from Quito to Bogotá. Federmann, whose desertion of von Speyer had gotten him in bad with the Welsers, got nothing. Quesada, after a ten-year sojourn in Europe, returned to Bogotá with a couple of honorary titles and became an influential elder citizen of the colony. In 1569, aged about sixty-nine, he set out with 500 men to hunt *el hombre dorado*. After two years of wandering the Orinoco region he returned with twenty-five survivors and spent his remaining decade writing.

What had become of the gilded man of the Cundinamarca area? When the men of the three parties began to fraternize, those of the parties of Quesada and Federmann soon heard the tale from Belalcázar's men and scoured the country looking for the source of the story. They soon found Lake Guatavitá, a circular mere about a mile in diameter on a mountaintop amidst towering peaks a few miles north of Bogotá. But no gilded man.

The fact was that some years before, the zipa of Bogotá had extended his sway over the Chibchas of Guatavitá, with the result that the ceremony had gone out of use.

But this explanation was much too simple and disappointing for the gold-mad Spaniards. The idea that they had just cleaned up the last respectable loot in the whole vast continent would have been more than flesh and blood could bear. Instead of being dropped from consideration and filed away with other historical curiosities, the gilded man was moved from the Cundinamarca plateau two or three hundred miles eastward to the forests of Meta, through which the River Meta flows east on its way to join the Orinoco. Moreover his wealth was increased until instead of being powdered with gold on the day of his accession he was powdered every day; instead of being the only person so treated it was said that he and all his officers and sub-chiefs were likewise gilded. Finally the term *el dorado* was expanded from meaning a gilded man to a gilded country: El Dorado, where gold was as common as dirt, just waiting for gallant Spaniards to come and take it.

In the early 1530's Diego de Ordaz, a former companion-in-arms of Cortés, in exploring the Orinoco, heard of a large lake in the Meta country, near which lived a dense population of Indians with much gold. (After a little experience with Europeans the Indians had learned that the quickest way to get rid of their unwelcome visitors was to tell them that some other tribe over the horizon had lots of gold.) Thus little Lake Guatavitá began to evolve into that phantom inland sea of northern South America which survived the Dorado legend by a couple of centuries.

Ordaz himself never got to that country, becoming involved in quarrels with his fellow *conquistadores* about the boundaries of their respective bailiwicks, but later explorers—Herrera, D'Ortal, and von Speyer—did, the last reaching the borders of Ecuador and determining that there were no lake and no civilized Indians in Meta.

But still the legend would not down. In 1539 Francisco Pizarro's half brother Gonzalo Pizarro set out from Quito with over 200 Spaniards, 4000 Indians, and a large herd of animals to find El Dorado and, if possible, a land of cinnamon as well. His party almost froze to death in the passes of the Andes, suffered from terrible storms and earthquakes, and finally struggled through to the headwaters of the Curaray River in northern Ecuador. The Curaray flows into the Napo, which flows into the Marañon, which in turn becomes the Amazon when it gets into Brazil.

Pizarro's men found a tree with cinnamon bark and hopefully named the place *Canela* ("cinnamon") but the material occurred in negligible quantities and the party ran short of food. They built a small ship, using the shoes of their dead horses for nails, their ragged shirts for caulking, and so on. Pizarro put his lieutenant Francisco de Orellana aboard the ship with fifty-three men and instructions to accompany him down the river, keeping a sharp watch for anything edible.

But the stream swept the unwieldy craft along at six knots, much faster than Pizarro could struggle along on shore. Orellana halted and waited but Pizarro did not come up, and being in a parlous condition with regard to food himself Orellana finally abandoned his commander and sailed downstream all the way to the Atlantic Ocean, where he arrived in 1541.

Now, Orellana had with him a Dominican friar named Carvajal who chronicled the journey. In the course of his narrative Carvajal set afloat another legend, that of the American Amazons. He said that below the mouth of the Río

Negro they had one of their many fights with Indians whose food they stole, and that this time Indian women took part in the fight. This is plausible by itself. He also repeated a probably false story that he was told, to the effect that these women were not members of the tribe that the Spaniards fought, but were sent from another rich and powerful tribe consisting entirely of warrior women who consorted from time to time with the men of other tribes to reproduce their kind, just as did the original Amazons of Greek legend. Columbus had heard a similar story in the Antilles, and Nuño de Guzman had gone ravaging through northwestern Mexico looking for the Amazons.

The original Greek Amazons first appear in Homer's *Iliad*, where in Book VI the Trojan Glaukos tells the Achaean Diomedes how his ancestor Bellerophon defeated the Amazons when the latter invaded Lycia in southwestern Asia Minor. The Amazons supposedly lived in their capital of Themiskyra on the river Thermodon in Asia Minor and raided all the neighboring countries. They showed up in numerous myths, as in the one where Theseus kidnaped Antiopë, the sister of the Amazon queen Hippolytë, and carried her off to Athens. The Amazons invaded Attica in retaliation but were defeated in a battle wherein Antiopë fell fighting at the side of Theseus.

The name "Amazon" is Greek for "no-breast" and was supposed to refer to a custom of cauterizing or otherwise destroying the right breast so that it should not interfere with the drawing of a bow. Another tribe of Amazons in North Africa was described by Dionysios Skytobrachion and is preserved in Diodoros of Sicily. Dionysios carefully distinguished these from the Asiatic Amazons and told how under their Queen Myrina they had conquered the neighboring Atlantioi and the latter's enemies the Gorgons. If the Asiatic Amazons have any historical basis, it is probably the armed priestesses of the Hittite mother-goddess, who lived in large temple communities all over Asia Minor in the days before Greek history began.

At any rate, when Orellana got to the court of the king-emperor and told his tale, the people of the court ridiculed his Amazons, though credulous enough in other respects. Nevertheless the fighting Indian women gave the name of "Amazon" to the river, much as the imaginary eastern island of California on medieval maps, inhabited by warrior women in golden armor, became the land now known by that name.

As for Pizarro, he gave up and struggled back to Quito with his remnant afoot (for they had eaten their horses) practically naked and carrying rusty swords whose leather scabbards they had also eaten. Soon thereafter both Pizarro brothers met violent ends.

At the same time another expedition was setting out in the opposite direction. When von Speyer died, leaving the fief of Venezuela without a director, the Bishop of San Domingo as interim administrator appointed one of Speyer's knights, the young Philipp von Hutten of Württemberg, to head the next search for El Dorado. In 1541 von Hutten left Coro on the coast of Venezuela with a hundred-odd horsemen, and the young Bartholomäus Welser, of the Augsberg Welsers, as one of his officers. Like several of his predecessors he followed the golden mirage east and south until he reached the chief town of the powerful Omagua tribe near the Japura River, which flows eastward through southeastern Colombia on its way to join the Amazon. Hutten led a charge into the midst of the town, but the Indians, not at all terrified, swarmed out, and von Hutten and his men had to cut their way to safety through an army of 15,000 Indians.

On returning to Venezuela von Hutten was astonished to learn that a Spaniard, Juan de Carvajal, had been appointed governor of Venezuela, for the Spaniards were getting ready to terminate the Welsers' fief, as they soon did. This Carvajal instituted a reign of terror in Coro and then, fearing lest von Hutten might interfere, tried to arrest the latter on his return to the settled part of the colony. An impending battle between the adherents of Carvajal and von Hutten was averted by an agreement to live and let live. Hutten resumed his march towards Coro—but then Carvajal, coming up behind him, pounced on his camp at night, seized and disarmed the whole party, and had the heads of von Hutten and Welser hacked off with a rusty machete. Shortly thereafter a magistrate with a few soldiers arrested Carvajal, whose head in due course rolled in the dirt too.

The next Dorado-hunter was a young man in his early twenties, Pedro de Ursua, who had made a reputation in the highlands of Colombia by his campaign against the warlike Muso Indians. He tried to end this campaign by inviting the Muso chiefs to his camp for a parley and then having them all murdered, but instead of being pacified the Musos fought more fiercely than ever.

About this time the royal officers in Bolivia, Peru, and Ecuador were perplexed to know what to do with the horde of turbulent adventurers who, with the subjugation and extermination of most of the Indian tribes and the drying up of the stream of loot, were left without an occupation save that of hell-raising and preying on the other colonists. Somebody had the bright idea of collecting them all in one grand final search for El Dorado, rumors of which, stimulated by exaggerated accounts of the Omagua capital invaded by von Hutten, were flying thicker than ever. And

Ursua, a feckless and frivolous youth, impressed them as the ideal leader for such a razzia. If anybody could be counted upon to lose the whole gang of rascals he could.

A flotilla of boats was accordingly built on the Rio Llamas, which flows down the eastern slope of the highest Peruvian Andes into the Huallaga, which flows into the Marañon-Amazon.

Trouble, as was to be expected, started almost immediately. Some of the men murdered Ursua's lieutenant Ramiro. Ursua lured the murderers out of their hiding places by a promise of immunity and had them hanged. As the flotilla floated farther and farther downriver, finding no gold but plenty of alligators and mosquitoes and occasional naked Indians making a precarious living with their blowguns, the men became more and more dissatisfied with never-ending promises. A sinister Basque named Lope de Aguirre formed a plot to kill Ursua and his lieutenant. This they did and made another young knight, Fernando de Guzman, their commander.

Guzman, however, really wished to pursue El Dorado, while the sceptical Aguirre meant to embark upon a piratical career, seize a suitable part of the continent, and build up an independent nation. So Aguirre and his adherents shot Guzman and Aguirre proclaimed himself "General of the Marañon."

For some time thereafter the movements of the gang are obscure. They may have followed Orellana's route to the mouth of the Amazon, or they may have gone up the Negro from its junction with the Amazon to the world's oddest river, the Cassiquiare. Now it is well known that no river in the world divides, one branch going into one watershed and one into another—with the one single exception of the Upper Orinoco. The Orinoco does so divide, in the southern panhandle of Venezuela. The right-hand fork turns north to become the great main Orinoco and so flows into the ocean; the left fork, the Cassiquiare, flows across country into the Amazon watershed where it joins the Guaiania, which flows into the Negro, a major tributary of the Amazon.

But not even that exhausts the peculiarities of these rivers. The Negro is so called from the blackness of its water, which in a water glass looks something like weak tea. Between the Guaiania and its junction with the Amazon the Negro is joined by the Branco or "White" River, and the "White" and "Black" waters flow along side by side for a considerable distance without mixing. Perhaps here the Negro should be called the Rayado—The Striped River!

Anyway in 1561 Aguirre and his cutthroats swooped upon the island of Margarita, off the coast of Venezuela halfway between Trinidad and Caracas. He ruled in sanguinary style for two months, causing the governor and his officers to be slain; then he invaded the Venezuelan mainland. But his daily murders had caused even his own men to become disaffected. They stole away at every chance, and when a smaller Royalist force appeared the remainder deserted Aguirre, whose bloody career was ended by a volley of musketry.

By now eastern Colombia, southern Venezuela, and the adjacent parts of Brazil had been crossed and recrossed without sign of El Dorado. The myth was therefore moved still further east, to the Rio Branco Valley in the northern panhandle of Brazil and the adjoining parts of southwestern Guiana, where the Essequibo and its many tributaries rise to flow north to the ocean.

In 1584 Antonio de Berrio (or Berreo) set out from Bogotá to westward to find El Dorado. The first time he turned back, but the second time he won through to the

Orinoco watershed and sailed down that imposing stream to the sea. In the course of this journey he heard more tales of the gilded: that the fabulous wealth in question was to be found in the city of Manoa, located on the great lake or inland sea called Lake Manoa or Parimá. He sent his campmaster, Domingo de Vera, back to Spain to raise a full-scale expedition for Manoa. Vera sailed from Spain in 1595 with a fleet of ships and more than 2000 people, many times the force Columbus had had. They landed at Trinidad, went on to Santo Tomé, and plunged into the brush in all directions. In a few months they were nearly all dead from disease, snakebite, starvation, Indians, and other normal hazards of the Venezuelan jungle.

By a curious coincidence, in the same months that Vera put to sea from San Lucar, Sir Walter Raleigh sailed from Plymouth on a freebooting expedition of his own. He in his turn landed on Trinidad long enough to burn and loot the town of San José and to seize Antonio de Berrio, who was at that time governor of Trinidad and who filled his captor's ears with rumors of Manoa and its lake. Raleigh started up the delta of the Orinoco with a fleet of small boats, though he would have done better to take a full-sized ship, as the bayous of the delta soon gave way to the wide deep river itself. He had not gone far, however, before news of an approaching Spanish force sent him back to his ships and home to England, where he wrote *The Discovery of the Large, Rich, and Beautiful Empire of Guiana, with a Relation of the Golden City of Manoa, which the Spaniards call El Dorado, etc.* In this book he told how at Manoa:

> . . . when the Emperor carowseth with his captayns, tributaries and gouernours—all those that pledge him are stripped naked, and have their bodies anoynted al ouer, with a kind of white balsamum; that then they are anointed all over, cer-

taine seruants of the Emperor hauing prepared gold made into a fine powder blew it thorow hollow canes upon their naked bodies untill they be al shining from the foote to the head and that in this sort they sit drinking by twenties and hundreds and continue in drunkenes sometimes six and seven daies together . . .*

Raleigh was also told of the headless Ewaipanomas who "are reported to have their eyes in their shoulders and their mouths in the middle of their breasts. . . ." These are of course our old friends the African Blemmyes of Pliny and Mela. Who first put them in the New World we do not know, but apparently somebody who noticed that the Amazons had preceded Columbus across the Atlantic thought it only reasonable that other Old-World figments should have done likewise. And a map published by Theodore de Bry in 1599 shows the backlands of Guiana occupied by the great inland sea of Parimá, on whose north shore stands the golden city of Manoa, and south of which roam the headless men.

There were a few other hunts for El Dorado, all with the same story of extravagant hopes, frightful hardships, and scanty survivors. Raleigh made another descent on South America, in 1617, having been let out of jail by his enemy King James I on the strength of some wild promises of finding gold without trespassing upon Spanish soil. He found no gold and did trespass, and after a brush with James's Spanish friends that cost the life of one of his sons he crowned the many follies of a long and active life by returning into the clutches of James who promptly had his head cut off.

Thereafter the false glitter of El Dorado slowly dwindled until few took it seriously. Lake Parimá, however, had now become a fixture on the maps of northern South

* Quoted in J. A. Mansó's *The Quest of El Dorado*, in *The Bulletin of the Pan American Union*, XXXIV, No. 5 (May 1912) p. 615.

America and remained so for two whole centuries. The reason that this misapprehension was not cleared up sooner lies in the nature of the country. The supposed lake lay somewhere along the divide between the Amazon and Orinoco watersheds. In fact the Orinoco and other rivers were supposed to issue from it.

Now, in the first place, the whole Amazon-Orinoco region is one of the hardest on earth to travel about. It is the largest continuous tropical rain forest on earth, much bigger than that of the Congo despite the fact that away from the rivers it is interrupted by sizable streaks and patches of open savannah and prairies. The area is one of the world's rainiest, and when the skies are not raining they are often overcast, so that one gets only an occasional chance to navigate by sun or stars. As the equator runs right through the middle of the area, the climate is one of constant steaming heat.

Land mammals are rather small and sparse, nor are they especially dangerous. The only formidable carnivore, the jaguar, though the third largest of the cat family, seldom attacks men unprovoked. Vampire bats are annoying but no great menace. The most conspicuous elements in the fauna are birds and mostly arboreal mammals: a screeching, chattering, scrambling horde of parrots, toucans, monkeys, squirrels, ant eaters, sloths, pangolins, coatis, kinkajous, ocelots, porcupines, and so on. The reptiles include several poisonous snakes. The southern relative of the alligator, the cayman, though numerous, is seldom large enough to be dangerous. More to be feared in the rivers are the electric eels and the small big-toothed fish, the piranhas, which can reduce a wounded man or animal who falls among them to a skeleton in a matter of minutes. The real dangers of Amazonia are not those of vertebrate animal life so much as those of insects and bacteria. The region swarms with billions of buzzing, biting, burrowing, and stinging pests.

One can die in many ways in that region: succumb to exhaustion in trying to hack one's way through the suffocatingly thick and entirely inedible vegetation, or get stuck in one of the bottomless swamps, or get lost, or be stranded or drowned by the rising of one of the rivers, or run out of food and starve, clash with the natives or come down with one of the innumerable diseases of one of the world's unhealthiest areas—for those not immune to its peculiar maladies.

As for lost Lake Parimá, not only was it where nobody would go strolling for fun, but it was placed along the divide between the Amazon and the Orinoco watersheds where all streams were too small to be navigable. For the country along the navigable streams was opened up early; for centuries small ships have plied the sluggish Orinoco and Amazon and their main tributaries, all now dotted with towns and villages. But when one nears the margins of the watershed, where streams are small and swift with many rapids, one comes into little-known or unknown country.

Thus Lake Parimá (or Manoa or Guaiana or Rupununi) though shorn of golden cities and headless savages, lingered on the maps until in 1800-02 Baron von Humboldt plowed through 1700 miles of jungle to prove that it did not exist; that there were in fact no large lakes in that region at all—though the rivers' nasty habit of flooding hundreds of square miles might give that impression to the casual visitor. The names Rupununi and Parimá are now firmly attached to rivers of that region. And while he was about it, Humboldt investigated the unique Cassiquiare River and proved that it does, alone of all the streams of the earth, flow across the divide between two major watersheds—though the country is so flat that to locate such a divide would tax the abilities of the ablest surveyor.

As for the original Lake Guatavitá, the source of all these rumors, the Spaniards made several attempts to drain it but were unsuccessful until an Englishman undertook the task in the twentieth century. Several golden objects were found in the mud of the bottom, of archeological interest but no fabulous value.

Old legends die hard anywhere and South America is no exception. To this very day stories of lost cities, lost races, rich mines, white Indians, Pygmies, warrior women and dinosaurs left over from the Mesozoic Era buzz about the ears of the traveler as thickly as do the insect pests of that arthropodally rich continent. Small wonder that novelists have taken advantage of that opportunity and sometimes it is hard to tell whether a story cropping up somewhere is based on a "straight rumor" (if there is such a thing) or on a confused recollection of a fiction story which gained verisimilitude by being tied up with such rumors.

But during the last sixty years there has been a kind of geographical separation. The rumors usually center on the Matto Grosso, while the fiction stories center upon Mount Roraima which, strange to say, acquired political fame first.

From the place where the boundaries of British Guiana, Venezuela and Brazil come together, the Brazilo-Venezuelan boundary curves 300 miles to westward before turning south to inclose the Venezuelan panhandle of Amazonas Territory. This 300-mile stretch follows the Sierra Pacaraima, a low range rising into a number of flat-topped mesas isolated from the surrounding land by cliffs of extraordinary steepness. At the junction of British Guiana, Venezuela, and Brazil stands Mount Roraima, rising perpendicularly 4000 feet from the plain to a height above sea level of 8600 feet. In plan the table-land is about nine by three miles in dimensions and the area is about twelve square miles. The top is rather bare and rocky, and one of the mountain's odder features is the singular Töwashing Pinnacle that stands at the south end of the four-mile southeast wall. Near-by stands the similar but smaller Mount Kukenam.

Then, 150 miles west of Roraima, in Venezuela, stands another mountain of the same kind but much larger: Auyantepui, also about 8000 feet high but with an area of 300 square miles. And 300 miles southwest of Auyantepui the Guiana Highlands end in Mount Duida, of a size and shape comparable to Auyantepui. Duida is crowned by a thick forest, whereas Auyantepui is bare and rocky like Roraima. Moreover, because of its size, Mount Duida supports a considerable river system which has cut the top into so many deep clefts and ravines as to make exploration extremely difficult.

Both Duida and Roraima have long been known. Roraima was discovered over a century ago by Sir Robert H. Schomburgk, a German-British traveler one of whose exploits was to survey the disputed boundary between British Guiana and Venezuela.

Britain had obtained British Guiana from the Netherlands in the settlements following the Napoleonic wars, and along with it they also acquired a standing dispute with newly independent Venezuela over the boundary. As nobody lived along the boundary except Indians, and as nobody else had ever been there save occasional adventurers and prospectors, some uncertainty about the line was inevitable.

In 1840, then, Schomburgk surveyed a line, ending it squarely on Mount Roraima, though he did not ascend the mountain himself. The Venezuelans refused to accept the line and for sixty years continued, when not internally occupied with revolutions and civil wars, to denounce and threaten Great Britain and to appeal to the United States in the name of the Monroe Doctrine to take their side. In 1895 this appeal led to strained relations between the United States and Great Britain, but in 1899 an international arbitration commission decreed a modified version of the Schomburgk line as the final boundary, and that verdict stands to this day.

In the meantime Roraima's cliffs had been scaled in 1884. Another Anglo-German, Sir Everard F. im Thurn, and a companion named Perkins wormed their way up one of the clefts in the face to the top, and later an explorer named John Quelch, though sick at the time, dragged himself to the top and camped there for nine days. More recently several scientific expeditions have climbed Mount Roraima, Mount Duida and Auyantepui to study their life forms. They are hardly impressive—mice, squirrels and the like—but of scientific interest because they are closely related to those of the Venezuelan Andes hundreds of miles to the west and not to those of the plains and forests around the mountains.

Mount Roraima's entry into literature coincides with the time when the political boundary dispute was at white heat, 1897. This was when President Cleveland had just sent Congress a message saying that if Great Britain seized the disputed territory without an attempt at arbitration the United States would regard the act as one of war against itself. The British Crown Agents in the meantime prepared a set of postage stamps for British Guiana showing Mount Roraima. In Venezuela feelings ran somewhat higher than in Washington and London, the Venezuelans claimed the land clear to the Essequibo River, putting the mountain well inside their republic.

In that year the British writer Frank Aubrey published a novel entitled *The Devil-Tree of El Dorado*. The book, admittedly a fiction story, carried a preface *Shall Roraima Be Given Up to Venezuela?* Aubrey did his best to arouse British opinion in support of a strong stand on this question on the grounds that all sorts of fascinating creatures might be found on the unscaled top of the mountain. Apparently he was unaware of the fact that Roraima had been climbed at least twice even then.

After this political introduction the author got down to his story which identified Manoa, El Dorado and Mount Roraima as one and the same and which strikes a modern reader as being "strictly pulp." Two young Englishmen, Templemore and Elwood, set out to explore Roraima. In the jungle a jaguar jumps on Elwood, but a mysterious stranger pulls the cat off, kills it with a knife, and nurses Elwood back to health. The stranger is Monella, a bearded giant with a mysterious past and a saintly manner, of whom they have already heard.

Monella guides the party to a cave in the side of Roraima which communicates by a tunnel with the plateau above, where they find a lake on which stands a city whose roofs and towers gleam with gold. Monella tells them that this is Manoa, a city of pre-Egyptian origin. They approach the city in time to see a gilded noble make a murderous attack upon a beautiful girl. Elwood shoots the attacker and learns that he has saved the daughter of King Dranoa from the son of the wicked high priest Coryon.

Thanks to their science the Manoans live for many centuries. They have two religions, that of a White Brotherhood and that of a Black Brotherhood headed by Coryon and centering around a man-eating tree, like a vegetable octopus, to which victims are sacrificed. Traditions tell of the time when Roraima and the neighboring mountains were merely islands in Lake Parimá. After fights, plots, imprisonments, escapes, and battles (carried on to the accompaniment of egregiously corny dialogue) Monella turns out to be an exiled Manoan king; Coryon is eaten by his own tree; Elwood is united to the princess; and Templemore leaves the mountain for civilization just as an earthquake blocks the tunnel.

Much better known is the second Roraima novel, Sir Arthur Conan Doyle's *The Lost World* (1912). The narrator in this story is a young journalist, Malone, who is sent to interview the eccentric Professor George Edward Challenger to find out about the latter's claims of having discovered a plateau in South America harboring animals supposed to have been long extinct.

The interview, like everything connected with Professor Challenger, is stormy and ends with Malone's being thrown bodily out of the professor's house. But then Challenger, having proved to himself that he could get rid of an "obnoxious journalist," invites Malone back in, and some weeks later the journalist finds himself a member of a party on its way to the South American mesa. The other members of the party are Challenger himself, his main critic, the acidulous Professor Summerlee, Lord John Roxton, a sportsman, and assorted Brazilians to tote the gear.

Doyle is careful to leave the location of the mountain vague though it is plain enough that he has Mount Roraima in mind. The party ascends a northern tributary of the Amazon and when the mesa is finally reached it has a semidetached pinnacle just like Roraima. The party climbs the pinnacle and gains the inaccessible plateau by felling a tree on the pinnacle so that it bridges the gap. On the plateau they find assorted dinosaurs, even ichthyosaurs and plesiosaurs swimming in a lake—no such landscape ever existed, not even in the geological past. The life forms, evidently assembled for dramatic effect only, originally existed in at least three continents and four geological periods. There are even two types of humanoids present, modern South American Indians and "ape men" of a type *Pithecanthropus* was thought to be in the books Doyle probably read for the purpose. (We now know that *Pithecanthropus* was much more "human" than originally thought but a life form which probably fits the description existed in South Africa.)

The party of explorers then takes part in a campaign in which the ape men are nearly exterminated, finds a means of escape from the plateau and returns to London with a crated live pterosaur to prove the story. *The Lost World* is one of Sir Arthur Conan Doyle's best stories, action is fast, humor sparkles throughout and Professor Challenger has become one of the immortal characters of science fiction. Just because this story is so good, any other lost-world story sounds like an imitation. And as for Mount Roraima itself it had to be left alone by other writers for the same reason.

For several reasons, South American rumors don't die easily. One is the memory of the old civilizations—there might really be some old centers which have not yet been rediscovered. Another is the simple fact that there is a rather large patch of "unexplored" land left and it is by its very location more promising than unexplored territory of similar size in Antarctica.

Still another one is the custom of certain tribes of Amazonia of cutting symbols on boulders. They are highly stylized pictures of fish, lizards, insects, men, maps of sections of the nearest river and similar subjects. Nikolaus Hortsmann, a German surgeon, was probably the first to mention them, he noticed them on rocks along the Rupununi River in 1739. Later, in 1852, the great English botanist Richard Spruce found great numbers of them on the Rio Uaupés (or Río Vaupés, one of the sources of the Río Negro), copied them and started the branch of anthropology concerned with the study of this culture trait of the Amazonian tribes. Theodore Roosevelt found more of these petroglyphs on the Río Duvida in 1913 (mostly interlocking circles and inverted W's) and ethnologists have watched modern Indians carving them.

To the mind of the credophile, however, the idea that savages might have cut these signs for religious or tribal reasons would be much too simple. They look to him like "hieroglyphics," and to them he attributes an Egyptian, Phoenician, Sumerian, Etruscan, Cretan, Hindu, or other exotic origin. Thus for several decades a French prospector, Apollinaire Frot, between spells of wandering the Brazilian wilderness, filled the ears of all who would listen with his stories of cities buried in the jungle and mysterious inscriptions in Old-World tongues. He wrote Braghine the Atlantist: "The results of my investigations are so striking that I am afraid to publish them." Alas! Frot died during World War II, taking his secrets, if any, to the grave. And several South American savants like Onffroy de Thoron the philologist and Bertoni the ethnologist have gone off on similar tangents.

Before getting excited over such remarkable identifications of these inscriptions, it would be well to remember that if anybody devises a set of symbols consisting of simple linear figures he is practically certain to hit upon something that resembles a symbol from another set, like one of the civilized alphabets. For example the syllable *su* in the Japanese *kata-kana* syllabary looks like a kind of Z and the Chinese character for *djung* ("middle") looks like a Greek *phi*, although there is no historical connection between these sets of symbols.

But now for that last "unexplored" piece of South America, the Matto Grosso. The words mean "great forest" and the Brazilian state that bears this name has about twice the size of Texas, over half a million square miles. The southern half of the state is fairly well known; it is cattle country where the Borero Indians wear shirts and sometimes read newspapers. It consists mainly of the *pantanal* or flood plain of the River Paraguay and its tributaries: a grassy savannah broken by circular patches of dense forest called *caapões*. When the rivers rise they flood the flat portions of the plain for thousands of square miles but leave the slightly higher caapões unflooded which is why trees can grow on the latter but not on the plain. The region has a numerous fauna of modest size: jaguars as big as small lions, tapirs, deer, peccaries, giant otters, wild dogs, armadillos and so on, all now dwindling because of cattle grazing and hunters.

The state capital, Cuyabá, though the most isolated of Brazil's state capitals, is a fairly modern town with respectable schools and newspapers and possesses the odd distinction of being the world's ipecac capital. A few miles to the north of Cuyabá there are the low Parecis Mountains, the divide between the Paraguay and the Amazon watersheds. North of the mountains rise the main southern tributaries of the Amazon, looking on the map like branches dividing into twigs dangling down from the main river. The whole area is nearly uninhabited except for Indians: Anauquas, Apinages, Aravotos, Bakiris, Calapalos, Camayuras, Carajos, Chavantes, Gayapos, Jurunas, Nambicuaras, Suyás, and others you probably never heard of: thinly scattered tribes of a few hundred persons each. Most of them go completely naked and trim their hair to a soup-bowl cut with sharpened mussel shells. The women raise a few simple crops while the men hunt with blowguns.

In disposition they range from the amiable Carajos and Camayuras to the fierce Chavantes who kill all strangers on general principles and preserve their heads, though without shrinking them as do the Jivaros of Ecuador. When the Brazilian government, in setting up a chain of airfields across the region a few years ago, sent the aviator Antonio Brasilio to fly over the Chavante villages and drop gifts in an endeavor to make friends, the Chavantes sent up an antiaircraft barrage of arrows, one of which went through Captain Brasilio's wing-tip. Then they burned the gifts.

In general the Indians' good will varies inversely with the amount of contact they have had with *caraibas* (non-Indians). The ferocious Chavantes are said to have got that way as a result of being enslaved by early Spanish gold seekers to work in their mines.

Such is the remaining land of lost cities. It is not strictly correct to speak of it as "unexplored" because it has been traversed many times and in recent years flown over in all directions. The courses of the main rivers are now pretty well known, though those for some of the smaller streams are still doubtful, and between the rivers there are still many spots and slots of territory that have yet to feel the explorer's foot.

In 1743 a party of six Portuguese, a dozen Negro slaves, and a train of Indians set out from Minas Geraes into the interior to look for some fabulous mines, knowledge of whose location had perished with their mestizo owner in 1622. These people sent out a report by an Indian runner to the viceroy at Bahia, telling how on the central plateau they had sighted the ruins of an immense city made of great stone blocks, and had also caught glimpses of a couple of white Indians. The report even included copies of the hieroglyphs they said that they had found engraved on the stone of the city.

After this report nothing more was heard of this party. The report lay unheeded until unearthed about a century ago, when the Brazilian government sent an unsuccessful expedition to follow in the footsteps of their predecessors.

Then in the early 1900's the Krupps of Essen, convinced that this or another lost city existed in the western part of the Matto Grosso, organized a large expedition with pack animals, guides, and Indians. They spent $500,000 of their armaments profits on this project, but the Indians vanished at their approach and showered them with poisoned arrows, and eventually they were defeated by logistics. That is, since neither explorers nor pack animals can live on the country, they must carry nearly all their food and can go no farther than this fuel will take them, though in sore straits an expedition can stretch its tether a little by eating its pack animals as the latter's loads are consumed.

Then in 1913 that most versatile of American presidents, Theodore Roosevelt, went down the Río Duvida or River of Doubt (then represented on maps by a dotted line) to determine its true course. He took with him one of the outstanding characters of modern Brazil, Colonel (now General) Candido Mariano da Silva Rondon, explorer and Indian administrator. They struggled through 900 miles of wilderness, enduring the usual calamities of disease, boatwreck, and starvation until they issued into the Madeira River. One man perished in the rapids; another was murdered when he caught a third stealing food, and the murderer escaped into the bush. In recognition the Brazilian government renamed the River of Doubt the Río Roosevelt.

Then in 1925 came the Fawcett expedition, which became even better known than that of Roosevelt and Rondon and which might be taken as the culmination of all tales of lost cities and unknown lands in South America.

Lieutenant Colonel Percy Harrison Fawcett, D. S. O., F. R. G. S., was a British artillery officer, then nearing sixty. In his youth he had served in Ceylon, Malta, and Hong Kong, as well as at home, and gone exploring in Morocco. In 1906 his government had lent him to Bolivia to act as boundary commissioner to help fix the line between Bolivia and Peru. In the course of this work he nearly starved to death on the Río Verde, and later on the Heath River he braved an hour-long bombardment with six-foot arrows from the warlike Guarayos until by shouting words from a phrase book he convinced them that his intentions were friendly.

When he had completed his surveying assignment he retired from the army with the rank of major and gave himself up to Brazilian exploration until World War I, when he was called back and brilliantly commanded a brigade of heavy artillery. After this war he went back into retirement and exploration.

To judge from what has been written about him, Fawcett was a man of great physical energy and endurance, infinite courage, and intense drive: hasty, ardent, impatient, and inclined to be brusque and overbearing with "natives." The easygoing Brazilians found his enthusiastic strenuousness a little horrifying. A man of great versatility, he was also a competent artist and yacht designer.

Moreover he possessed a strong mystical or credophilic tendency: a seer of visions and a dreamer of dreams. He dabbled in Spiritualism and lent if anything too ready an ear to those tales of treasure and prodigy that are South America's chief invisible export. In his youth, as a gunner lieutenant in Ceylon, his interest had been aroused by mysterious inscriptions that he saw on a rock while rambling around the jungle with a native guide looking for the alleged buried treasure of the Kandyan kings. He became a devotee of the cult of the lost Atlantis and later, responding to South America's ever-buzzing *khurafas*, became convinced that the lost city of the 1743 expedition, either Atlantis or one of its offshoots or colonies, lay in the northeastern Matto Grosso, somewhere between the upper Xingú and Araguaya River regions. On the maps of the time this area was shown as occupied by the Sierra do Roncador or Snoring Mountains.

Fawcett also credited other tales. Thus in 1910, in an address before the Royal Geographical Society of London, he told of a rumored race of white-skinned, red-haired, blue-eyed Indians called Morcegos or "bats" from their nocturnal habits. He said:

> There may be curious things hidden in the forests of the Amazon basin. There are rumors of old ruins and strange animals—of tracks huge and unrecognized. Fables gather, of course, around unexplored places, but we must not forget that the African pigmy and the okapi were long discredited.*

Writing in 1916 he told how on one of his trips he almost reached the country of a race of cannibals covered with black hair all over, who lived in trees like monkeys and dispatched all visitors with clubs. "Beyond these ape-like people are, according to my informants, 'houses of stone'! . . . Can it be the lost 'City'?" † In speaking of the anaconda, the big sluggish South American relative of the python, he credited it with a "weird cry," which would

* P. H. Fawcett, *Explorations in Bolivia*, in *The Geographical Journal*, XXXV, No. 5 (May 1910) p. 522.
† P. H. Fawcett, *Penetrating the South American Jungle*, in *Travel*, XXVII, No. 3 (July 1916) p. 62.

raise one of a herpetologist's eyebrows, and claimed to have killed one sixty-five feet long, which would certainly hoist the other.

Such was the fascinating Colonel Fawcett. In 1919 he went back to South America and set out from Cuyabá to find his Atlantean city, his arboreal anthropophagi, his white Indians, his pygmies, and his leftover dinosaurs. He was defeated by floods and the defection of his Brazilian *camaradas*, a class whom many explorers have denounced for cowardice, meaning that they display an invincible aversion to risking their lives for the whimseys of crazy foreigners.

Then in 1924 he set out again from England, this time with the backing of the Royal Geographical Society, to map the unknown land in the neighborhood of the Paramántinga (or Paranátinga) and Tapajos Rivers, and to seek the other and more fascinating things that he believed the Matto Grosso to contain. Some Brazilians suspected that he was also looking for the alleged lost Gold Mine of the Martyrs, unworked for two centuries since its Portuguese discoverers were killed by their Indian slaves. With Fawcett went one of his sons, Jack, and a friend of the latter, a young photographer named Raleigh Rimell. Fawcett believed in small parties traveling light and fast.

They journeyed northeastward from Cuyabá into the watershed of the upper Xingú. Fawcett was purposely vague about his destination, for, as he wrote his friend Ahrens in Cuyabá a couple of months before he started,

> I am not giving you any closer information as to locality because I don't want to encourage any tragedy for an expedition inspired to follow our footsteps under the impression that it is an easy matter. . . . It must be understood that it is, on the face of it, a highly dangerous undertaking.*

* G. M. Dyott, *Man Hunting in the Jungle*, p. 88.

He got to the military outpost of Bakiri, or Posto Simões Lopes (where Rimell was suffering from an infected foot) and from there headed into the wilds. From Dead Horse Camp, forty miles northeast of Bakiri, he sent back his mules and his *camaradas*, both of which had proved useless for his purpose. With the Brazilian helpers he sent another letter to Ahrens, stating: "Do not count on any more dispatches. It may be possible, but the recent trouble with the Indians makes it precarious. . . . It is risky, of course, and we may get killed."

Then he went on with three Bakiri Indians. On the Kuluseu River he found a pair of bark canoes whose owners had hidden them in a creek while calling on friends in the jungle. Fawcett coolly appropriated these canoes and continued on down the river in them until he reached the Anauqua village. Here he sent the three Bakiris back upriver with the canoes. On the way these Indians met the owners, some Anauquas, highly indignant about Fawcett's making free with their property.

Then Fawcett headed eastward towards the Kuluene River (another tributary of the Xingú) and vanished.

When no word came from the intrepid visionary for months, his friends and backers began inquiring after him. In 1927 an engineer, De Courtville, said that he had met a mysterious bearded white man in the jungle whom he identified with Fawcett. Spiritualist mediums gave out spirit interviews in which they said that Fawcett was kept captive by Indians who had made a god of him, and other colorful stories. Finally a rescue party was organized in 1928 by a British naval officer, Commander George Miller Dyott, who also had explored in South America.

Dyott, with four young Americans, followed Fawcett's trail to the Anauqua village, overland eastward towards the

Kuluene, and down that river. The Indians agreed that Fawcett and his companions had been murdered but disagreed as to the culprits: the Calapalos blamed the Anauquas and the Anauquas blamed the Suyás. An Aurá Indian accused Aloique, the Anauqua chief—or at least so it seemed through the linguistic barrier, as Dyott had but a few words in common with the Indians and had to depend largely on sign language. Dyott also saw, in Aloique's hut, a suitcase which he took to be Fawcett's, and saw tied around the neck of one of Aloique's children a brass plate bearing the name of the firm of W. S. Silver & Co. of London, which had furnished Fawcett with his equipment.

Dyott concluded that Aloique was the murderer, though his suspicion seems to have been largely motivated by a violent dislike that he took to the chief, and which in turn seems, as far as one can judge from his narrative, to be based upon nothing more than Aloique's wary and reticent manner. Later Aloique agreed for a large bribe to show Dyott the place where Fawcett had been buried, but changed his mind and faded away into the jungle, and Dyott's food supply did not permit him to try to hunt down the spot by himself.

Dyott and his party went on down the Kuluene in boats. The word that there were caraibas who gave presents for the asking had got around among the tribes, and when the explorers camped on a sandbar the entire Camayura (Dyott spells it Kamaiula) nation and some other Indians descended upon them in canoes, all shouting the Indian equivalent of "gimme!" When Dyott's knives and beads gave out the brown-skinned horde became threatening. To avert a repetition of Fawcett's disaster Dyott made a speech promising a general distribution of gifts next morning, after which his party would depart upriver. Then when all the

Indians were asleep that night, Dyott and his party quietly loaded their boats and took off downstream, leaving the Indians when they awoke to paddle furiously in the wrong direction after their deceivers.

That should have settled the question, but still rumors buzzed out of the Brazilian bush. Missionaries and travelers reported hearing that the Fawcetts had settled down among this or that tribe and that Fawcett or his son had begotten children of Indian women—infants who, in cheerful defiance of the laws of heredity, were always described as blond and blue-eyed. One is tempted to think that for a time there was a fad among the upper Xingú Indians to pass off any albino or half-breed children among them as Fawcett's offspring. And Mrs. Fawcett averred that her husband must be alive because she kept getting telepathic messages from him through mediums.

Rumors and search parties continued during the next decade. Nobody found Fawcett, though Koch-Gruenberg's party saw a grave which they were told was Fawcett's. A man who identified himself as Stephan Rattin, a Swiss trapper, showed up at the British consulate in São Paolo with a curiously inconsistent story of meeting a skin-clad white captive in an Indian village, who said that he was a British colonel (without giving his name) and entrusted Rattin with an appeal for help. All Rattin wanted was a little money to outfit a rescue expedition; if that was not forthcoming he would undertake the project himself. He departed on his search and was seen no more, though whether he too perished in the jungle or whether the whole episode was a mere money-getting act we do not know.

Furthermore an Indian inspector picked up a theodolite compass in good condition and gave it to a missionary who forwarded it to Mrs. Fawcett, and some inferred that Fawcett had sent this compass out from his place of durance as a means of communicating with the outside world. In 1933 the well-known expedition of Fleming and Churchward produced a couple of travel books but no Fawcett, having failed to reach his last camp and having foundered on the common rocks of quarrels and food shortage. One of the books was Peter Fleming's best-selling *Brazilian Adventure*, wherein the expedition is described in a tenor of inflexible jocosity.

If these abortive expeditions accomplished nothing else, they at least did demonstrate that the Snoring Mountains do not exist.

Finally, in 1951, the answer wafted out of the Matto Grosso. A bearded Brazilian Indian agent, Orlando Vilas Boas, after patiently questioning the Calapalos on and off for five years, persuaded them, on a promise of no revenge, to tell the whole story. Fawcett had failed to give them all the presents he had promised and had struck an Indian named Cavicuiri. Therefore the Calapalos had massacred the three whites with clubs between the Kuluene and the Río das Mortes (River of Deaths) a tributary of the Araguaya farther east. Cavicuiri had ambushed Fawcett while others dispatched the young Britons, who had lagged behind the rest. The young men's bodies they had thrown into a lake, but Fawcett, whom they regarded as chief, they had formally buried with the machete with which he had tried to defend himself. Komatzi, the new Calapalo chief, led Vilas Boas to the grave and had his men dig up the bones and machete.*

* According to newspaper reports from England, the identification of the skull as Fawcett's has been doubted; the dental work on the teeth of the skull allegedly fails to match the dental records for Fawcett. If true, the Fawcett mystery is still unsolved, but so far no real evidence has been presented for that contention.

Perhaps Fawcett had run into a situation like that which Dyott had experienced with the Camayuras and, lacking Dyott's tact, had tried to bull his way through. Still, no matter how exasperating the Indians prove themselves, to hit one is a mad thing to do, for while they can be friendly enough if carefully handled they will go to great lengths to avenge any injury or insult. This is not mere vindictiveness, either, but a consequence of the fact that on such a primitive social level there is no law-enforcement machinery, so that fear of retaliation is the only real deterrent to evildoers. General Rondon, now retired, guessed that perhaps an additional source of friction was Fawcett's insistence that the Calapalos should guide him into the country of the dreaded Chavantes to the east.

So ended the last great hunt for El Dorado-Atlantis-Manoa. With the rapid opening up of the Matto Grosso by air and the increasing attention which the Brazilian government appears to be giving its Indian wards, the remaining unknown patches will not be unexplored long. There is no compelling reason why such ruins should not exist, though by now the Matto Grosso has been flown over often enough so that if such cities existed they would probably have been seen.

CHAPTER X

The Shape of the Earth

WHETHER YOU WENT TO SCHOOL IN EUROPE OR IN THE UNITED States you probably had a history book with a picture in it showing Christopher Columbus at the court of Ferdinand and Isabella. In this picture—any of several that have been painted by different artists—a clean-shaven ascetic-looking Columbus usually stands erect in the middle, orating, while to one side a cluster of bearded wise men whisper behind their hands and sneer. You almost certainly have a vague recollection that Columbus was supposed to be arguing that the earth was round, whereas King Ferdinand's philosophers averred that the earth was flat.

And if Queen Isabella is in the picture too, she is probably fingering her jewels which, the popular story goes, she later pawned to make the voyage possible.

The main trouble with these ideas is that they are totally wrong. As for Isabella's jewels she never pawned them but is merely said to have offered to do so if necessary. And what Columbus and the doctors were disputing hotly and at great length was not the *shape* of the earth. They were all agreed from the outset that the earth was a sphere. The discussion concerned its *size*—and, as events proved, the king's philosophers were right and Columbus wrong. Their ideas of the size of the earth were much nearer the truth than Columbus's belief which took it to be much smaller than it is.

Not that it is important, but for the sake of a clean sweep, we are not even sure about the external appearance of Columbus at those meetings. We can guess reasonably well what he wore because of our general knowledge of fashions of that time at the Spanish court. But fashion did not decree the style (or absence) of beard generally and whether Columbus was clean shaven or wore a beard on those occasions is simply not reported.

Well then, if not Columbus, who did first proclaim, in the teeth of a conservative opposition, that the world was round?

Nearly all primitives and barbarians, unless they have been told otherwise by civilized men, believe that the earth is the shape it looks: a flat disk under a hemispherical blue dome. Plainsmen who lived in sight of a range of lofty mountains naturally supposed that the sky bowl rested upon those peaks. As the sky looks the same distance off in all directions, most people also assumed that they lived at the center of the world disk or that the center was some real or imaginary object not far away. In Greece the center of the world was thought to be either Mount Olympus or else the sacred rock, the "navel stone" at Delphi.

The topography of the landscape did influence speculations about the shape of the earth even after urban civilizations arose and ideas became more sophisticated. Thus the Babylonians believed in the customary floating round disk. The Egyptians favored a rectangular earth like a long and narrow room with Egypt in the middle of the floor, taking up most of it and separated by a meager border of seas and deserts from the four walls. The drawn-out length of the Nile Valley obviously influenced their concepts.

The thinkers of India worked up perhaps the gaudiest world scheme. The center of their earth was the legendary Mount Meru, 80,000 miles high with the gods on top and surrounded by the Central Enchanted Ocean of equal depth. Around Mount Meru were disposed seven concentric circles of ocean and seven of golden mountains, decreasing in depth and height, respectively, as one went outward from the center. In the outermost ring-ocean lay the four main inhabited continents: Virat-deha with its calm virtuous inhabitants to the east; Jambudvipa with "us" (that is, the Hindu and Buddhist philosophers) to the south; Godhana with its round-faced beefeaters to the west; and huge Uttara Kuru to the north. The whole is inclosed in a hollow iron sphere, and there is an infinite number of such sphere-universes.

At least the sages of India never did anything on a petty scale. Reading their speculations about thousands of universes, continents with dimensions of tens of thousands of miles, and cycles of millions of years, one wonders if, having invented the symbol for zero, they became intoxicated with their discovery and started throwing many-zeroed numbers about in sheer exuberance.

Greek thought about the shape of the earth began in Ionia, now the west coast of Turkey. The earliest of the Greek philosophers who expressed an opinion on the subject was great Thales of Miletos, incidentally also the first man to predict an eclipse correctly. Thales, however, merely took over the Babylonian idea of the floating disk, apparently the prevailing idea at the time he flourished which was during the first half of the sixth century B.C., that is, from 600 to 550 B.C.

After him came three other Ionians who would be easier to keep distinct if they had not been named Anaximandros, Anaximenes and Anaxagoras, respectively. They form a chain, their lives overlapping with that of Thales and each other. Anaxagoras, the last of them, went to Athens where he became a friend of Perikles, knew Socrates, and died at a high age in about 430 B.C.

Anaximandros of Miletos devised an earth closer to the facts than the floating disk: a drum-shaped object, one-third as thick as it was broad in diameter, poised in space with us living on one of its flat surfaces. Moreover he taught that there were many such worlds, some always coming into existence while others disappeared. Anaximandros went on to propose organic evolution and to undertake the first world map. There had been maps before him, in Babylonia and elsewhere and the cartographic art is even known to some primitives. But this was the first map of the whole known world. For data Anaximandros quizzed sailors who put in to Miletos.

It was probably Anaximandros's map of which the regent Aristagoras had a bronze copy made when he went to European Greece in 499 B.C. to ask help against the Persians. He stirred the cupidity of the Spartans with his map and his account of the riches of Asia Minor and finally King Kleomenes asked how far it was from the Ionian coast to the Persian capital.

"Oh," replied Aristagoras, "a journey of maybe three moons."

"What, you are proposing to lead the Lacedaemonians on a three months' journey from the sea?" cried the king, who had never contemplated such a distance and felt acutely uncomfortable with the thought of that much land between him and the shore. "Get out of Sparta!"

Aristagoras and his map had better luck in Athens, for the Athenians sent a force to help the Ionian cities in their revolt against Persian rule. The revolt was not successful. Miletos was destroyed in 494, and the Persian kings used the intervention of the European Greeks as a pretext for invading Greece. Such is the influence one unworldly scholar can have.

The second Anax, Anaximenes (also of Miletos before its destruction) devised another earth: a flat rectangle, like a blanket, held up by compressed air. There were other theories, too, such as that of Archelaos of Athens that the world had the form of a saucer. Leukippos, who taught the great atomist Demokritos, accepted the cylindrical earth of Anaximandros. By the latter part of the fifth century B.C., when Anaxagoras was at Athens, the spherical earth was fast coming into acceptance among educated men.

But who suggested it?

It was not Aristotle, as one can often read; the idea was older, since it appears quite clearly, as we'll see, in the writings of Aristotle's teacher Plato. As for a still higher age we have the word of the doxographer Diogenes Laërtius (of the third centry A.D.) that Alexander Polyhistor in the first century B.C. said that " he found in the Pythagorean memoirs the following tenets," namely that there are four elements "fire, water, earth and air; these elements interchange and turn into one another completely, and combine to produce a universe animate, intelligent, spherical, with the earth at its center, the earth itself too being spherical and inhabited round about. There are also antipodes, and our 'down' is their 'up'." *

* Diogenes Laërtius, *Lives of Eminent Philosophers*, VIII, i.

This would seem a plain enough statement—except that Diogenes is giving a third-hand account of a man who lived 800 years before his time: Pythagoras of Samos, mathematician, philosopher, and eccentric genius-at-large, who after a lifetime of travel, study, and adventure settled in southern Italy to found a cult with curious customs like a tabu against eating beans. And as Diogenes drew largely from one Aëtios who wrote about 100 A.D., drawing heavily in his turn upon the writings of Cicero's erudite but careless and credulous friend Poseidonios, we have to take the statements of Diogenes with caution. For instance the theory of the four elements is usually credited, not to Pythagoras, but to the later Empedokles.

Moreover Poseidonios was a leader of the Stoics, who had the reprehensible habit of "accommodation." That is, to lend authority to their teachings they ascribed their own opinions to earlier philosophers, just as contemporary politicians cite George Washington on subjects that Washington never heard of.

When we turn to original philosophical works the situation is not much better because the earliest such works that have come down in their original form are Plato's dialogues and Aristotle's voluminous lecture notes. The earlier works by Anaxagoras and others survive only fragmentarily in quotations and citations by Plato, Aristotle, and later writers.

Plato alluded to the earth's shape twice. In *Phaidon* his "Socrates" says that he saw a man reading a book by Anaxagoras, and "I imagined that he would tell me first whether the earth is flat or round," but when he tried to read the book he found it so confused that he could make neither head nor tail of it. Later in the same dialogue Socrates says that "my conviction is that the earth is a round body in the center of the heavens, and therefore has no need of air or any similar force as a support . . ." (Plato, *Phaedo*, 97, 108.)

Of course Plato's "Socrates" is to a large extent a ventriloquist's dummy, and the dialogues are fictions intended to express Plato's ideas. Nevertheless it seems safe to infer, first, that the roundness of the earth was a live controversy in the time of Socrates, and that Anaxagoras, though he had clearer ideas about the sun and moon than his predecessors, had no clear notion of the shape of the earth.

Then in *Timaios*, the character after whom the dialogue is named mentions "Earth, our nurse, which is globed around the pole that stretches through all . . ." (Plato, *Timaeus*, 40.)

By the time Plato's pupil Aristotle (around the middle of the fourth century B.C.) got his sharp dialectical teeth into the subject he could not only affirm that the earth *was* round, but also give reasons—some good and some bad—and estimate its size. It must be round, he said, because that is the shape a body naturally assumes when all parts of it tend in towards the center; because of the curvature of the earth's shadow on the moon during lunar eclipses; and because of the change in the altitude of stars as one goes north or south. He added that "mathematicians who try to calculate the size of the earth's circumference arrive at the figure 400,000 stadia." * That is, about 46,000 miles—nearly twice the actual circumference but not bad for a first approximation. Unfortunately Aristotle neglected to mention the names of these "mathematicians" nor did he give a résumé of the arguments for and against a round earth. He merely stated that the floating island earth of Thales had to be rejected for the obvious reason that earth doesn't float.

* Aristotle, *On the Heavens*, II, 14. There were several stadia; Aristotle probably meant the Attic one of about 607 feet.

So all we can say is that the spherical earth was fully accepted among literate people during the time designated by the three names Socrates—Plato—Aristotle. And except for a later theological recession the spherical earth stayed accepted from then on. The arguments at the time of the so-called age of discovery—this cannot be repeated too often—did not deal with the shape, but with the size.

As far as the Greeks were concerned this was also the next step. Having convinced themselves about the shape, they undertook to measure it. A method for measuring the earth was perfectly clear to the Greeks of Aristotle's time. If you know how far place A is north of place B in miles you only have to measure the altitude of the north celestial pole (or the altitude of the sun) from both places at the same time on the same day. You take the difference in altitude in degrees—or let's say you find the difference to be 3 degrees. That is the 120th part of 360 degrees, the full circle. Now if point A were 180 miles north of point B the full circle would measure 120 times 180 miles which makes 21,600 miles and that would be the circumference of the earth.

Although the classical scientists did not have optical instruments for their measurements they probably had more trouble with distances on the ground than with angles in the sky. They had only such unreliable data as the statements of sea captains and of caravan leaders; presumably Aristotle's mathematicians had used some such method.

The first calculation of the earth's size about which we have reliable information is somewhat more recent than Aristotle. It is that of Eratosthenes of Kyrenë, who became librarian of the Library of Alexandria when that great institution was flourishing under the early Ptolemies. In browsing through the 700,000 manuscripts of the library he came across a report that 5,000 stadia up the Nile at Syenë (modern Aswan) there was a well whose peculiarity was that at noon on the day of the summer solstice the sun shone directly down into it, so that when one looked over the edge one could see the sun's reflection shining in the water below.

Evidently at Syenë the sun was directly overhead at noon on that day. Next time Midsummer's Day rolled around, Eratosthenes measured the shadow of a vertical pole and found that the sun was $7.2°$ from the zenith. As this is one-fiftieth of a circle, the earth's circumference had to be fifty times the distance from Alexandria to Syenë, or 250,-000 stadia.

So says the main source, the first-century astronomer Kleomedes, but without indicating which stadion Eratosthenes used. With the Attic stadion the circumference is 28,800 modern English statute miles; with others, anywhere from 23,400 to 35,000. Others (Pliny, Strabo, Vitruvius, Heron) say that Eratosthenes gave the circumference as 252,000 stadia without explaining the discrepancy. In one place Pliny says that Eratosthenes's 252,000 stadia equal 31,500 Roman (29,000 English) miles. Elsewhere it is indicated that Eratosthenes used a stadion of 516.73 feet which gives a circumference of 24,850 miles—a phenomenally close result. If this is what he computed, his accuracy was the result of the happy accident of his errors' canceling out.*

At any rate this was the best estimate for many centuries. Eratosthenes's successor and critic Hipparchos increased the circumference to 278,000 stadia. Then came Poseidonios who taught Cicero at Rhodes. There the star

---

* The true circumference is about 24,900 miles. It is not known whether Eratosthenes took into account or even knew the fact that Aswan is not due south of Alexandria but about 200 miles east of it.

Canopus barely clears the southern horizon, whereas at Alexandria, about 345 miles south, it comes well up into the sky. Poseidonios measured its maximum altitude at Alexandria and got 7.5 degrees. Actually that star rises to only 5.25 degrees for the latitude of Alexandria, but because of refraction near the horizon it looks higher than it is. As 7.5 degrees is 1/48th of a circle, Poseidonios asserted that the circumference of the earth was 48 times the north-south distance from Rhodes to Alexandria. The original of his work has not survived and the writers who cite Poseidonios vary in their interpretations: Kleomedes saying 240,000 stadia; Strabo, 180,000. The latter figure proved more influential if less correct, being adopted by the great Claudius Ptolemy. But with either the Attic or the Egyptian stadion it gives much too small an earth.

A little over 900 years later Harun al-Rashid's two eldest sons had the usual civil war to determine who should succeed their late father as Caliph. After the second son, Abdallah al-Ma'mun, had graciously received his brother's head from his victorious general he settled down as Caliph to become a notable patron of the arts and sciences. Among his projects was to try once more to settle the question of the earth's size by sending a crew of surveyors jouncing across the desert on camels to shoot the sun simultaneously from Palmyra in Syria and Sinjar in Mosul. Their result was 76.4 miles per degree, compared with the 57.5 of Poseidonios and the actual 69.1. This result was published by al-Farghani ("Alfraganus") and was transmitted to the non-Arabic speaking world by Roger Bacon.

And now we get to Columbus.

Columbus based his argument on two factors. One was the size of the earth as a whole. The other was the size of the European-Asiatic land mass. Greek geographers, with

Anaximenes in the lead, had held that the "land" (Asia with its European peninsula) was generally rectangular in shape, being wider in east-westerly direction than from north to south. It is also for this reason that Hipparchos, when he invented the longitude-latitude frame of reference for es-

Figura prodigiof. Draconis alati . ex Musco Cardinalis Barberini . apud Terrentium Lynceum .

FIG. 18. One of the dragons supposed to live in caves beneath our feet. Picture from *Mundus subterraneus* by Athanasius Kircher. The original belonged to the collection of *curiosa naturae* of Cardinal Barberini. Unfortunately it has not been preserved.

tablishing the position of a place, called the east-west measurements "longitude" (length) and the north-south measurements "latitude" (breadth).*

If you have a sphere with a large and roughly rectangular land mass on it, it is obvious that the ocean between the east and west coast of that continent will be the narrower,

* These words, of course, are those we use and which are of Latin derivation. Hipparchos used the Greek equivalents.

the smaller the sphere. Or, if the size of the sphere is given, the larger the land mass. Columbus, being at the western end of that land mass, in Spain, and desiring to make the distance to the eastern end look as short as possible, used both approaches.

For the sphere he adopted the figure of 76.4 Arabian miles per degree of al-Farghani. The Arabian mile is 1.346 ours, but Columbus asserted that the short Roman or Italian mile was meant and figured a circumference of 18,800 miles (our type) which is less than three-quarters the real size.

Of the various estimates of the size of the land mass Columbus adopted the largest. Or rather he took assorted figures from the works of Ptolemy and others and juggled them to get a whopping big one of his own: a length of 14,700 miles from the coast of Portugal to that of China— nearly twice the fact. As he once wrote on the margin of a book: "The world is but small; the dry part of it is six parts, the seventh only is covered by water. Experience has shown it, and I have discussed it in other letters, with quotations from the Holy Scripture, with the situation of the Terrestrial paradise, which the Holy Church has approved." *
With this statement Columbus repeated one of the arguments advanced in favor of *Terra australis* although he himself does not seem to have been interested in that problem.

Columbus, at the court of Ferdinand and Isabella, argued for an ocean 18,800 minus 14,700 miles wide, 4000 miles in round figures. He reached land after some 3000 miles of travel which confirmed him in his opinions about the size of the earth and the size of the main land mass, as well as of having reached the other end of that land mass. He became a fanatic who would listen to no arguments that

* Quoted in *The Geographical Conceptions of Columbus* by G. E. Nunn, p. 10f.

it might be unsuspected land. He was certain that it was Asia. It was Asia! *It was Asia!* IT WAS ASIA!!! On his second voyage when he had almost circumnavigated Cuba he made all his crew sign a deposition that it *was* Asia—Vote *Ja,* or else!

Which, of course, did not make it Asia and shows at the same time that Columbus felt some faint doubts himself. Geographers argued the matter for a few decades until the return of the surviving one of Magellan's ships in 1522 proved Eratosthenes right and Columbus wrong. So Ferdinand's philosophers—or their ghosts—had the last laugh after all.

Of course there are always a few people who simply refuse to accept a fact they happen not to like and are willing to substitute the most tortuous fantasies for a simple reality. The reality that the earth is a sphere is not an exception.

As has been mentioned in passing, the flat earth came back to respectability for some time with the Christianization of the Roman Empire. But most of the time the argument was rather negative; "those who, having once erred and consistently persevere in their folly" think that the earth is spherical. This contradicts both Scripture and common sense. Most of the time, however, it was only said what one should not believe, not what one should. In that respect Kosmas, the sixth-century monk who had voyaged to India, was more explicit than most of the others. Kosmas undertook not only to refute the pagan notion that the earth was round, he also asserted that the Tabernacle built by Moses was an exact model of it. The resulting fig-

ure was much like the shoebox universe of the Egyptians
of Pharaonic days over a thousand years before:

> We have said that the figure of the earth is lengthwise
> from east to west, and breadthwise from north to south, and
> that it is divided into two parts: this part which we, the men
> of the present day, inhabit, and which is all round encircled
> by the intermedial sea, called the ocean by the Pagans, and
> that part which encircles the ocean, and has its extremities
> bound together with those of heaven, and which men at one
> time inhabited to eastward, before the flood in the days of
> Noah occurred, and in which also Paradise is situated.
>
> Kosmas, *The Christian Topography of
> Cosmas*, ii (p. 33, Hakluyt Soc. Ed.).

This box was divided horizontally into two stories by
the firmament, the upper being full of "the waters that are
above the firmament. The sun and moon revolved around a
great mountain in the north, it was the shadow of that
mountain which we called night." Had Kosmas heard about
Mount Meru when he was in India as a young man?

Similar barn universes of two or three stories were
preached by Severian of Gabala and by Diodorus of Tarsus,
but the influence of these Easterners was limited and did not
penetrate to the West which in that age had forgotten how
to read Greek. In the West the most erudite upheld the
spherical earth while the common people accepted the visi-
ble flatness, provided that they thought about it at all.

Just one amusing idea may be mentioned here. Some
thinkers of the early Middle Ages seem to have been convinced by the arguments in favor of the spherical earth but
felt unable to accept the idea of the antipodes. Possibly
influenced by the round land mass of the earliest Greek
thinkers they succeeded in combining the round oikou-
menë, the sperical earth, and the nonexistence of antipodes

all into one. They postulated that the world consisted of two spheres, one of land and one of water. If the two were perfectly concentric all land would be covered by water, drowned in a shoreless ocean. But if the two spheres were not quite concentric a circular island would appear above the water: the known inhabited world. The question of the antipodes then ceased to exist, for on the other side of the earth the ocean would be deepest.

Centuries later Nicholas Copernicus demolished this fancy by pointing out that Egypt, near the center of the supposed world island (Jerusalem) was washed by the Red and the Mediterranean Seas, whereas it should be high and dry, thousands of miles from salt water.

While the thinkers of the time prior to the great voyages of discovery still had some reason on their side—usually adherence to Scripture, or their interpretation of it—all the later revivals of the flat earth have been strictly screwball antics. The most recent and certainly the most notorious of them was that of Wilbur Glen Voliva, ruler of the Christian Catholic Apostolic Church of Zion, Illinois, from 1906 to his death in 1942.

The founder of this cult was a noisy little Scot named John Alexander Dowie who left his Congregationalist ministry in Australia to found a faith-healing society. In 1888 he set out for England to organize a branch, but in passing through the United States he sensed greener pastures and presently set up his church in Chicago. Persecution caused him to move to Zion, thirty-five miles north, where he reigned for nearly two decades by virtue of hortatory gifts, commercial shrewdness, and adamantine opposition to all vices, in which he included tobacco, oysters, medicine, and life insurance.

Dowie's downfall began when he proclaimed himself

Elijah III (that is, the second reincarnation of Elijah, the first having been John the Baptist) and tried to take New York City by storm. He descended upon the sinful metropolis with eight trainloads of followers and rented Madison Square Garden for a week. The New Yorkers came to see the wonder man, but found somebody who looked like Santa Claus mouthing a tedious spate of vituperation in a rich Edinburgh brogue. They got bored and trooped out in droves, leaving the prophet screaming threats and insults.

To seal his doom Dowie had been selling "stock" (actually promissory notes bearing 10% interest) to pay interest on stock already sold. Inevitably the laws of arithmetic caught up with him. While Dowie was away in Mexico buying an estate to which he intended to retire, Wilbur Voliva, using the power of attorney with which Dowie had imprudently trusted him, led a revolt of the cult's officials and at one stroke stripped Dowie of power and pelf. Elijah III died soon after.

The bushy-browed and austerely handsome Voliva had started as an Indiana farm boy, gone into the ministry of the Christian Church, and deserted that for Dowieism. Under his rule Zion's formidable blue laws were screwed even tighter, so that anybody caught smoking or chewing gum on the muddy streets was liable to be thrown in the hoosegow. After his coup he reorganized the bankrupt community so successfully that by 1930 he was making $6,000,000 a year from Zion's industries, which included not only Dowie's original lace factory, but also a paint factory, a candy-bar factory, and other establishments. But the depression of the 1930's broke his control of these industries, and a lot of Methodists and other heathen moved into Zion and in 1935 swept his partisans out of the municipal offices. After Voliva's death the cult continued on more conventional lines, and now sinners can buy cigarettes in Zion without fear of the Bastille.

Voliva's cosmogony comprised a disk earth with the north pole at the center and a wall of ice around the edge. Those who traveled around the earth (as Voliva himself did several times) were merely following a circular path around the center of the disk. When asked what lay beyond the ring-wall of ice that corresponded to the Antarctica of the wicked, he retorted that: "it is not necessary that we know," and when taxed with the fact that on his map the Antarctic circle (and with it the coastline of Antarctica) would be 43,000 miles long whereas those who did circumnavigate Antarctica found much smaller figures, he simply changed the subject.

Virtually all of the "earth changers" of the last two centuries differed from Voliva in two respects. They were far less successful in business and also far more inventive than just to advocate the return to the flat earth of pre-Platonic philosophy.

Early in the nineteenth century a synthesis of contemporary (more or less) speculations and recent fantasies erupted into one of the strangest "scientific theses" in the history of science. The eruption began with five hundred printed letters sent out to all the members of Congress, the presidents of all the American universities and learned societies, and some outstanding European scientists. They read:

> St. Louis, Missouri Territory
> North America
> April 10, A.D. 1818

To All the World:
    I declare the earth is hollow and habitable within; containing a number of solid, concentrick spheres; one within the

other, and that it is open at the poles twelve or sixteen degrees. I pledge my life in support of this truth, and am ready to explore the hollow, if the World will support and aid me in the undertaking.

Jno. Cleves Symmes,
Of Ohio, late Captain of Infantry.

There was a separately printed postscript reading:

N. B. I have ready for the press a treatise on the principles of matter, wherein I show proof of the above positions, account for various phenomena, and disclose Dr. Darwin's "Golden Secret."
My terms are the patronage of This and the New Worlds.
I dedicate to my wife and her ten children.
I select Dr. S. L. Mitchell, Sir H. Davy, and Baron Alexander von Humboldt as my protectors.
I ask one hundred brave companions, well equipped, to start from Siberia, in the fall season, with reindeer and sleighs, on the ice of the frozen sea; I engage we find a warm and rich land, stocked with thrifty vegetables and animals, if not men, on reaching one degree northward of latitude 82; we will return in the succeeding spring.

J. C. S.

Also attached was a certificate of sanity! Despite this the modern reader has the feeling that the choice lies somewhere between paranoia and schizophrenia. Typically Symmes, who could talk for hours about his new world, never succeeded in arranging his argument in coherent form and producing a book in favor of his thesis.

But first this strange phenomenon has to be identified as a man. He claimed to have been (and probably was) a descendant of one of the early Puritan settlers. He was born in 1780 in New Jersey, joined the army in 1802 as ensign, distinguished himself in the War of 1812 for bravery, in 1816 was discharged with the rank of captain. So much for his career.

The idea of "concentric spheres" must have been on

his mind for some time when he wrote the circular letter. Once he vaguely stated that it came to him while he was looking at Jupiter through a telescope. Like fifty-seven other people he thought that he had found the explanation of gravity by assuming a fine "elastic fluid" pushing in concentric spheres, thus forcing everything into such shape.

Consequently he declared it to be a natural law that everything was hollow, as witness the bones of animals and birds, the hairs on our heads, the stalks of wheat and other grasses . . . hence the planets must be hollow too. In the case of the earth there were five such hollow spheres one inside the other, all habitable inside and out and all equipped with large polar openings so that the inhabitants of each sphere could travel to every point on the inside as well as the outside, like an ant walking up the outside of a goldfish bowl, over the rim, and down the inside. He spent hours talking about the exotic races and fearsome monsters that he believed to inhabit various parts of these shells.

About the outer shell on which we live, Symmes guessed it to be between 1000 and 1500 miles thick. At both poles were circular openings which he called "verges," each surrounded by an icy hoop. Once you got past that hoop the climate became warm so that it would be simple to sail over the verge from "complete convexity outside to complete concavity inside."

The diameters of the verges were about 2000 miles for the northern one and 3000 for the southern. Although the verges were truly circular they were not concentric with the poles; their planes, which were parallel to each other, formed an angle of 12° with the axis of the outer shell. The northern verge was "highest" (in latitude) over Europe, and the Svalbard Archipelago, whose largest island is Spitsbergen, was right on the edge of the verge. This had to be so because some Norse fishermen lived in Spitsbergen. In northeastern Siberia (then almost unexplored) the northern verge came farthest south, so that the best way to enter it would be to sail north through Bering Strait and then proceed northwest.

All this was explained carefully in the lectures that occupied most of the rest of Symmes's life, in slow and tedious speech with an occasional fumbling for the right word. Symmes planned his lecture tours like political campaigns, with publicity releases to the newspapers ahead of time and press conferences afterwards. He hardly required proof of his assertions; he *knew* that they were true, and his personal honor as an officer and a gentleman should have sufficed anybody else. It was all in accordance with natural law, he asserted: did not unconfined smoke assume the shape of concentric spheres? (It doesn't, but then he never made an experiment to see.)

The American public, loath to doubt the word of a minor national hero, did not know quite what to say. The French Academy, less impressed by Symmes's patriotic trappings, ridiculed him. But the Russians, eager to explore their enormous Siberian territory, showed genuine interest. They actually offered Symmes a post on an expedition to northeastern Siberia. But, ironically, before the expedition was organized, Symmes succumbed to the less arduous rigors of the Canadian winter climate during a lecture tour in 1829, died, and received military burial.

He left behind several barrels full of newspaper clippings and notes, and, probably, the little wooden model of the Symmes globe now in the Academy of Natural Sciences at Philadelphia. His son, Americus Vespucius Symmes, believed in the theory and tried without notable success to assemble the notes into coherent form. He added the surmise that, when the verge was passed, the Lost Ten Tribes of Israel would probably be found dwelling on the inside of the outermost sphere.

Several others believed in the theory also; one P. Clark defended it in an article in the *Atlantic Monthly* for April, 1873, and in 1868 a professor W. F. Lyons published a book of his own, called *A Hollow Globe*. In that book he reiterated the Symmes theory—minus the smaller concentric spheres inside—without mentioning Symmes's name at all.

Since Symmes never wrote a book on his thesis himself we can't know which sources he used. That he had read widely, especially works on natural history and exploration, is clear from quotations from his lectures which appeared in newspapers. And actually his hollow earth fantasies were merely the climax of a long tradition.

This tradition had started so early in antiquity that its origin cannot even be traced any more. But the oldest pieces of literature still extant all hint at the tradition of a separate world beneath our feet, presumably inhabited by the dead. When Gilgamesh, the legendary hero of the ancient Sumerian and Babylonian epos, goes to visit his ancestor Utnapishtim, he seems to go down. When Odysseus comes to the extreme West, he brings a special sacrifice to strengthen the spirits of the dead so that they can emerge from below and speak to him. Generally Greek mythology of the classical period taught that there was an underworld of the dead, ruled by Pluto, and that the divine smith Hephaistos had his workshop under the volcanoes.

Plato, in his dialogue *Phaidon*, organized these beliefs into an impressive picture of happenings below. After saying that the earth is a sphere at the center of the universe (the first mention of the round earth doctrine in any original writing) he went on to tell about "passages broad and narrow in the interior of the earth" and "huge subterranean streams of perennial rivers, and springs hot and cold, and a great fire, and great rivers of fire, and streams of liquid mud . . ."

Early Christian belief adopted the underground land of the dead, but restricted it to sinners and pagans. Later on, Christian folklore appropriately consigned the legendary relics of pre-Christian times to the underworld too. The gnomes live in the mountains and plague the miners who inadvertently disturb them, and their ruler King Laurin maintains a fabulous castle inside a mountain. Germanic folklore even banished Venus underground and names one mountain, the Hörselberg in southwestern Germany, as the place where access to her realm might be had.

Just as Plato had organized mythological fragments into one vast philosophical concept of the interior of the earth, so Dante Alighieri organized the Christian thinking into one vast impressive picture of hell in the interior of the earth. As one went underground through the always yawning gate one passed circle after circle of punishment until at the bottom, in the very center of the earth, the three worst sinners of all history were permanently tortured by Lucifer himself.

Some 350 years after Dante the ideas about the underworld entered a new phase. If the first phase had been that of underground gods and their helpers and the second that of damned souls and the imps and devils who tormented them, the next phase was speculation about subterranean life on a material plane, special and terrible underground life forms.

European folklore had developed a special monster which was given the classical name of "dragon" although that word originally meant nothing more unusual than a big snake, for example a python. All folklore dragons of Europe were always associated, in some manner, with caves. Folklorists were quite puzzled by this association until a paleon-tologist, Professor Othenio Abel, pointed out that this asso-ciation could easily be explained as direct experience of the original storytellers. For centuries Europeans had been com-ing across caves and had often found curious skulls and bones in them. Where such skulls had been preserved—if only in the form of drawings—they could be identified as skulls of *Ursus spelaeus*, the enormous cave bear of the Pleistocene. Racial memory apparently did not reach back to the cave bear but it was easy to see that this was the skull of a big and unknown carnivore.

So there were the dragons, associated with caves. There were the cave legends: Tannhäuser entering the Hörselberg through a cave, knights and peasants blundering into King Laurin's realm through caves and mines, Dante entering Hell through a cave. Caves might be physical gates to a physi-cal subterranean world.

And that suspected physical subterranean world was then described by the learned and imaginative Father Athanasius Kircher, S.J. The title of his work is *Mundus Subterraneus*, (The Subterranean World). It is an enormous book of two big folio volumes, lavishly illustrated with expensive copper plates, dedicated to Pope Alexander VII and published at Amsterdam in 1678. There is a special chapter *de draconibus subterraneis* (about the underground dragons).

Kircher has been much criticized later. True, he did ac-cept purest hearsay as incontrovertible evidence; he even sometimes manufactured evidence. But he had learning and imagination and sometimes he hit the nail on the head. In the case of disease, for example, Kircher warned people to stay away from anything dirty. *Omne putridum ex se et sua natura vermes generat*, he wrote; "everything putrid, by its very nature, generates worms." He made it clear that he did not mean "worms" in the present zoölogical sense, either. He meant small animals generally, and added that disease might be caused by such creatures so small that they could not be seen! He had guessed, correctly, at the rôle of bacteria in disease. He also invented the magic lantern and advanced stimulating if wildly erroneous theories about Egyptian hieroglyphics.

As for the subterranean world he has a lot of new ideas too. Volcanoes are evidently fed from a central fire in the middle of the earth, and some springs seem to be interconnected underground. With so many subterranean connections it is obvious that there must be many other passages and spaces not filled by lava or water. And there live the dragons.

Now and then a poor dragon blunders into the outer world, emerging from a cave. Then it causes great trouble, eating the farmers' herds and the farmers themselves until some knight gains immortal honor by slaying it. Needless to say he cites cases: of the dragon which appeared on Rhodes and was slain by Deodatus of Gozon; of the dragon which devastated the Swiss landscape until a peasant named Winkelriedt, who had been condemned to death, was offered a chance to get off and a bonus as well if he would encounter the dragon with a sword. He slew the dragon all right, but died because some of the beast's blood splashed on him.

As Plato's *Phaidon* had marked the climax of the first phase of belief in a subterranean world and Dante's *Divine Comedy* that of the second, so Kircher's weighty volumes were the culmination of the third.

But during the eighteenth century still another phase appeared which may be called the Literary Phase, although some speculation of scientific nature was mixed into it. One of the earliest literary works was a book by a Frenchman who "preferred to remain anonymous," as they phrased it in those days. It appeared in 1723 and bore the title: *A Narrative of a Voyage from the Arctic Pole to the Antarctic Pole through the Center of the World,* being everything the title promised. This pure adventure story was followed by the Chevalier de Mouhy's *Lamékis, ou les voyages extraordinaires d'un Egyptien dans la Terre intérieure* (1737) which was one of the utopias which were then establishing themselves as a special branch of fiction. There the Inner World served as a safe retreat for a community of sages of Egyptian descent. In 1741 there followed *Nicholas Klim* by Ludvig Baron von Holberg* who is regarded as the founder of Danish literature.

For its setting it had small planets inside a hollow earth, receiving light from an interior sun. And this setting was influenced by some scientific speculation of the time, fleetingly referred to in one of the best known stories of that type, Jules Verne's *Voyage au Centre de la Terre* (1864). Jules Verne operated with the device of an old manuscript and had his usual three heroes descend through the extinct crater of the volcano Snäffel's Yökul in Iceland. The three, a professor, his nephew and an Icelandic guide, know that they are following the proper path, for every once in a while they find on the rock the runic initials A. S., those of the author of the manuscript, one Arne Saknussen. The explorers sail across a subterranean sea in which ichthyosaurs and plesiosaurs are fighting fiercely, something they probably never did in the surface seas back in Jurassic times. The party finally reappears at the surface by way of an eruption of Stromboli, a volcanic island

---

* Originally written in Latin as *Nicolai Klimii iter subterraneum;* it was quickly translated into Danish, but not by its author. Although hardly known in English-speaking countries *Nicholas Klim* is slightly more popular in Scandinavia than *Alice in Wonderland* is in the United States.

in the Lipari group, the islands of Aiolos, dispenser of the winds.

Jules Verne usually stated in his stories whose theories he was following, but in this particular novel he did not do so. He merely dropped a hint about "the ideas of an Englishman" concerning an internal sun. This Briton was the mathematician and physicist Sir John Leslie. Nor was he the only one to harbor unusual ideas about the interior of the earth. Sir John Leslie, Dr. Edmund Halley (of the comet) and the German mathematician Leonhard Euler, three contemporaries who worked on many of the same problems, all speculated about the possibility of the earth's being a hollow sphere. And if the earth was hollow, there might be a separate fiery core or miniature sun in the center of the hollow ball. Leslie supposed two such bodies which he named Pluto and Proserpina. Leonhard Euler was satisfied with just one while Dr. Edmund Halley proposed something more complicated by far.

In 1692 he published an article in the *Philosophical Transactions* of the Royal Society of London in which he tried to explain the observed motion of the magnetic poles by peculiarities of the structure of the earth as a whole. He assumed that the earth consisted of three concentric hollow spheres, without any openings and with a hot spherical core in the center of the whole. He then assumed that the outer sphere may not rotate at precisely the same rate as the inner spheres, which minute difference in rotation, in his opinion, caused the magnetic poles to shift position.

Scientific circles seem to have been somewhat reluctant to comment on Dr. Halley's elaborate theory; a very few scientists endorsed it, the majority seems to have been more interested in Halley's chart of the deviations of the magnetic needle than in his ideas about the reason for them. But a few outsiders were impressed with the idea, among them Cotton Mather who described it with approval in chapter 24, "Of Magnetism," of his book *The Christian Philosopher*, which appeared in London in 1721. This work may have influenced Symmes.

The writers of the eighteenth and nineteenth centuries seem to have been more impressed with Sir John Leslie's simple hollow sphere with an internal sun or two than with Halley's complicated arrangement of several concentric spheres. The theme has returned once more in our century in the Pellucidarian stories of Edgar Rice Burroughs: *At the Earth's Core; Pellucidar;* and so forth, which are among Burrough's commercially less successful efforts. Burroughs was a romantic primitivist of the stripe of Jean Jacques Rousseau, who in the eighteenth century inflicted on the world the myth of the noble savage, never having met any savages himself. In the Pellucidarian tales Burroughs, by depicting a race of semi-civilized intelligent reptiles, indulged his Rousseauism to the full. The result is rather silly. In *The Moon Maid* Burroughs went further and attributed this hollow form to the moon as well as the earth.

There have been a great many stories based on the hollow-earth theme, such as *The Eye of Balamok* by Victor Rousseau (Emanuel), author of the better-known *Messiah of the Cylinder*. In this typical example an Australian mining prospector, lost in the central desert, finds his way into the interior of the hollow earth where he discovers the descendants of the Atlanteans living a colorful life; he engages in various fights, flights and conspiracies and finally wins a princess and flies off with her on the back of a tame pterosaur. These hardy remnants, the Atlanteans, have turned up (in fiction, that is) practically every place you can think of—the Sahara, the

Arctic, the Antarctic, the bottom of the oceans (usually under glass domes) and on the planet Mars. It was simply inevitable that somebody would locate them inside the earth as well.*

Thus Symmes, though he did not say so, had had quite a lot of earlier material to go by. But the idea of the hollow earth permitted one more development. Symmes had still left us on the outside and merely added others on the inside. The next development was to put *us* inside. Apparently the first to voice this thought was an American physician, Cyrus Reed Teed. He claimed that that "truth" had been divinely revealed to him in 1869 when he was a young man.

> The sun, moon, planets, and stars are not large bodies as they are supposed to be, but are focalizations of force which, being substantial but not material, is susceptible of transmutation to materialization and dematerialization, properties of metamorphosis which maintain a constant combustion and consequently a radiation of the ethereal essences which the combustion incessantly generates. . . .
>
> The moon and planets are reflections of vision; the moon, of the earth's surface, the planets, of mercurial discs floating between the laminae of the metallic planes. . . .
>
> At the very center of the egg [the universe] is an excentric momentum comprising an astral nucleus positively and negatively electro-magnetic. This forms the central phys-

* The short novel *The Coming Race* by Lord Bulwer-Lytton may be mentioned here although it is not strictly a hollow-earth novel. The hero finds a race of supermen living an utopian existence in large underground caves. The caves are infested with dragonlike monsters (*vide* Kircher) but the subterraneans control an invincible force called *vril* which they direct to blast the monsters and also to enlarge their caves when necessary. The story ends on an ominous note, suggesting that the subterraneans have plans to take over the surface of the earth. Madame Blavatsky, ever hospitable to chimeras, adopted *vril* as a part of her bizarre cosmogony so that it has remained a fixture in the Theosophical world picture ever since. The Atlanteans, she averred, propelled their aircraft by means of *vril* jets.

ical star. . . . It moves around an ethereal cone, the apex of which is toward the north, and the base of the cone toward the south.

"Koresh," *Fundamentals of Koreshan Universology*, pp. 3f.

If some of this about "ethereal essences" and "excentric momenta" sounds like gibberish, your critical sense does not deceive you: it *is* gibberish. Nevertheless Teed made it plain what he meant. We never see this "central physical star"; instead, the atmosphere acts like a set of lenses to focus an image (which we do see) on the surface of the earth. The central star's movements account for day and night and the seasons. Every 12,000 years the ecliptic suddenly rotates through 30°, causing the "sun" to look like a continuous band encircling the earth, and such a catastrophe is now imminent.

The shell of the universe is about 100 miles thick and composed of seven layers of metals, five of rocks, and five of geological strata. Teed devoted much space to railing at the "so-called scientific doctrine" of scientists like Oliver Lodge, and the "gigantic fallacy and farce of the benighted Copernicus"; on the other hand he rejected the "vagaries" of the British-Israelites and accepted a modified doctrine of evolution. In 1894 he set up a celibate, communistic colony at Estero, Florida, near Fort Myers, called "Koreshan Unity." * The cult spent much time sailing out into the Gulf of Mexico in a sloop and traveling about with surveying instruments to prove Teed's hypothesis. Teed died in 1909, his admirers who had accepted his word that he was immortal laid him out on a cypress plank on the banks of the Estero River and waited for weeks for his resurrection. The dampness of a

* The name *Koresh*, under which Teed wrote several of his books, is Hebrew for *Cyrus*—or rather both are ultimately derived from the Persian *Kurush*.

river bank and the Florida heat are both encouraging to microorganisms and the grim nonsense finally found its end by way of a hurricane. Afterwards some of the cultists killed themselves but others carried on and at last accounts there are still a few left.

Quite similar to Teed's ideas was the *Hohlweltlehre* or Hollow Earth Doctrine which appeared in Germany in the late 1920's. Its chief proponent was a most unimpressive looking typical burgher by the name of Karl Neupert, but there was some internecine strife about who had originated the idea. Offhand one would, of course, assume that somebody in Germany had plowed his way through Teed's writings, but this does not seem to be the case. It was autochthonous nonsense, with much pseudoscientific argument and only a small amount of scriptural quotations thrown in.

Neupert, who died during the Second World War, declared that the earth was a spherical bubble. Geographers had measured its dimensions correctly and also drawn correct maps, but under the mistaken assumption that they were on the outside of a sphere while they actually walked the inside of this bubble. Under our feet is an infinity of rock, over our heads three bodies move about near the center of the bubble: the sun, the moon, and the "phantom universe," a darkblue sphere with little lights on it which we mistake for stars. Night is caused by the phantom universe's obscuring the sun for part of the earth, eclipses by the shadow of the phantom universe falling upon the moon.

The error of orthodox geomorphy is caused by the assumption that light rays are straight, whereas they are all curved with a radius of a quarter of the earth's radius, violet rays more sharply than red rays. In one treatise Neupert proclaimed: "Old folk-tales often speak of the time when God still walked the earth. We know that the earth-universe expands; even Einstein admits that. What is more logical, then, than to take the old folk-tales at face value and assume that they refer to a time when the earth-universe was smaller and the distance from the central luminosities to the surface less than it is now?" And:

> Certain German naval circles [in World War II] believed in the *Hohlweltlehre*. They considered it helpful to locate the British fleet, because the curvature of the earth would not obstruct observation. Visual rays were not suitable because of refraction; but infrared rays had less refraction. Accordingly a party of about ten men under the scientific leadership of Dr. Heinz Fischer, an infrared expert, was sent out from Berlin to the isle of Rügen to photograph the British fleet with infrared equipment at an upward angle of some forty-five degrees.
>
> G. P. Kuiper, German Astronomy During the War, in Popular Astronomy, June 1946.

It did not work. Equipment failure, no doubt.

For a climax we have to return to Columbus, who, for a while, thought that he had modified the shape of the earth, but in a different manner than is ascribed to him in grade school.

Kosmas Indikopleustes as well as other churchmen had occasionally referred to the terrestrial paradise which led a phantom existence on the margins of medieval maps. Eden, the reasoning ran, must have existed on earth and when the Lord expelled Adam and Eve He probably did not lift it into heaven. For if He had, why did He order a watch-angel with a flaming sword to guard the entrance? Therefore Eden must still exist on earth.

Kosmas placed Paradise on the eastern side of the rectangular strip of land that ran around the edge of the floor of his box universe. Other Christian thinkers who had absorbed pagan fancies looked for it in the North among the happy Hyperboreans, or in the West in the Islands of the Blessed, or the Fortunate Isles or the Hesperides. Or else in the South among the blameless Ethiopians. The majority opinion, however, swung to the East and an anonymous Ravennese geographer who wrote about 650 A. D. explained the lack of definite travel reports about it by assuming a vast impassable desert in the East behind which Eden lay inviolate.* Even before Spain and Portugal began exploring, the location in the extreme East had become customary, the theological reason given was that Paradise was located in the place where the rays of the rising sun would touch the earth first on the Fourth Day.

Ranulf Higden, a fourteenth-century English historian, gave a whole chapter to the terrestrial paradise. Its existence, he said, was proved by "narraciones of storyes," "testimonies of men experte," "waters flowenge from hit," and "the olde fame berrethe testimonye to the existence of Paradise"; that is, as men had believed in it for 6,000 years it must be true. It could not be elevated to the height of the moon, as some said, because there would be no air or water up there to enable its luxuriant vegetation to grow. "If hit be seyde that hit is in a manner contiguate to oure place habitable, then hit scholde appere that the erthe were not rownde, as hit is describede of discrete men, but longe." The roundness of the earth, however, is proved by the shape of its shadow during lunar eclipses. "Wherefore prudent men conclude that Paradise Terrestrialle is in the extreme parts of the este. . . . For hit is the pantre or place of alle pulchritude, where

* Dante, in placing Paradise on top of the mountain of Purgatory no doubt thought that he was indulging in poetic license when he put that enormous mountain in the point antipodal to Jerusalem (which would be about 1000 miles south of Tahiti in the Pacific).

the trees of euery kynde loose not theire beaute, floures fade not, hauenge in hit pleasaunte frute." *

The location of Paradise in the extreme East has left a trace in a spot where one would not expect it, in zoology. That a certain group of birds bears the collective name of Birds of Paradise is directly due to this reasoning.

Higden's contemporary, the peripatetic Franciscan Marginolli, claimed to have almost attained Paradise in Ceylon which does have a luxuriant vegetation capable of evoking thoughts of Paradise in the mind of a man coming from Europe. Marginolli visited Ceylon's Adam's Peak on which he saw the footprint Adam had made upon his expulsion. The Mount of Eden was, Marginolli reported, only forty miles away and even higher than Adam's Peak. He would have seen it but for the constant mists and he could hear the four sacred rivers plunging down the precipice in the distance.

One hardly needs to mention that John de Mandeville in his book of travel lies said that he too almost reached Eden but turned back because he knew that so sinful a man as himself would never be admitted.

It remained for Columbus actually to find Paradise. When he was coasting the Orinoco region on his third voyage, he suspected the nearness of Eden from the pleasantness of the climate, and his surmise was startlingly confirmed when he shot Polaris and found its distance from the north celestial pole to be 5° instead of the correct 3° 25′.† His explanation was that he must be nearer the stars than when he had made his earlier observations, so that the circles they described around the pole looked larger. He concluded that the earth

---

* Ranulf Higden, *Polychronicon*, I, x (anon. fifteenth-cent. translation).

† That is, correct in his time. Now the distance is less than one degree, and the pole is almost at its closest approach to the star.

. . . is not round in the form they describe, but that it is in the shape of a pear which is round everywhere but where the stalk is, for there it is higher; or that it is like a very round ball, on one part of which is placed something like a woman's breast, and that this part of this stalk is the highest and nearest the heavens, and it is below the equator and in the Ocean Sea at the end of the Orient.

S. E. Morison, *Admiral of the Ocean Sea*, II, p. 283.

And what could this bump be but Paradise?

Poor Cristóbal!

One of the greatest seamen and explorers the world has ever known, he seemed doomed to trip over his own feet whenever he tried to do any serious thinking. He had, incredibly, shot the wrong star!

And after his time the terrestrial paradise was quietly laid to rest with the one-eyed Arimaspians.

Epilogue

WHETHER THE PEOPLE WHO SETTLED IT WERE MORE PRACTICAL
in their outlook than those who invaded South America, or
possibly because the North American landscape and its life
forms more closely resembled the lands where the settlers
had come from, comparatively few legends grew up among
the whites in North America. True, the Spaniards ranged
the Southwest looking for the golden cities of Cibola and
Quivira, but these were minor adventures, big only in the
mileage covered. There were a few spine-tingling rumors:
thus Lewis and Clark looked forward to finding the Great
Salt Mountain expected to be 180 miles long, and Thomas
Jefferson, whose secretary Meriwether Lewis had been, hoped
that his protégé would come upon a live mammoth. And at
least the second of these rumors had a certain reasonableness
about it. A salt mountain would be washed away by the rains
quickly, but the mammoth might have survived in northern North America.

But it was just in North America that a strange legend
formed and not at some time in an illiterate past, but more
or less within our own twentieth century. That legend centers around Mount Shasta in Siskiyou County at the northern
end of California, a beautiful mountain which is the second
tallest peak in the United States, towering to more than
14,000 feet above the level of the near-by Pacific Ocean.

The story, still passionately believed by small groups of

people and still endowed with some general currency, has it that a strange race lives on the slopes of the tall mountain, practicing strange rites and having contact with the outside world only on rare occasions.

Just because the Mount Shasta legend formed so recently, tracing it to its original source is no problem at all. It began, incredibly enough, with an occultistic novel, published in 1894 under the title *A Dweller on Two Planets*. Its author called himself "Phylos the Tibetan"—"Phylos" is just about the most un-Tibetan-sounding name you could find—although his real name was Frederick Spencer Oliver, not to be confused with his contemporary, the novelist Frederick Scott Oliver.

The story tells that the narrator was wandering about Mount Shasta, then a considerably wilder place and a more plausible site for arcane mysteries. One day he accidentally met a Chinese named Quong. The narrator says that he shared with many Californians of the time a virulent anti-Chinese prejudice, looking upon them as a benighted, degenerate and sinful race. Quong, however, cured him of this fixation and also demonstrated supernatural powers by taming bears and pumas by merely speaking to them, as St. Francis is alleged to have done with a wolf. It transpires that Quong is no mere coolie, but one of the Masters of a group of magi who preserve the wisdom of the ages in their headquarters on Mount Shasta. These supermen induct the narrator into their brotherhood and take him on a tour of the planet Venus in his spiritual body—hence the title of the book.

This story has become fairly important in the history of American cults and pseudo-science. As a novel it belongs in the group of lost-continent fantasies where it easily holds the record for tediousness. For more than three decades nobody paid much attention to it, but then several people, not connected with each other and some even rivals, began making use of it all at once. Until that time one cannot speak about a "Mount Shasta Legend," as one badly written fantasy novel hardly constitutes a tradition in itself.

One of those who utilized it was the late Guy Warren Ballard, alias Godfré Ray King, a long thin, fanciful, histrionic person born in Kansas in 1878, who spent many years as a Spiritualist medium. His wife, Edna Wheeler Ballard, alias Lotus Ray King, had been a clerk in an occult bookshop. Together they formed the "I AM Movement" also known as Ballardism and described as a caricature of Theosophy. Since Theosophy itself has been defined by K. T. Behanan (in his book *Yoga, A Scientific Evaluation*) as a "caricature of Eastern thought and Western science" little needs to be said about Ballardism, except for Ballard's use of Oliver's Mount Shasta story.

It has to be mentioned first that the Ballards adopted a historical character as their Mahatma, namely the slippery eighteenth century occultist and industrial promoter, the Comte de Saint Germain. According to Ballard's doctrines, Saint Germain is one of a hierarchy of Ascended Masters, of whom the Ballards were the Accredited Messengers. In his *Unveiled Mysteries* Ballard told (or rather cribbed from Oliver) how while wandering Mount Shasta on "government business" he had met Saint Germain and had been taken on a series of tours of the world and through past ages. He explored lost civilizations in the Sahara Desert and at the bottom of the Amazon, and saw himself and his wife as they were in former incarnations. At one rendezvous Saint Germain converted a panther to vegetarianism, just as Oliver's Quong had done.

Other elements of his doctrine Ballard borrowed from Theosophy, Christian Science, Rosicrucianism, and the

Swamis who comprise one of the more picturesque elements of the fauna of California.

At the same time that Ballard was launching his cult, Cervé's *Lemuria, the Lost Continent of the Pacific* (1931) was published by the Rosicrucians (AMORC) of San Jose, California. In his book Cervé dropped dark hints of mysterious inscriptions at Klamath Falls and unaccountable lights at night and other prodigies around Mount Shasta, which was revealed as being infested with diffident, long-haired persons of angelic aspect, speaking with English accents. There were also boat-shaped aircraft, buzzing around the mountain and rumors of mystic rites. Lemurians!

Well, one good hoax deserves another, and in 1932 the Shasta legend reached definitive form in a feature story in the Los Angeles *Times*, a sheet normally distinguished for its zealous political and economic conservatism. One Edward Lanser wrote of how when he had been riding on the Shasta Limited enroute to Portland, the train wound around Mount Shasta and:

> Gazing upon its splendor, I suddenly perceived that the whole southern side of the mountain was ablaze with a strange reddish green light. A flame of light that grew faint, then flared up with renewed brilliance.
>
> My first conjecture was a forest fire, but the total absence of smoke discounted that theory. The light resembled the glow of Roman candles.
>
> Then the rising sun dimmed the color of the scene, and gradually, as the train crept north, the weird phenomenon was lost to view. The thing intrigued me; yet I felt unable to discuss what I had seen with anyone. . . . Convinced that I had not been the victim of a mirage, I later asked the conductor about the mysterious pyrotechnics. His answer was short but enticing.
>
> "Lemurians," he said. "They hold ceremonials up there."
> Lemurians!
> The fact that a group of people conduct ceremonials on

the side of a mountain is not of exceptional interest, but when these people are said to be Lemurians, that is startling, for the continent of Lemuria, like the lost Atlantis, disappeared beneath the ocean ages ago, and the Lemurians have long since been known as an extinct race.*

Eager to learn more, Lanser inquired round about the Shasta region and learned that:

. . . the existence of a "mystic village" on Mt. Shasta was an accepted fact. Business men, amateur explorers, officials, and ranchers in the country surrounding Shasta spoke freely of the community, and all attested to the weird rituals that are performed on the mountainside after sunset, midnight and sunrise. Also, they freely ridiculed my avowed trek into the sacred precincts, assuring me that an entrance was as difficult and forbidden as an entrance into Tibet.

It appeared that although the existence of these last descendants of the ancient Lemurians have been known to Northern Californians for more than fifty years, only four or five explorers have penetrated the invisible protective boundary of this Lemurian settlement; but no one has ever returned to tell the tale. . . .

Just then I learned that the existence of Lemurian descendants on Mt. Shasta was vouched for some years ago by no less an authority than the eminent scientist, Prof. Edgar Lucien Larkin, for many years director of the Mt. Lowe Observatory in Southern California.

Prof. Larkin, with determined sagacity, penetrated the Shasta wilderness as far as he could—or dared—and then, cleverly, continued his investigations from a promontory with a powerful long-distance telescope.

What the scientist saw, he reported, was a great temple in the heart of the mystic village—a marvelous work of carved marble and onyx, rivalling in beauty and architectural splendor the magnificence of the temples of Yucatan. He saw a village housing from 600 to 1000 people; they appeared to be industriously engaged in the manufacture of articles necessary to their consumption, they were engaged in farming the sunny slopes and glens surrounding the village—with miracu-

---

* The Los Angeles *Times*, May 22, 1932, quoted in Lewis Spence's *The Problem of Lemuria*, p. 104ff.

lous results, judging from the astounding vegetation revealed to Prof. Larkin's spy-glass. He found them to be a peaceful community evidently contented to live as their ancient forebears lived before Lemuria was swallowed up by the sea.

In their nightly ceremonies the Lemurians celebrated their escape from Lemuria to "Guatama," * as they call America. From time to time they enter the neighboring towns, "tall, barefoot, noble-looking men, with close-cropped hair, dressed in spotless white robes" to buy lard, sulphur, and salt with nuggets of gold. They also contribute generously of these nuggets to worthy causes like the Red Cross, though they seem never to have learned English.

> The really incredible thing is that these staunch descendants of that vanished race have succeeded in secluding themselves in the midst of our teeming State and that they have managed through some marvelous sorcery to keep highways, hot-dog establishments, filling stations and the other ugly counterparts of our tourist system out of their sacred precincts.

A story not without a certain fey charm, and it is almost too bad that there is not a word of truth in it. Most of Mount Shasta is a state preserve and public camping ground, and campers and state forest officials roam freely over Shasta all the time without meeting Lemurians, in nightgowns or otherwise. Any reader may go camp there himself to see. There is no "Shasta legend" current in Siskiyou County. Miss Edith Mirrielees, editor of *The Pacific Spectator* and a person of long experience, wide acquaintance, and profound sagacity, who grew up in sight of Shasta, assures us that the people who actually live in that region never heard of such a thing.

And far from being an "eminent scientist," Larkin was just an elderly occultist who until his death in 1924 ran the Mount Lowe Observatory near Los Angeles. You have no doubt heard of the Mount Wilson Observatory (now run in

* This is of course the name of the founder of Buddhism.

conjunction with the Palomar Mountain Observatory) and have a vague picture of Larkin twirling the knobs of the hundred-inch telescope and peering at distant galaxies. But the Mount Lowe Observatory had nothing whatever to do with the great scientific institution of Mount Wilson. It was a tourist attraction operated by the Pacific Electric Railway in conjunction with its Mount Lowe Inn, reached by a steep and winding ride on the railroad's electric interurban cars from Los Angeles. Larkin (and later his son) showed the hotel's guests the stars through a small telescope until in the 1930's the telescope mechanism broke down and the inn burned, so that the installation was abandoned.

The whole story is evidently just an imaginative expansion upon the hints dropped by Cervé in his book, with perhaps assistance from something Larkin wrote. The motto would seem to be the French *l'audace, toujours l'audace,* or to give an English paraphrase, "Enough gall will get you a fast buck."

And so we come to the end of our tale of geographical legends, or, we might say, of subjective geography—the geographies that people of other times and places have believed in. Indubitably these imaginary landscapes were more brightly colored, livelier, and more romantic than the real thing. It's a little sad that they do not exist in fact—who would not trade, for Terra Australis with its golden cities and giant parrots, the real South Pacific with its millions of square miles of empty heaving water and whistling winds? Colonel Fawcett may have been, as Clifton Fadiman once described him, "a gallant crank with a mania for legendary cities and buried treasure," self-deceived and doomed to frustration even if the Calapalos had not killed him. But wouldn't it have been wonderful if he *had* found a tribe of White Indians lurking in the ruins of a genuine Atlantean city?

However, if these things had turned out to be true we would just take them for granted by now. Plenty of real wonders have made a stir when discovered, the gorilla, the Pygmies, okapis and Congo peacocks of the African Ituri forest, the geysers of Yellowstone Park, the redwoods of California, Grand Canyon, the Victoria Falls and the real ruins of Babylon, Angkor Wat and Copán. But now we just know they exist.

And so, no doubt, it would have been if all the other wonders had turned out to be true. The headless Ewaipanomas would not only have been scrutinized by scientists as a strange life form, they would have been corrupted by traders, demoralized by tourists and dragged from their habitat by showmen. Prester John's kingdom would be appealing to the United Nations to halt Russian aggression. The dinosaurs of the Matto Grosso would be brought close to a second extinction by hunters before belated and half-hearted attempts were made to save them. And Atlantis would be just one more set of dates and outlandish kings' names to be forced into the brains of unwilling school children, to be forgotten as quickly as possible after graduation.

So, perhaps it is better that these things exist only in print. That way they afford enjoyment of the mental pictures they evoke and provide the pleasure of tracing down their histories to see how they came to be.

Bibliography

HISTORY OF GEOGRAPHY:

BEAZLEY, C. RAYMOND: *The Dawn of Modern Geography: A History of Exploration and Geographical Science.* (3 vols.) London (Murray), 1897–1903.

BROWN, LLOYD A.: *The Story of Maps.* Boston (Little, Brown), 1949.

BUNBURY, EDWARD HERBERT: *A History of Ancient Geography; Among the Greeks and Romans from the Earliest Ages till the Fall of the Roman Empire.* (3 vols.) London (Murray), 1883.

DICKINSON, R. E. AND HOWARTH, O. J. R.: *The Making of Geography.* Oxford (Clarendon), 1933.

FIRESTONE, CLARK S.: *The Coasts of Illusion: A Study of Travel Tales.* New York (Harper), 1924.

HEIDEL, WILLIAM ARTHUR: *The Frame of the Ancient Greek Maps.* New York (American Geographical Society), 1937.

HOURANI, GEORGE FADLO: *Arab Seafaring in the Indian Ocean.* Princeton (Princeton University Press), 1951.

KEY, CHARLES E.: *The Story of Twentieth-Century Exploration.* New York (Knopf), 1938.

SPILHAUS, MARGARET WHITING: *The Background of Geography.* Philadelphia (Lippincott), 1935.

THÉVENIN, RENÉ: *Les Pays Légendaires.* Paris (Presses Universitaires de France), 1946.

TOZER, HENRY FANSHAWE: *A History of Ancient Geography.* Cambridge (Cambridge University Press), 1897–1935.

WROTH, LAWRENCE C.: *The Early Cartography of the Pacific.* (Bibliographical Society of America) 38/2, 1944.

Most of the classical authors quoted or mentioned, like Aristotle, Diodorus Siculus, Herodotus, Hesiod, Homer, Pausanias,

Pliny, Strabo, Vitruvius, Cleomedes, Heron of Alexandria are available in the *Loeb Classics* series which can be found in any library.

WORKS PERTAINING TO SPECIAL THEMES:

CHAPTER I. (ATLANTIS)

BESSMERTNY, ALEXANDRE: *L'Atlantide; Exposé des hypothèses relatives à l'énigme de l'Atlantide.* Paris (Payot), 1935. (A translation of Bessmertny's *Das Atlantis-Rätsel* by F. Gidon.)

BJÖRKMAN, EDWIN: *The Search for Atlantis.* New York (Knopf), 1927.

BRAGHINE, COLONEL ALEXANDER P.: *The Shadow of Atlantis.* New York (Dutton), 1940.

BRAMWELL, JAMES GUY: *Lost Atlantis.* New York (Harper), 1938.

BRASSEUR DE BOURBOURG, ABBÉ CHARLES ETIENNE: *Manuscrit Troano: Etudes sur la Système et Langue des Mayas.* (2 vols.) Paris (Impériale), 1869.

CHURCHWARD, JAMES: *The Children of Mu.* New York (Washburn), 1933.

———, *The Sacred Symbols of Mu.* New York (Washburn), 1931.

———, *The Lost Continent of Mu.* New York (Washburn), 1926.

DE CAMP, L. SPRAGUE: *Lost Continents: The Atlantis Theme in History, Science and Literature.* Philadelphia (Prime Press), 1952.

DONNELLY, IGNATIUS T.: *Atlantis: The Antediluvian World.* New York (Harper), 1882, 1949.

GATTEFOSSÉ, JEAN AND ROUX, CLAUDIUS: *Bibliographie de l'Atlantide et des questions connexes (Géographie, Ethnographie et Migrations anciennes . . .).* Lyon (Bosc et Rious), 1926.

LANDA, DIEGO DE: *Landa's Relación de las Cosas de Yucatan.* Cambridge, Massachusetts (Peabody Museum), 1941.

LE PLONGEON, AUGUSTUS: *Queen Móo and the Egyptian Sphinx.* London (Trübner), 1896.

———, *Sacred Mysteries among the Mayas and Quiches 11,500 Years Ago.* New York (Macoy), 1886.

MARTIN, T. HENRI: *Etudes sur le Timée de Platon.* (2 vols.) Paris (Lagrange), 1841.

Scott-Elliot, W.: *The Story of Atlantis*. London (Theosophical Publishing House), 1896.
———, *The Lost Lemuria*. London (Theosophical Publishing House), 1925.
Silbermann, Otto: *Un Continent Perdu: l'Atlantide*. Paris (Genet), 1930.
Spence, J. Lewis T. C.: *Atlantis in America*. New York (Brentano), 1925.
———, *The History of Atlantis*. London (Rider), 1926.
———, *The Occult Sciences in Atlantis*. London (Rider), 1926.
———, *The Problem of Atlantis*. New York (Brentano), 1924.
———, *The Problem of Lemuria*. Philadelphia (McKay), 1933.
Stewart, John Alexander: *The Myths of Plato. Translated with Introductory and Other Observations*. London (Macmillan), 1905.
Warmington, Eric H.: *Greek Geography*. London (Dent), 1934.

CHAPTER II. (THE ODYSSEY)

Abel, Othenio: *Die vorweltlichen Tiere in Märchen, Sage und Aberglauben*. Karlsruhe (G. Braun), 1923.
Bérard, Victor: *Did Homer Live?* New York (Dutton), 1931.
Bonsor, George: *Tartesse*. New York *(Hispanic Society of America)*, 1922.
Butler, Samuel: *The Authoress of the Odyssey, where and when she wrote, who she was, the use she made of the Iliad, & how the poem grew under her hands*. London (Cape), 1897, 1922.
Carpenter, Rhys: *Folk Tale, Fiction and Saga in the Homeric Epics*. Berkeley (University of California Press), 1946.
Draheim, H.: *Die Odyssee als Kunstwerk*. Munster i. W. (Aschendorff), 1910.
Geddes, William D.: *The Problem of the Homeric Poems*. London (Macmillan), 1878.
Hennig, Richard: *Die Geographie des Homerischen Epos*. Leipzig (B. G. Teubner), 1934.
———, *Von rätselhaften Ländern*. Munich, (Delphin-Verlag) 1925.
Lang, Andrew: *The World of Homer*. London (Longmans, Green), 1910.
Leaf, Walter: *Homer and History*. London (Macmillan), 1915.

Murray, Gilbert: *The Rise of the Greek Epic.* Oxford (Clarendon), 1924.

——, *The Wanderings of Odysseus.* (In *Quarterly Review,* No. 403, pp. 344–370) London, 1905.

Scheffer, Thassilo von: *Homer und seine Zeit.* Vienna (Karl König), 1925.

Scott, John A.: *The Unity of Homer.* Berkeley (University of California Press), 1921.

Shewan, Alexander: *Homeric Essays.* Oxford (Blackwell), 1935.

Smith, William (ed.): *Dictionary of Greek & Roman Geography.* (2 vols.) Boston (Little, Brown), 1857.

Thompson, J. A. K.: *Studies in the Odyssey.* Oxford (Clarendon Press), 1914.

CHAPTERS III AND IV. (THE EAST AND SINDBAD)

Burton, Richard F.: *The Book of the Thousand Nights and a Night.* (17 vols.) London (Burton Club), 1886.

Hourani, George Fadlo: *Arab Seafaring in the Indian Ocean.* Princeton (Princeton University Press), 1951.

Spargo, John Webster: *Virgil the Necromancer (Studies in Virgilian Legends).* Cambridge (Harvard University Press), 1934.

CHAPTER V. (PRESTER JOHN)

Brunet, G.: La Légende du Prêtre Jean. Bordeaux, 1877.

Hennig, Richard: *Terrae Incognitae,* vol. II. Leiden, Holland (Brill), 1937. (An annotated collection of original old travel reports in German translation.)

Komroff, Manuel (ed.): *Contemporaries of Marco Polo.* New York (Liveright), 1928.

——, *The Travels of Marco Polo.* New York (Liveright), 1930.

Mandeville, Sir John: *The Voiage and Travayle of Sir John Maundeville, Kt., which treateth of the Way to Hierusalem; and of Marvayles of Inde, with Other Ilands and Countyes.* London (Pickering & Chatto), 1887.

Oppert, Gustav: *Der Presbyter Johannes in Sage and Geschichte.* 2nd ed. Berlin, 1870.

Sanceau, Elaine: *The Land of Prester John.* New York (Knopf), 1944. (Description of Ethiopia).

Zarncke, Friedrich: *Der Priester Johannes.* Leipzig, 1876.

CHAPTER VI. (LOST TEN TRIBES)

BARON, DAVID: *The History of the Ten "Lost" Tribes. Anglo-Israelism Explained.* London (Morgan & Scott), 1915.

ERITH, LIONEL E. P.: *The British-Israel Fallacy.* London (Mowbray), 1921.

GARTENHAUS, JACOB: *The Ten Lost Tribes: A Discussion of British Israelism.* Atlanta (Home Mission Board), 1938.

GODBEY, ALLEN H.: *The Lost Tribes a Myth.* Durham (Duke University Press), 1930.

HANAN, ARCHDEACON DENIS AND ALDERSMITH, H.: *British-Israelite Truth.* London (Covenant Publishing House), 1891, 1932.

HOWLETT, REV. THOMAS R.: *Anglo-Israel.* Philadelphia (Spengler & Davis), 1896.

KOHUT, GEORGE ALEXANDER: *The Lost Ten Tribes in America.* Portland, Oregon (Jewish Tribune), 1909.

POOLE, REV. W. H.: *Anglo-Israel, or the Saxon Race Proved to be the Lost Ten Tribes of Israel. . . .* Detroit (Winn & Hammond), 1889.

ROSE, GEORGE LEON: *Real Israel and Anglo-Israelism.* Glendale, California (Rose), 1942.

STRAUB, WALTER L.: *Anglo-Israel Mysteries Unmasked: The Pyramids Re-explored and the Prophecies Re-examined.* Omaha (privately printed), 1937.

CHAPTER VII. (TERRA AUSTRALIS)

JASTROW, JOSEPH: *The Story of Human Error.* New York (Appleton-Century), 1936. A symposium.

RONNE, FINN: *Antarctic Conquest.* New York (Putnam), 1949.

VILLIERS, ALAN: *The Coral Sea.* New York (Whittlesey), 1949.

CHAPTER VIII. (THE WESTERN OCEAN)

ABU AL-FIDA: *Géographie d'Aboulféda (traduite de l'Arabe en Français).* (2 vols.) Paris (Nationale), 1848.

AELIANUS, CLAUDIUS: *His Various History.* London (Dring), 1665.

CHATTERTON, E. KEBBLE: *Sailing Ships: The Story of their Development from the Earliest Times to the Present Day.* London (Sidgwick & Jackson), 1909.

CLOWES, G. S. LAIRD: *Sailing Ships (Their History and Development).* (2 vols.) London (Science Museum), 1930.

COLUM, PADRAIC: *The Voyagers (Being Legends and Romances of Atlantic Discovery)*. New York (Macmillan), 1925.

GIBSON, CHARLES E.: *The Story of the Ship*. New York (Schuman), 1948.

IDRISI: *Géographie d'Édrisi*. (2 vols.) Paris (Société de Géographie), 1840.

RICHARDSON, R. C. AND ROMOLA: *The Sailing Ship (Six Thousand Years of History)*. New York (McBride), 1947.

CHAPTER IX. (GOLDEN MEN AND AMAZONS)

BANDELIER, ADOLF F. A.: *The Gilded Man (El Dorado)*. New York (Appleton), 1893.

CHURCHWARD, ROBERT: *Wilderness of Fools*. London (Routledge), 1936.

DYOTT, GEORGE MILLER: *Man Hunting in the Jungle*. Indianapolis (Bobbs-Merrill), 1930.

FLEMING, PETER: *Brazilian Adventure*. New York (Scribner), 1934.

HAGEN, VICTOR WOLFGANG VON: *South America Called Them*. New York (Knopf), 1945.

ROUSE, IRVING: *Petroglyphs*. (In Bull. 143, Vol. V Bureau of American Ethnology, pp. 493–502.) Washington, D. C. (Smithsonian Institution).

WILKINS, HAROLD T.: *Mysteries of Ancient South America*. London (Rider), 1946.

CHAPTER X. (SHAPE OF THE EARTH)

BABCOCK, WILLIAM H.: *Legendary Islands of the Atlantic: A Study in Medieval Geography*. New York (American Geographical Society), 1922.

CHATTERTON, E. KEBBLE: *Sailing Ships: The Story of their Development from the Earliest Times to the Present Day*. London (Sidgwick & Jackson), 1909.

GIBSON, CHARLES E.: *The Story of the Ship*. New York (Schuman), 1948.

KIMBLE, GEORGE H. T.: *Geography in the Middle Ages*. London (Methuen), 1938.

MORISON, SAMUEL ELIOT: *Admiral of the Ocean Sea: A Life of Christopher Columbus*. Boston (Little, Brown), 1942.

———, *Portuguese Voyages to America in the Fifteenth Cen-*

tury. Cambridge, Massachusetts (Harvard University Press), 1940.

NUNN, GEORGE E.: *The Geographical Conceptions of Columbus*. New York (American Geographical Society), 1924.

WRIGHT, JOHN K.: *The Geographical Lore of the Times of the Crusades*. New York (American Geographical Society), 1925.

EPILOGUE. (MOUNT SHASTA)

BALLARD, GUY WARREN: *Unveiled Mysteries*. Chicago (Saint Germain), 1939.

CERVÉ, WISHAR S.: *Lemuria, the Lost Continent of the Pacific*. San Jose (Rosicrucian Press), 1931.

OLIVER, FREDERICK SPENCER: *A Dweller on Two Planets, by "Phylos"*. Los Angeles (Borden), 1894, 1940.

SPENCE, J. LEWIS T. C.: *The Problem of Lemuria*. Philadelphia (McKay), 1933.

INDEX

(Italicized numbers refer to captions or illustrations.)